■

Parables
of
Possibility

Parables
of
Possibility

The American Need for Beginnings

Terence Martin

Columbia University Press   New York

Columbia University Press
New York   Chichester, West Sussex
Copyright © 1995 Columbia University Press

Library of Congress Cataloging-in-Publication Data
Martin, Terence.
    Parables of possibility : the American need for beginnings /
Terence Martin.
        p.   cm.
    Includes bibliographical references and index.
    ISBN 0–231–07050–0
    1. American literature—History and criticism—Theory, etc.
2. National characteristics, American, in literature.   3. Politics
and literature—United States—History.   4. United States—
Civilization.   5. Openings (Rhetoric)   I. Title.
PS25.M37   1995
810.9—dc20   94–17486
                                                  CIP

Casebound editions of Columbia University Press books
are printed on permanent and durable acid-free paper.
Printed in the United States of America
c 10 9 8 7 6 5 4 3 2 1

For
Roy Harvey Pearce

Contents

Preface

This book explores the protean importance of a sense of beginning in American literature and culture. My organization
is topical, frequently cutting across genres and centuries so
that I may stress connections, continuities, habits of the
imagination. Edward W. Said observes that the fundamental matter of locating a beginning point became
"increasingly problematic" in European literature at the
end of the eighteenth century. No such problem beset
writers and public figures in the new United States. Historians of former colonies turned to dates of first settlement as the natural way of beginning their accounts. Joel
Barlow took 1492 as the year from which to project the
vision of *The Columbiad* centuries into the future. Fourth
of July speakers annually praised the Declaration of Independence as the birth document of the nation. What these
diverse forms of expression share is an assumption of
accessibility that allows them to locate points of founding
from which subsequent action flows.

Part 1 of what follows examines, first, the attempts to
"fix" a beginning that would serve the nation as a whole,
then the use of negation to strip away phenomena so that

one confronted beginnings both radical and atemporal in nature. The basic function of rhetorical negating in the years after the American Revolution was to wipe the slate clean of European history and institutions (sometimes with festival energy) and thus establish the conditions for a national identity. Out of an impulse to negate in order to possess came imaginative constructs that became signatures of a culture—political (as in Thomas Paine's *Common Sense*), transcendental (as in Ralph Waldo Emerson's *Nature*), utopian (as in Charlotte Perkins Gilman's *Herland*), even commercial (as in a variety of advertisements). Emerson's arguments against time and limitation, for example, are profoundly negative in strategy, made so by his faith in the self as partaker of the infinite. They are reminiscent (provocatively so) of the negative or apophatic discourse of Christian mysticism, which rigorously erases the finite as the way of knowing the Infinite. Although both Scotus Eriugena and Emerson breathed the cleansing air of a Neoplatonic tradition, there is an instructive difference between what is produced by the negatives of the apophatic theologian of the ninth century and those of the American writer of the nineteenth: if Eriugena had described a person in a series of dazzling negatives, he would have defined a saint; when Emerson characterized Thoreau in such a series, he defined (as he says) an American.

How beginnings function in works of American fiction—how they affect characterization, evoke certain kinds of description, and serve to organize experience—is the focus of my attention in part 2. What I call the negative character takes his and later her individuality from a rhetoric of negation that cancels out or nulls the conditions of relatedness that are conventional signifiers of identity. Negative characters, among them Huckleberry Finn, and Sylvie in Marilynne Robinson's *Housekeeping*, are asocial by conception: as figures in fiction, they enact the role of uncompromised American, measuring what our world has become by their detachment from it. They show us (frequently to our discomfort) the society in which we live by showing us the society in which they are unable to live.

Just as Thomas Paine embraced the prospect of beginning "the world over again," some American writers have made it their business to imagine the world over again, to reconstitute the story of the nation from a point inaccessible to history. With characteristic extravagance, Faulkner in *Go Down, Moses* sweeps the import of beginnings from Eden onward into the negative flow of an Augustinian dialectic concerning ownership and responsibility, innocence and guilt. An elemental sense of beginning, at times threatening in its austerity, at times exhilarating in its promise, gives authority to the developing contours of Willa Cather's narratives of the Nebraska prairie and the Southwest. In *The Deerslayer* Cooper provides an eloquent example of the manner in which narrative can join an otherwise inaccessible point of beginning to history—in this case "a world by itself" in which a youthful and innocent Natty Bumppo kills his first human being. In all cases, the writer appropriates a point of genesis to release the flow of narrative with its attendant conditions of sequence and time.

The concluding part of this study examines (again, in two chapters) the phenomenon and fate of inexhaustible beginnings. Bred by transcendent invocations of the infinite in the nineteenth century and by more than a century of westering expansion into what was seen as "empty" space, a sense of inexhaustibility guaranteed to Americans a unique purchase on the future—both individually and collectively. One who permits "no horizon to fall on the illimitable space," says Emerson in "The Protest," will have "immortal youth." One who makes "infinite demands" on life, writes Thoreau in "Walking," will "always find himself in a new country." With terms such as "infinite," "immortal," and "illimitable" these writers negate limits and thereby envision (and recommend) ideal states of existence forever unattached to previous experience. What Whitman adds is a temporal dimension. Standing steadfast at a moment of beginning, secure in his conviction that democracy has *time* to realize its promise, he repeatedly casts the problems of past and present into metaphors of preparation for the vindicating future.

In the face of mounting evidence that the resources of the nation—and of the Earth—are exhaustible, political figures in the twentieth century have faced increasing pressure to project visions of the future (substitute frontiers, policies for growth, programs for development), something Americans have never been without. And there is manifest difficulty: for our need for beginnings has remained intact while the traditional means of fulfilling that need have lost their efficacy. In its fullest dimensions, the American dream has been a yearning for the inexhaustible, unfulfilled now as never before. A painful, complex, but necessary process of recasting that dream, or perhaps replacing it with individual commitments to community and transnational perspectives on the world, may be what the coming century has to offer—a modus vivendi rather than an absolute beginning.

Quite obviously, the issues I am exploring, interdisciplinary as they are, intersect with previous studies of Adamic innocence, the frontier, the Neoplatonic tradition, and the achievement of individual writers. My debt to the scholarship that has been done on such topics and on the writers whose work I emphasize will be apparent in the pages that follow. What has come before has not only led me to the present inquiry but (together with my interest in negative structures) helped me to fashion an approach that will, I believe, bring something fresh and incisive to our understanding of literary achievement in its relation to American culture.

I should like to acknowledge my gratitude to the Guggenheim Memorial Foundation and to Indiana University for fellowships that supported my research—and to the staffs at the Ohio State University Library, the Indiana University Library, and the Lilly Library for directing me to relevant texts of which I was unaware. My special thanks go to Robert Middlekauff, Martin Ridge, and the Reader's Services Staff at the Huntington Library; their kindnesses and counsel in the early stages of this work helped me to get a surer grasp of its implications. I am also indebted to colleagues and friends who called significant material to my attention, among them Wallace E. Williams, Mary Burgan, Thomas Wortham, Stuart M. Sperry, Carolyn Mitchell, Paul John Eakin, Thomas Fick, Holly Witten Kondras, David J. Nordloh, Thomas Cooley, Cynthia Jordan, Steven Fink, and Christian Zacher. I am especially grateful to James H. Justus, whose ability to spot a passage of negative rhetoric at thirty feet and fathom its importance to my argument was a repeated source of comfort. To Jerome Loving and H. Daniel Peck, whose attentive reading of the manuscript eliminated some mushy spots and added expert perceptions, I offer my sincere appreciation. And to Barbara Martin, researcher on the spot, I give (once again) a wink and a smile.

Chapter 2 appeared in shorter form in *American Literature* 57 (1985): 1–22. An earlier version of chapter 3 appeared in *Toward a New Literary History: Essays in Honor of Arlin Turner*, ed. Louis J. Budd, Edwin H. Cady, and Carl L. Anderson (Durham: Duke

University Press, 1980), pp. 230–43. Part of chapter 4 appeared in *American Letters and the Historical Consciousness: Essays in Honor of* **xiii** *Lewis P. Simpson*, ed. J. Gerald Kennedy and Daniel Mark Fogel (Baton Rouge: Louisiana State University Press, 1987), pp. 158–76.

Parables
of
Possibility

**Part
One**

▌ 1

Fixing a Beginning

Toward Consensus   At the outset of his *History of New-
Hampshire* (1784), Jeremy Belknap remarks that America
is fortunate to have been discovered and settled at a time
when Europe was "emerging from a long period of ignorance and darkness." The vitality of the European mind in
recent centuries has resulted in major achievements, he
continues, among them the use of the magnetic needle,
the invention of printing, and the reformation of religion.
"To this concurrence of favourable causes, we are indebted
for the precision with which we are able to fix the beginning of this great American empire"—an advantage the
historians of other countries must do without because they
confront early periods of time either "disguised by fiction
and romance" or cloaked in "impenetrable obscurity."[1] The
double focus of Belknap's argument joins history and historian in productive combination: not only is the country
fortunate to have developed in these enlightened times
("It is happy for America" are the opening words of the
History); equally well off is the researcher, who can appropriate a beginning and thus endow narrative with definition and purpose.

Belknap's perception of the American past as unobscured and accessible anticipates the well-known observations of such nineteenth-century writers as Washington Irving, Margaret Fuller, and Nathaniel Hawthorne, who—from an opposite perspective—lament the difficulty of writing in a land without chivalry, ancestral wrong, or the twilight atmosphere that seemed the condition of legend and romance. More important for my present discussion, Belknap's assumption that being able "to fix" a beginning helps one to shape history reaches to the larger issue of the function of beginnings in human discourse. As Edward W. Said has demonstrated, beginnings impose a structure on experience; they fulfill a "primordial need for certainty" out of which comes a sense of form and coherence.[2] In both temporal and conceptual ways, beginnings satisfy what Wallace Stevens (in another context) calls a "rage for order." Thus, even Herodotus, who makes a distinctive kind of history out of what Jeremy Belknap would see as profound disadvantages, looks to the Persians for a point of departure that will help him convert tradition and hearsay into beguiling narrative. And Eusebius, early in the fourth century, asserts that anyone wishing to understand the Church must "go right back to Christ himself" and "start with the beginning."[3] Eusebius's predilection for taking narrative back to beginnings can be seen throughout his *History of the Church*, in his use of anecdote and source material as well as in overall conception. "Origen's story," he suggests characteristically, "deserves, I think, to be told right from the cradle" (239); "I will begin my narrative," he announces in book 7, with the valuable letters of Dionysius of Alexandria as a "starting-point" (287). The structure of the parts serves the structure of the whole: a series of individual beginnings reinforces the primary assumption of Eusebius's *History*.

Philosophers traditionally look to the idea of beginning as a manifestation of the absolute and thereby the occasion for a cosmology. Employing what he calls "the language of probability," Plato's Timaeus avers that the creator "made this world of generation." Finding that it was "not at rest," however, that it moved "in an irregular and disorderly fashion, out of disorder he brought order."[4] Meister Eckhart stresses the priority of an ideal creation that was made manifest in the Word. The modernity of Eckhart can be seen in his unorthodox ideas of simultaneity and perpetual beginnings: at the instant in which God existed and in which "he begot his coeternal Son," Eckhart writes, "he also created the world." Employing the double meaning of *principium* ("beginning" and "principle"), he contends that the *principium* "is always being born and has always been born."[5] The work of Edward Husserl likewise takes its impetus from a preoccupation with beginnings that makes him, in Said's words, the embodiment of "the perpetual *Anfanger*" or beginner. Husserl's effort, as Said writes, is "to seize the beginning proposing itself to the beginning *as* a beginning *in* the beginning."[6] It is Eckhart's quest of old, transposed to a world in which the sense of an absolute beginning has become problematic even while it retains its structuring potential.

Out of his concern to write narrative history, with its patterns of sequence and relation, Jeremy Belknap appropriates for his *History of New-Hampshire* a beginning that is temporal rather than absolute, proximate rather than remote. And he is not alone in taking pleasure at the accessibility of American beginnings. As John Daly Burk reminds his readers in *The History of Virginia* (1804), the "origin" of the colony has "nothing of the mysterious or marvelous about it." He can tell his story with relaxed authority because "the founders are scarcely out of sight."[7] At a meeting of the New England Society almost fifty years later, George S. Hillard measured the proximity of the Pilgrims with a clear note of satisfaction. "There are persons now living," he observed, "who have conversed with a venerable man, who remembered to have seen Peregrine White, who was born on board the Mayflower. By a fact like this we seem to be brought near to the event we are commemorating."[8] A sense of proximity is again the issue: Hillard's illustration personalizes a beginning he wants to bring home to the consciousness of his auditors. One can, of course, play wonderful games by stringing generations together in this way, perhaps none more acrobatic than that of Thoreau in *A Week on the Concord and Merrimack Rivers* (1849) when he demonstrates how close we are to a cluster of beginning moments: no matter how old the world seems, Thoreau muses, sixty one-hundred-year-old women, standing hand in hand, "would span the interval from Eve to my own mother." Their gossip, he goes on to say, "would be Universal History. The fourth old woman from myself suckled Columbus,—the ninth was nurse to the Norman Conqueror,—the nineteenth was the Virgin Mary,—the twenty-fourth the Cumaean Sibyl,—the thirtieth was at the Trojan war and Helen her name,—the thirty-eighth was Queen Semiramis,—the sixtieth was Eve the mother of mankind."[9] The desire to trace conception to a beginner has seldom been expressed with such arch flamboyance.

Most early American histories, both of individual colonies and of the nation, simply assume that beginnings are accessible—without elaborate strategies of claiming kin. Their initial claim (echoed in literary works of the early Republic) is one of "discovery." And whether or not Christopher Columbus is mentioned, what is discovered is the "New World." No matter that two formidable continents had existed for uncounted centuries before the arrival of European explorers; no matter that generations of human beings had fashioned societies and complex cultures on those continents. "Discovery" (then as now) is in the eye of the discoverer.[10] And the enabling perception of those who named territories New England, New France, and New Spain was that they had come to a New World. From this European perception of how they, the early colonists, were situated came the opposing term, *Old World*, and the powerful dialectic that fostered a sense of American identity during the first half-century of independence. From the Old World came a conception of the New, from the New a conception of the Old by means of which Americans (as we shall see in chapter 2) could announce what they were not and thereby proclaim their superiority.

Taking dates of discovery and first settlement as logical points of departure, early American histories move from the known to the known with a faith in the divine ordering of events that sustains their narrative structure. Although the writers are aware that civilizations rise, flourish, and decay, the organizing principle of their work is primarily linear rather than cyclical. Their subtitles, detailed and descriptive in the manner of the time, stake out boundaries with a clear sense of purpose. Belknap's study covers *One Complete Century from the Discovery of the River Pascataqua*. Benjamin Trumbull's history of Connecticut (1797) includes matters *Civil and Ecclesiastical, from the Emigration of Its First Planters in England, in MDCXXX, to MDCCXIII*. Displaying a similar taste for Roman numerals along with a broader national canvas, Abiel Holmes's *American Annals* (1805) presents *A Chronological History of America from its Discovery in MCCCCXCII to MDCCCVI*. And George Bancroft's more sophisticated *History of the United States* (begun in 1834) moves ambitiously *from the Discovery of the Ameri-*

can Continent to nineteenth-century issues and events. The "from-
to" convention in these and other titles serves the writers well: recognizing the beginning and end of one's narrative, framing at the
outset the entire history one proposes to tell, not only establishes
authority over one's material but suggests its continuity and interi-
or logic.

Although the occasions of first settlement and the voyage of
Columbus in 1492 became established starting points for American
histories, tales of pre-Columbian expeditions to the shores of the
New World lived a life of their own, sketchy but durable. With a
concern to establish the continuity of the American experience
with precision, Belknap examined what was known about the voyages of Eric the Red, Madoc the Welsh Prince, and Zeno in his
Biographies of the Early Discoverers of America (1798) and discount-
ed claims that Martin Behaim had discovered America before the
time of Columbus. Despite the pseudo-research that has at times
been devoted to these and other adventurers, the impulse to adopt
them as examples of a questing spirit has attracted writers as diverse
as William Carlos Williams and Samuel Eliot Morison.[11] So
enduring is our fascination with the idea of early visitors that it can
yield a knowing humor: a contemporary example furnishes Garrison Keillor's Lake Woebegon in Minnesota with the statue of the
Unknown Norwegian, complete with a runestone "which proves
that Viking explorers were here in 1381" and that eight of them
stopped for coffee "& a short nap."[12]

To a reader unschooled in alternative accounts of discovery, the
most surprising may be that given by Robert James Belford in his
*History of the United States, in Chronological Order, from A.D. 432 to
the Present Time* (1886). Not only does Belford begin with a year
that is strikingly unfamiliar in American history; he departs from a
European matrix and turns to Charles G. Leland's *Fusang; or, the
Discovery of America by Chinese Buddhist Priests in the Fifth Century*
(1875) for an account of the narrative of the Buddhist monk Hoei-
shin, which tells of a journey to a land of desert and cactus. (Predictably, but disappointingly after his unique beginning, Belford
leaps more than a thousand years to a conventional list of dates in
American history.) The work of dedicated offbeat researchers, one
might note, has added detail if not greater acceptance to the story
of Fusang. In *Pale Ink* (1972), for example, Henriette Mertz proposes the idea of "two Chinese expeditions to America—one in the

fifth century A.D. and the other in the twenty-third century B.C."

Mertz tentatively locates certain geographical features of Hoei-shin's narrative in the American Southwest, among them the Black Canyon of the Gunnison in Colorado and Palm Springs in California. More specifically, she suggests that Hoei-shin's "Sea of Varnish" might well be the La Brea Tar Pits in Los Angeles. Noting Mertz's efforts, Frederick Turner in *Beyond Geography* (1980) remarks that her study "explores the probability that the Chinese made regular visits to the Americas beginning about 2250 B.C."[13]

It was also possible, of course, to appropriate much earlier dates if they carried biblical sanction. Noah Webster's *History of the United States* (1832), one of the many accounts of the nation designed for school children, includes the story of our ancestors *from the Dispersion at Babel, to their Migration to America*. Both Thomas Prince and Samuel Whelpley move to the ultimate beginning for their histories—Prince in his ambitious *Chronological History of New-England . . . from the Creation* (1736), Whelpley in *A Compend of History, from the Earliest Times* (1808). As remote as these studies might seem from American beginnings, their manner of connecting Genesis to the story of colonial development combines assumptions of accessibility and continuity found in early national histories.

Prince informs us that he has adopted the model of historical presentation offered by James Ussher's *Annales* from the seventeenth century; by counting the ages of the patriarchs in the Old Testament, Ussher had ascertained that the world was created in the year 4004 B. C. Behind Ussher, of course, stands the example of medieval tomes, such as Richard of St. Victor's *Liber Exceptionum* (c. 1150), which cover a variety of subjects and trace the history of the world from its creation. Unlike Trumbull, Whelpley, or David Ramsey in his *History of South-Carolina* (1809), Prince has no United States to appear triumphantly at the end of his chronology, which comes only to the year 1633. By drawing on his personal collection of manuscripts and his knowledge of the Bible, however, he is able to argue that history has been moving toward New England as its ultimate achievement. Deeply influenced by the Puritan heritage he knew so well, Prince mistrusts "the specious Form" of narrative history because of its tendency to "raise the Imagination and Affections of the Reader" by means of rhetorical ornament. Accordingly, as he explains in his dedicatory letter to Governor Jonathan Belcher of Massachusetts, he has not only "taken the

greatest Pains to search and find" material for his historical work
but to present it in the form of "a *closer* and more naked *Register*,
comprizing only *Facts* in a *Chronological Epitome*, to enlighten the
Understanding."[14]

In a more secular time Prince might have mentioned the ratio-
nale for chronologies found in the editor's Preface to Belford's
History of the United States. One "unique merit" of Belford's compilation, the Editor notes, "is that it will never become antiquat-
ed." For dates, once known, are set in time, "fixed forever"; they
cannot be altered because of fashions in "historical criticism."
Thus, one need only to make additions to such works to keep
them current.[15] But Prince has a deep conviction about beginnings and the *direction* of history that keeps his detailed lists of
dates and events from being advertised as practical and open-
ended. The fundamental conception of his work implies a story of
success; if it comes initially from his assumption that New England marks the crowning achievement of history, it takes specific
shape from his sense of audience. Prince's regard for his readers is
strong, a functioning part of his scholarship: aware that many persons might like to learn how old the world was when "*This Part* of
the Earth came to be known to the *Other*," he provides a "Line of
Time" marked with "the Principal Persons, Events and Transactions, which had been running on from the *Creation* to the *Settlement of this Country*" (1:1). The Line of Time reaches back to
"YW 1 b" in Prince's initial list of dates—Year of the World 1,
beginning. In that year (near the end of the first week) the act of
creation concluded with Adam: the entry reads, "1m, 6d, Adam
CREATED." Prince tallies the years of the Biblical patriarchs
from Adam to the death of Moses and arrives at a total of "nearly
2553 compleat years." As he sees it, three great periods (each of
which features an authentic moment of beginning) make up the
history of the world:

1. From creation to the birth of Christ.
2. From the birth of Christ to the discovery of the New World.
3. From that point to the discovery of New England.

Also of great significance as a demarcating event is the Flood. In a
statement that might be considered sportive were it not for the

unremitting seriousness of his book, Prince says that although "*the Year of the World* 1656, is generally reckon'd to be the year of NOAH'S FLOOD," a careful arithmetic "unavoidably" brings "the *Beginning* of the FLOOD to the *Beginning* of the Year of the World 1657" (1:iii–iv).

With its insistence on a Line of Time running from the creation of Adam to the founding of New England and its emphasis on moments such as the Flood, the birth of Christ, and the discovery of America that divide history into monumental before-and-after segments, Prince's *Chronological History* anticipates the basic moves of later American histories and the confidence that one can fix a beginning with precision. Prince devotes the bulk of his study to the "most material Transactions and Occurrences" in New England, including such "REMARKABLE PROVIDENCES" as comets, eclipses, earthquakes, tempests, inundations, droughts, scarcities, and "epidemical Sicknesses." His plan is to list them "in the Order of Time wherein they happened, from the *Discovery by Capt. Gosnold in 1602, to the arrival of Governor Belcher in 1730*," a point that Prince's *History* never reached (1:iii). In doing so, he demonstrates the accessibility of beginnings by recording a number of "firsts"— among them the first execution in Plymouth Colony (the information taken from Bradford's *History of Plymouth Plantation*), the convening of the first General Court in Massachusetts, and "The *first* Recorded as Baptized in *Boston Church*"—"viz. *Joy* & *Recompence*, Daughters of Brother *John Milles*; and *Pitie*, Daughter of our Brother William Baulstone." He tells us, too, of the death of Isaac Johnson on Thursday, September 30, 1630, at "About 2 in the Morning" and adds details on Johnson's role in founding Boston that have been given to him personally by "the late chief Justice Samuel Sewall, Esq":

> Mr. Johnson was the principal Cause of settling the Town of *Boston*, and so of its becoming the *Metropolis*, and had removed hither; had chose for his Lot *the great Square* lying between *Cornhill* on the SE [and Tremont Street] . . . and on his Death-Bed desiring to be buried at the Upper End of his *Lot*, in Faith, of his rising in it, He was accordingly Buried there; which gave Occasion for the *first Burying Place* of this Town to be laid out round about his Grave.   (2:5,2)

Firsts were to become a kind of American hobby, beginnings in domesticated guise. In *The New Century Home Book* (1900), Frank A. DePuy lists hundreds of firsts in a chapter entitled "Beginnings of Things": he informs us that "air pumps were first made in 1650," that "silver dimes were first coined in 1796," and that "the first camp meeting was held near Russellville, Ky., in 1799."[16] More prominent is the concern for firsts articulated by Mark Twain and Nathaniel Hawthorne. In *The Innocents Abroad* (1869) Twain laments the antiquity of Rome, the visible presence of history piled on history, so that there is nothing for him to "discover," nothing to see or touch that others have not seen or touched before him. He prefers the opportunity of doing something "before *anybody* else": "To find a new planet, to invent a new hinge, to find a way to make the lightnings carry your messages. To be the *first*—that is the idea." Among Twain's heroes is Christopher Columbus, who "swung his hat above a fabled sea and gazed abroad upon an unknown world."[17] Out of profound respect for a history that offered access to *firsts*, Hawthorne used them as shaping points of departure that yield the tale: the showman in "Main-street" (1849) not only identifies the first settler of Salem but structures his panorama around the life of the first "town-born" child. And more than a century after Thomas Prince wrote of Isaac Johnson's death, Hawthorne made use of this same detail to establish the matrix of *The Scarlet Letter* (1850); near the outset of chapter I he refers to "the first prison-house, somewhere in the vicinity of Corn-hill," and to "the first burial ground, on Isaac Johnson's lot, and round about his grave, which subsequently became the nucleus of all the congregated sepulchres in the old church-yard of King's Chapel."[18] For Prince, early New England history gives importance to the rituals of christening and burial. For Hawthorne, visions of a new society "invariably" take account of death and evil. For Mark Twain, the New World is the antidote to the miasma of Roman history. And for Frank A. DePuy, the commencement of a new century is an appropriate time to recall how a variety of "things" began. As different as these writers are in perspective and purpose, all prize *firsts*.

Like Jeremy Belknap, Samuel Whelpley is concerned, in his words, "to fix" a beginning in his *Compend of History*. Like Prince he will trace "the great line of history" from creation to the present. The result is a series of beginning events that provide some organization for an otherwise baggy compendium. Finding "no evidence of a higher authority," Whelpley takes as his ultimate beginning the Mosaic account of "the creation of the world, and the origin of the human race." Although he does not calculate the precise date of the Flood, he does note its importance as a calamity that wiped out the known world and provided the occasion for a new start.[19] After describing the geography of North and South America, he explains that the new world discovered by Columbus "opened an inviting prospect to myriads in Europe," thus casting the idea of beginning into the form of opportunity, something inhering in the future. Finally, he defines the signing of the Declaration of Independence as a beginning both significant and personal: "A solemn instrument was drawn up, which declared, in strong but temperate language, the independence and sovereignty of the United States, and was published on the fourth day of July, 1776—a day ever memorable to the people of this happy country."[20] At times ponderous, at times pretentious, Whelpley's *Compend* nonetheless validates beginnings that had acquired privileged status by the first decade of the nineteenth century.

Despite the advantages consciously enjoyed by such historians as Belknap, Burk, and Ramsey, there were practical difficulties in writing adequate accounts of former colonies or of the new nation. Research, as always, depended on the availability of materials.[21] And not only were important public documents widely scattered; many of the letters and papers in private hands were not readily available. In his preface to *The History of New-Hampshire*, Belknap acknowledges his debt to public officials and "private gentlemen" for giving him access to original documents—letters, records, and personal papers. Thomas Prince comes in for special tribute: Belknap praises the generosity of the "indefatigable" pastor of the Old South Church in Boston, whose valuable library he used frequently "before the commencement" of the Revolutionary War.[22] Benjamin Trumbull describes his research into the history of Connecticut in a similar way, down to the detail of a journey to Boston to consult the "collection of the Reverend Mr. Prince," during which he "minuted every thing" pertaining to his subject.[23]

Historians were also concerned for the safety of materials that contributed to the story of colonial development. In 1809 David Ramsey warned that much early information about South Carolina was "already lost, and more is fast hastening to oblivion," recoverable only by means of traditional stories that grow fuzzy and imprecise.[24] The loss of documents by fire and the carelessness of persons who allowed original papers to be discarded as devoid of value led Belknap to call for a public repository for the safekeeping of records. Belknap's most eloquent complaint was levied against the British troops for destroying much of Prince's "noble collection of manuscripts" in 1775, an attack on what he saw as one of the sources of American history. It was, he said, an "irretrievable loss. Had we suffered it by the hands of Saracens, the grief would have been less poignant!"[25]

Although histories of individual colonies take dates of first settlement as logical (and approachable) beginnings, most employ a kind of textual pre-beginning, a perfunctory mention of Columbus or of John and Sebastian Cabot serving to introduce the idea of a new world and therefore a new colony. Writers who could not ignore the earliest explorers could subordinate them to matters that gave historical narrative an easy continuity of substance and spirit. Thomas Hutchinson's history of Massachusetts-Bay (1764), for example, moves directly to what Hutchinson sees as a suitable opening by alluding to beginnings he will not discuss: "The discovery of America by Columbus and of the northern continent by the Cabots, in the 15th century, and the several voyages of English and French, in the 16th, I pass over, and begin with the voyage made by Bartholomew Gosnold, an Englishman, in the year 1602, to that part of North America since called New-England." Belknap's *History of New-Hampshire* goes even farther: after pointing out the precision with which one can fix the beginning of American history, Belknap fastens immediately upon his subject with a brief word about the "voyager" John Smith and with no mention at all of Columbus, the Cabots, and Gosnold. More typically, Trumbull notes the discovery of the "western isles" and the "great continent of North America," then moves quickly to a consideration of the first planters of Connecticut. Similarly, the first sentence of Ramsey's *History of South-Carolina* tells us that "Columbus, by the discovery of America, introduced the old world to an acquaintance with the new."[26] A bare mention of the fact seems sufficient: in the same paragraph Ramsey describes the settlement at Port Royal in 1670, the beginning announced in his subtitle.

John Daly Burk likewise takes note of Columbus before he presents (in chapter 2) his account of the first settlers of Virginia.

Because it clarifies the problem historians of colonies had in dealing with Columbus, Burk's strategy for presenting a beginning is worth noting. At the outset he speculates at some length on the universal desire to know one's "origins" and to believe them "illustrious, or at least respectable." Whereas some people trace their ancestry to noble blood and others to deities, however, Americans take an "honester" pride in the courage of founders who are known figures of history. After a review of navigation in the ancient world, Burk traces the course of exploration in the fifteenth century and comes to 1492, the year in which "mankind were astonished by the discovery of a new world."[27] His speculation on the need for "origins" has brought him to a moment of beginning vast in implication for Western and world history. But Burk does not want to focus on the discoverer of the New World any more than Hutchinson, Trumbull, or Ramsey do, for the beginning he has reached falls outside the range of the story he proposes to tell. Because the figure of Columbus is necessary to a history in which it seems to have no part, the discovery of America functions less as a prelude to Burk's narrative than as a remote condition of its telling. The early settlers of Virginia and not the figure of Christopher Columbus (an Italian sponsored by the Spanish throne) embody the proper beginning for the history of what was now a state. Burk's assumption that "A correct History of Virginia, would be the history of North America itself," conflates colony and continent and thereby heightens the role of the "founders" he praises.[28]

As such historians as Daniel Boorstin, George H. Callcott, and David W. Noble have demonstrated, the American Revolution gave an impetus to the writing of national histories. The advantages were those of solidarity. The problems were those of perspective— or, to put the matter in another way, those of the historical imagination. For, in the words of the Austrian commentator Francis J. Grund, "America enjoyed the *political* existence of a nation before it had an *historical* one by geniture."[29] Gradually, and not without awkwardness, the effort to envision the country as a whole came to stress issues and themes common to all states. As part of this process, Christopher Columbus acquired privileged status as one who embodied a beginning. Some years after their studies of individual colonies, Benjamin Trumbull and David Ramsey wrote histories of the United States. Trumbull's title defines the scope of his study explicitly: *A General History of the United States of America*

(1810). And his subtitle—*Sketches of the Divine Agency, in their Settlement, Growth, and Protection*—characterizes the perspective that informs his narrative. Much more insistently than in his history of Connecticut, Trumbull adopts a traditional New England point of view and credits a beneficent Providence for the discovery and settlement of the New World. His thesis transcends such matters as nationalities and gaps in chronology and makes the voyages of Columbus and of John and Sebastian Cabot part of a divine and unassailably coherent plan for the new nation.

More secular in outlook, Ramsey's *History of the United States* (1816) credits Columbus with the momentous discovery of a new world, then adds a substantial footnote, virtually a synoptic essay, on the Admiral's life. Covering almost six pages, it provides an intelligent account of the four voyages, mentions the views of the humanist Peter Martyr, and even relates the story of Columbus standing an egg on end to support his claim of originality. Ramsey, in other words, gives us a great deal of information about Columbus (none of which appears in his history of South Carolina), but relegates his account to a footnote. Having acknowledged discoveries that amount to a pre-beginning for the United States and having shown a sensitive understanding of Columbus, he moves quickly to the Cabots in his main text and then to the "first permanent settlement on the coast of Virginia" in 1607. He comes, in other words, to a specific date and a localized subject that function (in this work) as the authentic beginning of American history. Happily, the means of nationalizing the specific occasion are at hand in the form of a conventional metaphor: the first settlers at Jamestown, Ramsey writes, "were the germ of the United States."[30]

Ramsey thus distinguishes two stages in the beginning of American history—the discovery of the New World and of North America (European events adapted to the story of the United States), then the important first settlement of Virginia. Both contribute to his narrative. Trumbull singles out the same stages as starting points and presents them as instances of the divine plan, part of a series of singular providences that brought the nation into existence.

As different as they are in method and purpose, Abiel Holmes's *American Annals* (1805) and George Bancroft's *History of the United States* reflect the developing consensus of how national histories might shape the story of the country. At the outset Holmes demarcates the ground he will cover: "A NEW WORLD has been discovered, which has been receiving inhabitants from the old, more than three hundred years." After giving the reader a cursory account of the voyages of Christopher Columbus, he proceeds to the present time, coming to "The United States of America" in part 3 of his *Annals* and recognizing the year 1776 as a beginning in its own right. "The Declaration of Independence," Holmes writes, "begins a new era in the history of America."[31] He does not pause to explore the assumptions, consequences, or philosophical background of the Declaration. For although the *Annals* is not a simple list of dates, not a strict chronology, its form flattens out the past, converting it to a record of events none of which receives extended treatment. Holmes's unit is the sentence; strategies of subordination and emphasis are excluded by a style that fastens on discrete facts. The first voyage of Columbus and the signing of the Declaration of Independence receive hardly more attention than the snowstorm in Georgia in 1800. Yet Holmes never courts the stance of coldness and remoteness Hayden White attributes to the annalists of seventeenth-century Europe.[32] The effect of his compilation is to domesticate American history, making local as well as national details available to readers and later historians. Thomas Jefferson admired the *Annals* for its accuracy and usefulness and sent Holmes material for a second edition, which appeared in 1829.

More detailed and more sophisticated than any of the narratives discussed in this survey, George Bancroft's *History of the United States, from the Discovery of the American Continent* employs what had become standard points of departure for the nation's history and gives Columbus a new position of importance. Defining a valid beginning for America remains essential: Bancroft discounts tales of the colonization of America by Northmen because they rest on narratives that are "mythological in form and obscure in meaning, ancient yet not contemporary." He develops a way of seeing the exploits of Columbus as both ancient *and* contemporary—and certainly not obscure in meaning. To Columbus, he writes, belongs "the individual glory" of discovering the New World. For the voyages of Columbus, "the most memorable enterprise in the history of the world, formed between Europe and America the communication which will never cease." Like Ramsey, Bancroft believes that the early settlements contain "the germ" of our institutions: because "the spirit of the colonies demanded freedom from the beginning," he writes, the "maturity of the nation is but a continuation" of its colonial youth.[33] Although his intellectual makeup differs markedly from that of Benjamin Trumbull, Bancroft (as Russel B. Nye makes clear) likewise sees history as the manifestation of a divine plan that will lead mankind to a future informed by truth, beauty, and justice.[34] The American Revolution was a magnificent part of this development and thus the beginning of a momentous era.

When the role of historian was converted to burlesque by Washington Irving, it retained all of its features—delightfully highlighted by parodic gesture. Indeed the very title of *A History of New-York, from the Beginning of the World to the End of the Dutch Dynasty* (1809) knowingly echoes the American tendency to tell the world over again that I shall examine in chapter 4. Out of a conviction that the early history of New York is "slipping from our grasp, trembling on the brink of narrative old age," Irving's persona, Diedrich Knickerbocker, undertakes his solemn and hilarious work, gathering the fragments still available, and—like his "revered prototype Herodotus"—pursuing "the chain of history" by invoking tradition when written records cannot be found.[35] The early history of most cities can no longer be recovered, Knickerbocker muses; "their origin, their foundation," is forever lost, buried beneath "the rubbish of years." New York would have met a similar fate, he claims, his language warming with a sense of mission, "if I had not snatched it from obscurity in the very nick of time, at the moment that those matters herein recorded were about entering into the wide-spread insatiable maw of oblivion—if I had not dragged them out, as it were, by the very locks, just as the monster's adamantine fangs were closing upon them forever" (27).

Knickerbocker's irreverence, as Jeffrey Rubin-Dorsky observes, is an essential part of the comic mode in the *History of New-York*.[36] In the passage just cited, the escalating pace of metaphor is likewise suggestive of gothic suspense and not far from the visual effects of later melodrama—the beautiful young scientist, eyes glazed with terror, sliding helplessly toward the gaping jaws of the monster, the timorous hero somehow managing a frenzied rescue so that her life and the secrets of Galaxy ZT4(O) will not be lost forever. An altered plan for Irving's *History* had set the conditions for such delightful excursions of style. As Irving remarked in the Author's Revised Edition of the work, his first idea had been to parody

Samuel Lathop Mitchill's *Pictures of New York* (1807), a statistical assessment of the resources of New York city already mentioned satirically in *Salmagundi* (1807–8). His later decision to burlesque the pretensions of some contemporary American histories opened up the possibilities of his subject in significant ways, allowing him (especially in book 1 of the *History*) to mock narrative conventions with the full force of his imagination. What William L. Hedges calls "the key to Irving's achievement" is the fully developed voice of Diedrich Knickerbocker, a curious blend of Sterne and Fielding endowed with impregnable seriousness and determined to investigate every aspect of the subject.[37]

Willing to overlook nothing in getting his history properly told, Knickerbocker's strategy is to relate Genesis, the Flood, and the discovery of the New World to the city of New York—something he does by means of a parade of pedantry and a relentless deadpan logic. After claiming that he will reclaim the vanishing past of the city, Knickerbocker turns to what seem remote periods of time. Book 1 of *A History of New-York* (overlooked by most readers in favor of more anthologized satirical portraits) parodies Thomas Prince's *Chronological History* in several ways, principally by relating cosmogony to the Dutch colony of which Knickerbocker is writing. The five chapters contain "DIVERS INGENIOUS THEORIES AND PHILOSOPHIC SPECULATIONS, CONCERNING THE CREATION AND POPULATION OF THE WORLD, AS CONNECTED WITH THE HISTORY OF NEW-YORK." Ever patient in his explanations, Knickerbocker assures the reader that it is "absolutely essential" to consider all such matters carefully, because "if this world had not been formed, it is more than probable, that this renowned island on which is situated the city of New-York, would never have had an existence" (36).

In his third chapter Knickerbocker adapts to his purposes the idea of a "line of time"—important to the histories of Prince, Whelpley, and others—by insisting on the "latent chain of causation" linking Noah to the city of New York. Irving does not make the vaulting claim of his friend James Kirke Paulding, who in *Letters from the South* (1817) argues that America was "the true hive from whence the earth was peopled" after the Flood, and that Noah was therefore an American.[38] His Diedrich Knickerbocker approaches the subject of historical cause and effect deliberately, in the role of meditative historian, confessing his astonishment that great events depend upon "obscure contingencies," that affairs "the most distant, and to the common observer unconnected, are inevitably consequent the one to the other." Many of his readers, Knickerbocker concedes, will wonder what connection Noah has with New York, "and many will stare" when told that the entire history of this quarter of the globe has taken its course from the fact that the patriarch had but three sons. His explanation follows: upon "becoming sole surviving heir and proprietor of the earth, in fee simple, after the deluge," Noah divided his territory among his children, giving Asia to Shem, Africa to Ham, and Europe to Japhet. A fourth son "would doubtless have inherited America," which would have been "dragged forth from its obscurity on the occasion," thus sparing historians and philosophers much conjecture concerning the discovery of this country. But Noah, "having provided for his three sons, looked in all probability upon our country as mere wild unsettled land, and said nothing about it; and to this unpardonable taciturnity of the patriarch may we ascribe the misfortune, that America did not come into the world as early as the other quarters of the globe" (46–47).

Once arrived at the subject of the New World, Knickerbocker bemoans the claims and counterclaims with which "unhappy historians overload themselves" in their endeavors to champion the true discoverer. He has no wish to investigate suppositions about Phoenicians, Carthaginians, Chinese, Norwegians, or "Behem [Martin Behaim] the German navigator." With characteristic disdain, he likewise refuses to discuss "the more modern claims of the Welsh, founded on the voyage of Prince Madoc in the eleventh century, who never having returned, it has since been wisely concluded that he must have gone to America, and that for a plain reason—if he did not go there, where else could he have gone?—a question which most Socratically shuts out all further dispute" (49–50). Irving is at his comic best in the first Book of the Knickerbocker *History*. His humor demonstrates a surprising knowledge of popular accounts of discovery (of Hakluyt's tale of Madoc, for example) even as it engages current debate. Only after searching out the relation of Creation, the Flood, and the discovery of America, three consensus beginnings revalidated by burlesque, does Irving turn to his account of the Dutch colony of New York.

Image and Name: Columbus and Vespucci   While historians
gradually domesticated 1492 as the date of a national beginning,
orators and poets began to fashion an image of Columbus according to American specifications. Among the most notable expressions of praise that clustered in these formative years were the ceremonies at the first Columbus Day festivities in Boston in 1792,
Philip Freneau's "The Pictures of Columbus, the Genoese" (1788),
and Joel Barlow's *The Columbiad* (1807)—initially written as *The
Vision of Columbus* in 1787. Alive with the buzz of implication in
their culture, functioning parts of what Claude Lévi-Strauss calls a
"hot" or "dense" period of history, these statements cast the navigator into durable symbols of progress and rebirth.[39]

On the tricentennial of his landing at San Salvador, the Admiral for the first time received official public attention. In New York
(on October 12), the Tammany Society, or Columbian Order,
sponsored a celebration that featured an oration on Columbus by
John Barent Johnson: the spirit of the courageous navigator, Johnson explained, lived on in the New World he had discovered. In
Boston (on October 23), the newly formed Massachusetts Historical Society conducted elaborate festivities praising both Columbus and Columbia, one a symbol of expansive destiny, the other of
nurturing and regeneration. Jeremy Belknap (founder of the society) began the ceremonies by characterizing the voyage of 1492 as
"a splendid instance of that remarkable prediction of the prophet
Daniel, chap. xii, ver 4. '*Many shall run to and fro and knowledge
shall be increased.*'" Then, in an ode written for the occasion, a choir
sang of the advent of freedom in the Western World. According to
Belknap, Columbus discovered America and "opened to the Europeans a new world." According to the ode, Columbus uncovered a
"Western World" that had been formed at creation and hidden
"from European eyes" during centuries of discord. "Fair Columbia
lay conceal'd" until, at the appointed moment, "Her friendly arms"
reached out to embrace those thirsting for "Freedom" and "pure
religion." Whereas Belknap praises a skillful and daring Columbus
who kindled "the spirit of enterprise and commerce" (including
the "detestable" practice of slavery), the ode attends to an
unspoiled Columbia ready to welcome "her adopted children."[40]
Whereas Belknap commends a steadfast discoverer, the ode
attends joyfully to the place discovered. And their complementary
accents exemplify the dual manner in which the events of 1492

came to be structured into the American experience: while Columbia could nourish and harbor, Columbus could serve as a symbol of ongoing expansion.

Philip Freneau's "The Pictures of Columbus" expresses a similar view of the navigator in a series of dramatic portraits. Freneau's Columbus is a visionary with practical resolve who sails on a voyage of discovery because he sees "blunders" on the maps, an arrangement of land he cannot accept. As he studies his charts (in the first portrait), Columbus is troubled with the "disproportion" sketched out before him. "Nature," he thinks, would not have positioned all the land in "one poor corner" of the world; there must be land elsewhere to balance "Asia's vast extent." Perhaps, he continues with prophetic instinct, in unknown "regions dwell / Forms wrought like man, and lov'd as well." Putting aside the existing maps, he draws "a new world" far to the west and wonders if God who hung this globe

> In the clear void, and governs all,
> On those dread scenes, remote from view,
> Has trac'd his great idea too.

Tired, finally, of speculation, Columbus the designer of "a new world" becomes Columbus the explorer, who declares "O'er real seas I mean to sail." If fortune will assist him in his "grand design," he thinks with a concluding surge of hope (and a curious possessiveness), "Worlds yet unthought of shall be mine."[41]

Rational dreamer that he is, Freneau's Columbus rejects the "disproportion" of European maps by invoking (for his own purposes) a medieval conception that God would have put more land than water on the globe because land was destined for the creation of human souls. Belknap secularizes the same idea both in his Columbus Day address and in his *Biographies of the Early Discoverers of America* (1798): convinced that the surface of the globe contained more land than water and aware of enlightened opinion in Europe, Columbus reasoned from the "immense quantity of land" known to be in the East the idea of a necessary "counterpoise in the west."[42] In one form or another such an explanation became the standard way of appreciating the Admiral's bold powers of mind. As early as 1736 Thomas Prince converted the westward lands to a continent in beginning the significant final section of his *Chronological History*:

> The united Continents of Asia, Africa, and Europe, have been the only Stage of History, from the CREATION to the Y C 1492. We are now to turn our Eyes to the West, and see a NEW WORLD appearing in the Atlantick Ocean to the great surprize and entertainment of the other. CHRISTO-PHER COLUMBUS or Colonus, a Genoese is the 1st Discoverer. Being a Skilful Geographer and Navigator, and of a very curious Mind, He becomes possess'd, with a strong Perswasion, that in order to Ballance the Terraqueous Globe & Proportion the Seas and Lands to each other, there must needs be form'd a mighty Continent on the other Side, which Boldness, Art and Resolution would soon discover.[43]

In his influential *History of America* (1777), the Scotsman William Robertson supplies even more detail about the judicious manner in which Columbus developed his plan: after considering "long and seriously every circumstance suggested by his superior knowledge in the theory as well as practice of navigation" and also assessing the "observations" of modern pilots as well as the "conjectures" of ancient writers, Columbus concluded that "by sailing directly towards the West, across the Atlantic ocean, new countries, which probably formed a part of the great continent of India, must infallibly be discovered." Moreover, because of "the wisdom and beneficence of the Author of Nature," it seemed likely that "the continent on this side of the globe was balanced by a proportional quantity of land in the other hemisphere."[44]

Whether it was simplified for schoolroom texts or adapted for poetic tribute, such a conception proved an effective way of appropriating ideas that could dramatize the beginning of new-world history. In Charles A. Goodrich's *Child's History of the United States* (1827), for example, chapters become "Lessons" designed for "a First Book of History for Schools." Precisely because it is elementary, unambiguous, and intended to instruct children about the "Discovery of America by Columbus," the initial lesson in this little volume assumes importance as culturally approved exemplum. After a brief recital of dates and events, Goodrich tells a story about the first voyage of Columbus. Prior to 1492, he writes, people did not know there was "any such land as America." How, then, did Columbus know? "He did *not* know. But he thought there must be, to balance the land in the Eastern continent." Although learned men ignored him, Columbus finally sailed westward, returned to Spain with his crew, and "told of the *new world* which they had dis- covered."[45]

American sketches of Columbus thus use the idea of counter-poise to minimize (and finally ignore) the intent of the original voyage. Subordinating the Admiral's desire to reach the Indies, Belknap identifies a strain of individualism that makes the Admiral an American by temperament. Goodrich (synoptically) and Freneau (in romantic detail) distribute their emphasis differently: their explorer is a man who set out in search of unknown lands he thought were there and found the New World. Finally, from Isaac Taylor in England comes a popular children's sketch of a navigator who sailed intentionally for the New World. All doubt of Columbus' goal is removed in *Scenes in America, for the Amusement and Instruction of Little Tarry-at-Home Travellers* (1821), which describes the manifold genius of the explorer and adds (with a curious sense of geography) that he "sailed five weeks" until he was "above 5000 miles distant from home." At last, Taylor concludes, "the object of all his hopes, labours, and sufferings" came into view: "On the morning of October 12 he distinctly saw stretched before him, the new world, after which his imagination had so long panted."[46] As Taylor's biographical sketch shows, the impulse to make Columbus both an intrepid and a romantic hero was not limited to the United States. But a nation that already thrived on a sense of beginning welcomed the tardy arrival of a Beginner who had conceived and set out to find their New World.

As dedicated to the subject as we know him to have been, Joel Barlow was not the first to write an epic about Columbus and a New World. *The Columbiad* (along with the earlier *Vision of Columbus*) was preceded by *La Colombiade, ou, la Foi Portée au Nouveau Monde*, written in 1756 by Marie-Anne DuBoccage. Each of these two poems shapes the figure of Columbus to its own purposes; each presents a vision of the future—bright with Renaissance (and subsequent) glory for France, stubbornly millennial for the new United States of America. Yet the epics differ radically in their enabling assumptions: whereas DuBoccage casts Columbus in the role of Crusader, Barlow portrays him as one whose "virtuous steps" were "Pursued by avarice and defiled by blood"; whereas DuBoccage sees Columbus's discovery as an adventure that energized an ongoing history, Barlow sees it as an event that fostered a national beginning.[47]

Despite its subtitle and a series of adventures that make Columbus seem like Indiana Jones approaching the Temple of Doom (in couplets), *La Colombiade* presents the discovery of America as a European event. The prophetic "Vision de Colomb" that comes in canto 9 reveals to the protagonist the vast consequences of his enterprise: at this point a world of Amazons, volcanoes, and demons gives way to a universe of high culture as DuBoccage lavishes attention on the coming age in Europe, particularly in France. To give specificity to her vision, the poet goes on a naming binge not unlike that of Barlow when he hails notable Americans. She mentions (among a host of others) Magellan, Francis I, Galileo, and (with exquisite chauvinism) Shakespeare—"qui est regardé," one reads in a note, "comme le Corneille des Anglois."[48] In addition to the "immortal" Voltaire, the French, Columbus learns, will boast a rival of Euripides (Racine), an Aristophanes (Molière), a Pindar (Rousseau), several Euclids, and sundry other geniuses. What we have in *La Colombiade* is a tribute to Old World consequences of New World discovery, with an unabashed gallic bias directing the accents of DuBoccage's poetic voice.

Whereas DuBoccage's *Columbiade* concludes triumphantly, Barlow's poem begins at a tragic end, with Columbus bemoaning treachery and "a world explored in vain" (1:97). As one who has already performed his deeds, who has been given "Chains for a crown, a prison for a world" (1:14), Columbus stands in the role of observer of the vision granted by Hesper, more qualified to be a reader of the American epic (as Roy Harvey Pearce suggests) than an actor in it.[49] But Barlow's Columbus is a decidedly active observer, curious, anxious to know more; to some extent Hesper's vision takes its loose, baggy shape because of his questions. In this poem, Europe has failed Columbus, who is (almost by that fact) absolved from crimes against the native population and reconstituted by the evolution of history. "The tribes he foster'd with paternal toil," Barlow writes at the outset, were "Snatcht from his hand, and slaughtered for their spoil," while "Slaves, kings, and adventurers, envious of his name / Enjoy'd his labors and purloined his fame" (1:9–12). By emphasizing the navigator's interest in histori- cal process, the poem proceeds to enlarge what Wayne Franklin calls "the plot" of Columbus's life to include an appreciation of the American Revolution and the early republic.[50]

The vision that Hesper parades before Columbus does not ignore Europe; such figures as Erasmus and Descartes come in for praise. But Barlow's political and geographical panoramas focus on America and carry with them imaginative and rhetorical habits characteristic of a nation that celebrated a sense of beginning as part of its identity. For one thing—naming: whereas DuBoccage writes out of, and about, a defined and *named* world, Barlow's "guardian Genius of the western continent" tells Columbus at the outset that this "happier hemisphere" was "Hesperia called, from my anterior claim; / But now Columbia, from thy patriarch name" (1:229–30). Hesper does use a number of North American place names. But the deep wonder of the continent lies in primal scenes that can be envisioned only by means of language that negates his- torical and mythical associations: to the eyes of an appreciative Columbus, Hesper evokes a vision in which

> . . . hills by hundreds rise without a name;
> Hills yet unsung, their mystic powers untold;
> Celestials there no sacred senates hold;
> No chain'd Prometheus feasts the vulture there,
> No cyclop forges thro their summits glare,
> To Phrygian Jove no victim smoke is curl'd,
> No ark high landing quits a deluged world.
>   (1:340–46)

Emory Elliott argues convincingly that Barlow's *Vision of Colum- bus* grew out of a resonant assessment of culture and self, while *The Columbiad*, produced after a lengthy separation from the United States during its formative years, embodies an effort both program- matic and anachronistic. Less confident in *The Columbiad* than he had been in *Vision*, caught between changing religious assumptions and Enlightenment attitudes, Barlow seems determined to assert "a collective national identity."[51] Yet these works, as Elliott reminds us, are two versions of the same poem. And in the final version of what

Cecilia Tichi terms a "worried-over" epic Barlow not only sharpens his emphasis on *firsts* and births and beginnings (the first peopling of America, "infant streams" developing into great rivers) but with studied determination salutes the advent of republican institutions in history—transforming Columbus into the aspirations of the world he discovered. After examining the text that Barlow used to convert *The Vision of Columbus* to *The Columbiad*, Tichi calls the poem "Barlow's great act of literary engineering."[52] It is an appropriate trope if only because Barlow made an epic originally embellished with a fawning dedication to King Louis XVI into a poem dedicated to Robert Fulton. And that, as one might surmise, signaled a commitment to some careful "engineering."

Commemorating an event in which Columbus played the principal role, Barlow's *Columbiad* thus focuses on consequences that exclude the protagonist from participation. The burden of the poem is to link event to consequences, to bring the protagonist to appreciate the distinctive merit of republican institutions and thereby become a kind of absentee hero because he made it all possible. At the end, interestingly, we do not see Columbus; rather, we hear Hesper telling him to complain no more "Of dangers braved and griefs endured in vain," of envy and "the frown of kings," but to "compose" his thoughts in the knowledge that he will be fulfilled by history (10:635–39). With this command (delivered with "a blissful smile") Columbus is subsumed by his vision, at once the occasion, the receptor, and the embodiment of Barlow's faith in the developing United States.

What was good for Christopher Columbus was bad for Amerigo Vespucci. The political and popular consensus that made Columbus's discovery of the New World in 1492 a privileged beginning had no use for the adventures of the rival from Florence. Charles A. Goodrich's *Child's History of the United States* is again useful in articulating the prevalent view with storybook clarity. In lesson 2, Goodrich takes his didactic narrative to the years after Columbus's famous voyage: "America now being discovered," he writes, "the news soon spread far and wide," and other men sailed in search of additional lands. Among them "was a man by the name of *A-mer-i-cus Ves-pu-cius*." He did not "discover much," Goodrich says bluntly. "But he told so *fine a story*, that America was called after him. It should have been called after Columbus."[53]

With this unwitting tribute to the power of narrative, Goodrich informs his young readers that "America" has been misnamed (by whom he does not say). His words express a long-standing attitude toward Vespucci that came to a head in the decades after the American Revolution. Almost a century prior to that event, Cotton Mather noted that "this vast Hemisphere" should "more justly . . . have receiv'd its *Name*" from Christopher Columbus than from Amerigo Vespucci.[54] But Mather's emphasis on a different kind of history in *Magnalia Christi Americana* made such a detail a minor concern. With feelings that ranged from disapproval to outrage, however, some later Americans blamed Vespucci for not telling the truth about his voyages. At bottom, and sometimes confusingly, the issue was over the name given to the New World, to the continent, and to the nation. Goodrich seems to be talking about the continent when he says that "America was called after" Vespucci, although the deliberate simplifications of his *Child's History* leave the matter ambiguous. David Ramsey is writing about the nation in his *History of the United States* when he tells us that Vespucci "robbed" Columbus "of the honour he so justly merited, of having the country called by his name." And Emerson shifts the context from the New World to the nation in *English Traits* (1856) when he devotes a few corrosive words to the career of St. George, concludes that the patron of England was an "imposter," then goes on to say:

Strange, that the New World should have no better luck,— that broad America must wear the name of a thief. Amerigo Vespucci, the pickledealer at Seville, who went out, in 1499, a subaltern with Hojeda, and whose highest naval rank was boatswain's mate in an expedition that never sailed, managed in this lying world to supplant Columbus, and baptize half the earth with his own dishonest name. Thus nobody can throw stones. We [the two nations] are equally badly off in our founders.[55]

In all such cases, the fact that the word *America* can designate both continent and nation creates an ambiguity for the writer—and for the reader.

In his *Biographies of the Early Discoverers*, Belknap rejected the claim that Vespucci had seen a continent before Columbus because "the evidence against the honesty of Amerigo is very convincing."

But Belknap accepted the naming of the New World as a fait accompli; because Vespucci "published the first book and chart" describing the new lands and "claimed the honor of first discovering the continent," the New World "has received from him the name of *America*."[56]

Samuel Whelpley was not so easily reconciled. His *Compend of History, from the Earliest Times* went through twelve editions from 1808 to 1870, carrying with it the most astonishing of all attacks on the name of the continent and a deep concern about the name of the nation. In his chapter on the United States, Whelpley includes a separate section entitled "Name." "The new world has been particularly unfortunate in all respects," he asserts, in "the matter of a name": it should "have been called *Columbia*—a name which yields to none in point of dignity, harmony, and convenience." Calling the new continent *America*, he continues, was "the greatest act of folly, caprice, cruelty, and injustice of the kind, that ever mankind were guilty of."[57] At one stroke it bestowed unmerited honor on Vespucci and deprived Columbus of deserved renown. Moreover, to adopt a name "which sounds but meanly in prose, and is intolerable in poetry, is an act of caprice and folly which can scarcely be thought of with any degree of patience." Happily, the word *Columbia* "will always reign in poetry, and in the pathetic and sublime of prose."

Whelpley focuses his initial complaint on the naming of the continent. When he considers the name of the nation, his argument takes on a note of bewilderment. He first contends that the nation should have a different name than the continent—not only to promote clarity but to establish a proper sense of national identity. Without benefit of transition, he then proceeds to the idea that the nation has no name at all since the words *United States* signify a collection of states and *of America* designate the continent of America. "Two favorable moments have passed," continues this historian (who, let us recall, had praised the signing of the Declaration of Independence as a beginning "ever memorable to the people of this happy country"), when "a name might have been given to the United States"—the first during the drafting of the Declaration, the second during the Constitutional Convention. Uncertain "when another time equally favorable will arrive," Whelpley hopes that it will be soon: for, as he says, "There are serious and urgent reasons why the United States should have a name."

So accustomed are we to thinking of "the United States," or "the United States of America," as a name that it is difficult to adopt the perspective of one who uses the same words with a totally different assumption about what they signify. To do so, however, is to see that for all his rhetorical excesses, Whelpley raises an issue of consider- able importance: for naming is a traditional feature of beginning, and a new nation in his view has existed for a generation without having been given a name. He is correct in saying that neither the Declaration of Independence nor the Constitution provides a name for the country. At a later time, Thomas Jefferson proposed to make ten states out of the land between the Ohio River and the Missis- sippi and to give them such names as Dolypotamia, Metropotamia, and Assenisippia. In the Declaration of Independence, however, Jefferson shows no intention of naming the country (perhaps it is just as well). The burden of the Declaration is to convert a group of united colonies to a group of united states—just as that of the Con- stitution is "to form a more perfect Union" among "the United States of America." Of our early national documents, only the Arti- cles of Confederation stipulates what might pass as a name for the country: article 1 states that "The Stile of this confederacy shall be 'The United States of America.'" In context, this is more a term of convenience than a name; and it is, of course, precisely the term to which Whelpley objects as inadequate.

How nations acquire names, Whelpley admits, is a matter both "intricate and obscure," probably the result of blind causes and the "energies of chaos." But one thing is clear: "No name was ever more unlucky, absurd, or unjust, than that of the new continent; nor is it ever to be hoped that the United States will ever obtain a name in a more rational way." Faint as it is, the only hope lies in the hands of "some illustrious *patriot*, who can brave the laughter of fools— the contempt of the wise—the arrows of the satyrist, and the deri- sion of the proud," and devise a name that will "force itself upon the world." In a footnote Whelpley offers his own suggestion in the form of a rhetorical question: "What reasonable objection could there be to calling this country FREDONIA? A name proposed by the greatest scholar in the United States—who *in Europe*, is con- sidered the luminary of this country."

Whelpley's anonymous tribute is to the same Samuel Latham Mitchill whose *Pictures of New York* Washington Irving once intended to parody in the Knickerbocker *History*. Obviously there was more to Mitchill than Irving acknowledged: a distinguished medical scientist who taught at Columbia and later became vice-president of the medical department at Rutgers College, Mitchill served as United States Senator from New York from 1804 to 1809. As a newly elected senator he proposed the name "Fredonia" for the nation, most notably in his Independence Day *Address to the Fredes, or People of the United States* (1804). In a note on the title page of his Address, Mitchill explains that "The modern and appropriate name of the people of the United States is FREDES or FREDONIANS, as the geographical name of their country is FREDON or FRE-DONIA, and their relations are expressed by the terms FRE-DONIAN or FREDISH." The penultimate stanza of the "Song" that was part of the celebration once again contrasted Old World and New—on this occasion mixing standard formulas with an up-to-date economic outlook:

> While war and misery attend
> The nations of the eastern climes;
> Here peace and happiness befriend
> The Fredes, most favoured people of the times.
> *Their* taxes and exactions oppress them hard and sore,
> While *yours* are small and easy, and likely to be lower.[58]

Although Mitchill's suggestion for an appropriate name for the nation did not find general support, twelve states have towns named Fredonia, Richard Emmons's epic poem celebrating the War of 1812 bore the title "The Fredoniad" (1827), and the Marx brothers film *Duck Soup* (1933) was set in a beleaguered country named (and spelled) Freedonia. Moreover, quite apart from Mitchill's effort, a concern to give the nation a suitable name has led a quixotic life of its own. Having decided that "America was discovered by Christovallo Colon," Washington Irving's meticulous Diedrich Knickerbocker announces that the "country should have been called Colonia." A member of the New York Historical Society proposed in the 1840s that the nation be called "America" and the continent "Columbia." And in 1846 Edgar Allan Poe asserted that "There should be no hesitation about" calling the country "Appalachia," an indigenous name that would point to a "magnificent" section of the land and "do honor to the Aborigines, whom, hitherto, we have at all points unmercifully despoiled, assassinated and dishonored."[59] Much later, in his history of American place names, George R. Stewart echoed the dissatisfaction of these writers and—surprisingly—their hope for a change: the manner in which the national name came to be accepted, Stewart believes, "was the worst misfortune in our whole naming-history." Like Whelpley before him, Stewart contends that "The United States of America" is both too long and too inaccurate to serve effectively as a name. Not only has it "consumed paper, ink, time, and energy. Its vagueness and inaccuracy have caused incalculable misunderstanding, and bad feeling." Taking a cue from the term applied to American soldiers in World War I and World War II, he suggests that an eventual "evolution of speech" might yield a substitute name, "possibly a derivation from the increasingly popular Yank."[60]

All things, of course, are possible. But some seem unlikely. One may as well indulge the wit of Garrison Keillor as contest seriously the name of the nation. As the citizens of Lake Woebegon realize sadly, Columbus simply "stumbled onto the land of heroic Vikings and proceeded to get the credit for it." Compounding the error, the place was named after another Italian, "who never saw the New World. . . . By rights, it should be called Erica, after Eric the Red. The United States of Erica. Erica the Beautiful."[61] Although no one has performed "Erica the Beautiful," patriotic song can have a powerful effect in validating the identity of a country. If the matter of a national name was not concluded by default in the final decades of the eighteenth century (and one logical alternative not effectively ruled out when New Granada became Grand Colombia in 1819), it was surely ratified by patriotic ritual when Samuel Francis Smith's "America" was sung at a Fourth of July celebration in Boston in 1831. On the birthday of the nation, Americans extolled the "sweet land of liberty" in which they lived. Fittingly, the words of the song did not (and do not) mention the name of the land.

Vespucci emerges from this brouhaha as a confidence man who invented a voyage to establish priority of discovery and then, somehow, gave the hemisphere his name. In whatever form, such charges stem from letters that were extremely popular in Europe and that brought the cartographer Martin Waldseemüller to put the name

"America" on the southern portion of his map of the New World in 1507. Along with the poet Martin Ringmann, Waldseemüller had been preparing a new edition of Ptolemy's *Cosmographiae Introductio* when he read Vespucci's accounts of four voyages to the New World (which he appended to his edition). After conventional descriptions of Europe, Africa, and Asia in chapter 9, Waldseemüller (or Ringmann, who had written a poem to honor Vespucci's discoveries) added the famous words:

> Now, these parts of the earth have been more extensively explored and a fourth part has been discovered by Amerigo Vespucci (as will be set forth in what follows). Inasmuch as both Europe and Asia received their names from women, I see no reason why any one should justly object to calling this part Amerige, i.e., the land of Amerigo, or America, after Amerigo, its discoverer, a man of great ability.[62]

Waldseemüller may have become aware that Vespucci's claims were not credited by experts; he omitted the name "America" from a second global map he issued in 1516. But the name stuck, perhaps for the linguistic reasons explored by Harold Jantz or the psychological reasons suggested by William G. Niederland.[63] When Mercator added it to the northern portion of his double cordiform map in 1535, he was both validating and extending the province of a name that had received general acceptance in Europe since it was given. Such a consensus, however, has never made Vespucci an American hero; throughout the history of the nation that ambiguously bears his name, he has suffered for his (or some other competitive Florentine's) elaborate fiction. As late as 1974, Samuel Eliot Morison referred to his "colossal" and "well-planned deception," and no Vespuccian parades or protests marked the quintennial festivities of 1992.[64]

Meanwhile, the image of a wise and stalwart Columbus acquired national authority in the first fifty years of the Republic. For many European painters and writers in the nineteenth century, as Hugh Honour observes, Columbus became "the archetypal man of genius," a figure solitary in his dreams, misjudged in his aspirations.[65] Although such writers as Irving, James Russell Lowell, and even Walt Whitman injected some of this romantic pathos into their work, Americans typically praised Columbus because of *what* he discovered: if one could say that Columbus discovered the New World, one could also say that he discovered America; and it was a short step to add that he hoped to do so. Yet, as we know, the Admiral never dreamed of, let alone "panted" for, a New World. Having shrunk his estimate of the size of the earth as represented on the Toscanelli map (with its own short measure of the earth's circumference) to make his voyage seem more feasible, Columbus sailed in 1492 with no conception of a continental land mass between Spain and India. Moreover, after frustrations and disappointments (and after the stress of leadership led him to claim in his third letter that he had been sailing uphill for a number of days), Columbus died with no realization of what lands he had reached. The enduring irony is that he is credited with having discovered, as Martin Waldseemüller put it, "Amerige, i. e., the land of Amerigo, or America." Of such anomalies are some beginnings made.

Orations and Anniversaries Once established, as recurrent Col-umbus Day festivities demonstrate, beginning dates could be commemorated. And with ready access to events closer in time and spirit than those of 1492, American orators seized on a variety of occasions as worthy of celebration. At a meeting of the New York Historical Society in 1809, Samuel Miller commemorated the bicentennial of Henry Hudson's discovery of New York in what had already become a typical manner. To contemplate any voyage of discovery, Miller reminds his audience, is to experience "high gratification" at the fulfillment of human aspirations. Moreover, proximity adds the zest of personal interest to philosophic appreciation. Important to all the world, Henry Hudson's discovery thus has particular interest "to AMERICANS" and vital meaning "to every citizen of our own STATE." For on this anniversary of "the DISCOVERY OF NEW-YORK" New Yorkers can experience emotions both "new" and "impressive" by saying specifically that a "great discovery" was made "on *this* day, or, on *this* spot."[66]

With its annual commemoration of the landing of the *Mayflower*, the New England Society likewise featured speakers who stressed proximity to and involvement with a significant and even unique beginning. George S. Hillard's three-generation jump back to the first Pilgrims was not the only way to show pride in the landing. In 1822 Philip Melancthon Whelpley recalled the drafting of the Mayflower Compact as "an event which has no parallel in the annals of the world. On that day a nation was born; on that day *the Pilgrims formed themselves into a perfect community,* social, civil, religious." Accordingly, when they landed, the Pilgrims "were a complete and well ordered community." Whelpley's interpretation of the Pilgrims' achievement allows him to focus on the very day of the landing with an ingratiating precision: "On the 22d of December, 1620," he announces, "the system began." Twenty-five years later, J. Prescott Hall turned to Greek mythology to make the same assessment. Just as Athena sprang "completely armed and all perfect" from the head of Jupiter, so "the first settlements of New England came into being" already formed and organized.[67] So accessible seemed the early details of colonial history that in an address delivered at the Broadway Tabernacle in 1839 Robert Charles Winthrop (a descendant of Governor Winthrop) could toy with a familiar strategy and humorously argue that there was some uncertainty over who first stepped on Plymouth Rock, Mary Chilton or John Alden, before conceding the honor to the lady, with a gallant rhetorical bow.

Ever ready to salute important moments of history, the citizens of Boston commemorated the victims of the Boston Massacre from 1771 to 1783 (prior to 1770 they had celebrated the drama of the Gunpowder Plot). The speakers on these annual occasions included James Lovell, John Hancock, and William Tudor. Frequently, the daylong ritual featured an elaborate *tableau d'histoire.* On the first anniversary of the Massacre, for example, the bells of the churches tolled from noon to one. Later, Dr. Thomas Gray delivered an oration that gave "a brief account of the massacre" and a "descant upon the nature of treasons." Finally, in the evening, "there was a very striking exhibition at the house of Mr. Paul Revere, fronting the old North-square":

At one of the chamber windows was the appearance of the ghost of Christopher Snider, with one of his fingers in the wound, endeavoring to stop the blood issuing therefrom. . . . In the next window were represented the soldiers drawn up, firing at the people assembled before them,—the dead on the ground, and the wounded falling, with the blood running in streams from their wounds,—over which was written, "FOUL PLAY." In the third window, was the figure of a woman, representing AMERICA, sitting on the stump of a tree, with a staff in her hand, and the cap of liberty on the top thereof; one foot on the head of a grenadier, lying prostrate, grasping a serpent; her finger pointing to the tragedy.[68]

As this account suggests, the first commemoration of the Boston Massacre dramatized that bloody incident less as a beginning than as an occasion for stirring up patriotic fervor. After the advent of the Revolutionary War and the signing of the Declaration of Independence, however, the Massacre became part of a larger panorama. As a result (in the words of William Cooper, the town clerk of Boston), "the immediate motives which induced the commemoration of that day do now no longer exist in their primitive force."[69] Because it had served its purpose, the citizens of Boston voted to replace the annual tribute to the victims of the Massacre with festivities honoring the Declaration of Independence—this at a town meeting at Faneuil Hall in March 1783, six months before the Treaty of Paris signaled an official end to the War. The majority of late eighteenth- and early nineteenth-century Americans would have concurred. For the Fourth of July, 1776, seemed at once more significant than the Fifth of March, 1770, more accessible than the Mayflower landing, and more *American* than Columbus's discovery of the New World: as the birthday of the United States, it was a genuine beginning and the first national event.

Much has been written about Independence Day orations, which began in 1777 and flourished for more than a century.[70] Although they all commemorated the same occasion, they were easily adapted to such local celebrations as the laying of cornerstones and the opening of canals and such divergent causes as those of abolition and temperance. In some cases their message seems surprising. In Conway, New York, in 1804, the Federalist congressman Samuel Taggart included severe criticism of the Louisiana Purchase in his tribute to the document composed by Thomas Jefferson. On July 4, 1863, the Copperhead W. M. Corry urged an audience in Canton, Ohio, to recognize the independence of the Confederate states. The formula

of most orations can be seen as early as 1787 in Joel Barlow's words
to the Connecticut Society of the Cincinnati. As came to be the custom, Barlow's address was preceded by a reading of the Declaration
of Independence—liberating text followed (in this instance) by a
patriotic homily in which the Declaration emerged as a document
that had "performed the miracles of the gods." Product of reason and
an enlightened people, the Declaration inaugurated a unique destiny, "a new task, totally unknown to the legislators of other nations."
Like almost all other speakers, Barlow issued a cautionary note in
the context of his tribute: with the Constitutional Convention delib-
erating in Philadelphia, he reminded his audience of the present
"alarming crisis," perhaps "the most alarming" that the new nation
(just eleven years old) had known.[71] It was an admission of difficulty that would be repeated throughout the years of American history
to characterize disruptions Barlow could not foresee.

To emphasize the unique quality of the national beginning,
Fourth of July orations tended to use rhetorical strategies similar to
those employed in other commemorative addresses—especially
those that envisioned the Pilgrims as a fully formed community at
the time of their landing in 1620. (This was neither a matter of
anticipating nor of *echoing* but of concurrent use: many of these
addresses overlapped in time; and there were, of course, a limited
number of favored arguments.) "No event more noble adorns the
annals of society," said the Reverend Henry Colman on July 4,
1826, the fiftieth anniversary of the Declaration of Independence—and the date of both Thomas Jefferson's and John Adams's
death. "We are met this day to celebrate the most august event
which ever constituted an epoch in the political history of
mankind"—thus spoke Edwin Forrest in 1838. As early as 1804
Samuel Taggart had marveled that a nation had been "literally born
in a day."[72] John Quincy Adams echoed this statement in 1821 as
he asked his audience to ponder the solemn and well-nigh mystical
fact that the United States had spoken itself "into existence as a
Nation." And on July 4, 1837, he portrayed the signing of the Declaration as the startling fulfillment of Biblical prophecy. " 'Who
hath seen such things?" Adams quoted from Isaiah:

"Shall the earth be made to bring forth in one day? Or shall
a nation be born at once?" In the two thousand five hundred

years that have elapsed since the days of that prophecy, no
such event had occurred. It had never been seen before. In the
annals of the human race, *then*, for the first time, did one People announce themselves. . . . The earth was made to bring
forth in one day! A nation was born at once![73]

This is grand stuff, with its updating of a Puritan faith in divine
favoritism, tribute to a beginning out of which a splendid history
should unfold. If such a history had not yet materialized, and every
speaker conceded that it had not, the solution lay in recalling the
principles of the Declaration of Independence (and, though the
matter receives less emphasis in these addresses, those of the Constitution). After enumerating the social evils that beset society in
1837, John Quincy Adams invited his audience to "review the principles proclaimed by the founders of your empire." The next year
Edwin Forrest must have drawn heavily on his abilities as an actor
in drenching a similar statement with saccharine rhetoric: "True it
is," Forrest admitted, "that a passing cloud has occasionally flecked
the serene brightness of our horizon"; but such momentary inter-
ruptions of serenity occur only "because we have sometimes deviat-
ed" from the noble aims of the Declaration. Even W. M. Corry,
admitting that "We have all been to blame for the catastrophe" of
the Civil War and urging the dissolution of the Union, prophesied
that "the great improvement of this mighty Anniversary will be, not
to indulge in vain regrets, but . . . in the light of the teachings of the
Declaration, to proceed with the work both of private and public
reformation, which alone can save our free institutions."[74]

Among the first to heighten the importance of the Fourth of July
by an infusion of sacralizing metaphors, Levi Woodbury (later
United States Senator from New Hampshire) insisted that the
"pageantry" of the day must shadow forth the "original design" of
the Declaration or "become mere moonshine." "Invigorating" the
"sacred principles" that proclaimed our liberties "thirty-nine years
since" is the fundamental purpose of the occasion. For this day
marks the anniversary of "our political creation," an event "Hal-
lowed by its martyrs and immortalized by its heroes." According to
Woodbury, the Fourth of July, 1776, "stood on the calendar of [our]
fathers next the day of our religious redemption." According to
John Quincy Adams in 1837, the day is "indissolubly linked with

the birth-day of the Saviour." According to Charles Sumner in 1845, it is the "Sabbath of the Nation."[75] For these speakers and others, the essential function of Independence Day orations was to recapture the spirit and the promise of the Declaration and thus encourage Americans to look backward in gratitude even as they looked forward in hope.

Frederick Douglass took a different and decisive step in his address to the Rochester Antislavery Sewing Society in 1852: "I do not hesitate to declare, with all my soul," he told his audience, "that the character and conduct of this nation never looked blacker to me than on this 4th of July!" Castigating a country that could celebrate Independence Day while endorsing the institution of slavery, Douglass nonetheless concludes on a note of hope. With gathering rhetorical power, he brings the authority of the Bible to bear on the principles of the Declaration and thereby appropriates for his purposes the promise inherent in radical beginnings—both theological and political: because "the fiat of the Almighty, '*Let there be light*,' has not yet spent its force," it is to be hoped that it will bring Americans to see that "'*all men are created equal.*'" The power of creational "light" (manifested in epiphanies of the human spirit) will destroy the "hideous monster" of slavery.[76] As the evidence indicates, whatever the moral or political stance of the speaker, the effort of these addresses was to strip away the failures of past and present so that the nation might begin again with original promise. "The country," Margaret Fuller insisted in an essay that captures the essence of Fourth of July ritual, "needs to be born again"—for its original promise has been tarnished and polluted by "the lust for power, the lust for gain."[77]

Fundamental to the rhythms of American life and expression, the impulse to reclaim the integrity of beginnings brought Independence Day addresses to take the form of latter-day and still vigorous jeremiads—"mediating between religion and ideology," as Sacvan Bercovitch observes, furthering the mission toward "continuing revolution."[78] Of all the "days" commemorated by American oratory, only the Fourth of July, 1776, could mark a beginning that yielded a recurrent purchase on the future.

Throughout the second and third decades of the nineteenth century, the language of personal memory began to give way to the rhetoric of public address in Fourth of July orations. In 1787, for example, Joel Barlow could observe that "the death of General

Howe has diminished the number of our brethren"; in 1804, Samuel Taggart could ask his audience to recall the emotions of 1776. In 1852, however, J. Murray Rush summoned up a time that was beyond the range of individual memory: "Seventy-six years have passed since the Declaration of Independence," he stated; let us carry ourselves "back to that period" when, "here in our own city, were assembled those great men who published it to the world."[79] Accompanying the inevitable movement from personal reminiscence to collective appreciation, the numerous references to Manifest Destiny and industrial progress in the middle years of the century support Daniel Boorstin's observation that after July 4, 1826, Independence Day addresses tended to affirm national purpose rather than simply to commemorate the birth of the nation.

Such a specific date, of course, is not absolute in application; rather, it functions as a convenient watershed for the student of American history, one given dramatic resonance by the fact that Jefferson and John Adams died on that day. The change to which Boorstin refers had begun some years before: in 1816 John Adams spoke of the "young gentlemen of genius" who frequently gave patriotic addresses, "describing scenes they never saw, and descanting on feelings they never felt." Their words, he felt, "are infinitely more indicative of the feelings of the moment than of the feelings that produced the Revolution." Were he fifty years younger with "nothing better to do," Adams says in a letter to Jedediah Morse, he would have orations devoted to the Boston Massacre and to Independence Day "collected and printed in volumes, and then write the history of the last forty-five years in commentaries upon them."[80] To read the work of later historians or the words of John Adams is to become aware of the protean nature of Fourth of July orations.

Yet the sense of having, possessing, a proximate and vital national beginning generated rhetorical habits that began early and helped to establish an enduring self-portrait of the nation. In a Fourth of July address delivered in the District of Columbia in 1809, Joel Barlow expressed his optimism in characteristic form, hailing the birth of the nation in 1776 and rejoicing that "we are yet in the morning of life": "The thirty three years of national existence which have brought us to our present condition . . . comprise an interesting portion of history. But they have only prepared this gigantic infant of a nation to begin its own development. They are only the prelude to the greater events that seem to unfold themselves before us."[81] The insistence on metaphors of youthful power, products of a beginning and often competitive vision, could sometimes take exaggerated form. The United States was not only a "gigantic infant," but, according to John Lowell in 1799, an "infant Hercules" and a "young and vigorous Samson." In 1826 Henry Colman adopted a more tempered trope when he announced that we were "as yet in the greenness of youth." And it was a sense that Americans were in "the period of childhood," at the "beginning of your national career," that gave Frederick Douglass a solemn and unflinching hope for a more enlighted future in 1852. But bombast was in season despite (perhaps because of) the seriousness of the problems confronting the nation; Edwin Forrest gloried in the image of a young United States as he asked his New York audience in 1838 to contemplate the years ahead: with abundant resources, with "the irresistible tide of emigration" pressing westward, "what bounds can the vision of the human mind descry to the spread of American greatness, if we but firmly adhere to those first principles of government which have already enabled us, in the infancy of national existence," to vie with the leading nations of Europe?[82]

Understandable, indulgent, and occasionally brash, such language converts the ideas of *youth* and *size* to those of *future* and *opportunity*. But one must watch one's addiction to analogical argument, as M. H. Abrams suggests in *The Mirror and the Lamp*, lest it lead to a hardening of the categories. In his Independence Day address in 1809, Joel Barlow announced confidently that we had arrived at a time "when, instead of looking back with wonder upon our infancy, we may look forward with solicitude to a state of adolescence, with confidence to a state of manhood." Fifty years later the image was virtually the same: speaking to a Newport audience on July 4, 1861, Henry James, Sr., delivered a scathing attack on slavery, deprecated the "mindless spread-eagleism" of much patriotic address, and defined the crisis of the Civil War as "the transition from youth to manhood." In the midst of a very different crisis in 1934, Henry Wallace began his book *New Frontiers* by saying that "The United States is like a boy eighteen years old, possessed of excellent health and a strong body, but so unsettled in his mind and feelings that he doesn't know what to do next."[83] One might conclude from this metaphorical evidence that the nation has never reached maturity; as a character in Oscar Wilde's *A Woman of No Importance* quips, "The youth of America is their oldest tradition. It has been going on now for three hundred years." More charitably, one might conclude that Americans had no wish to outgrow their romance with beginnings and the promise that attends them.

What John Quincy Adams termed the "annual solemn perusal of the instrument" (in 1821) was not, of course, the complete story of any Fourth of July celebration.[84] The day was obviously one of fun and rejoicing. As John Adams foresaw shortly after the signing of the Declaration of Independence,

> The 4th day of July, 1776, will be the most memorable epoch in the history of America. I am apt to believe that it will be celebrated by succeeding generations as the great anniversary festival. It ought to be commemorated, as the day of deliverance, by solemn acts to God Almighty. It ought to be solemnized with pomp and parade, with shows, games, sports, guns, bells, bonfires and illuminations, from one end of the continent to another, from this time forward forevermore.[85]

Although it is suffused with irony, James Fenimore Cooper's lengthy description of Fourth of July "exercises" in chapter 21 of *Home as Found* features most of the festivities Adams mentions. First comes the music—characteristically played (as Cooper insists) on inferior instruments by inept musicians. Then follows the oration, formula-ridden and narcissistic, delivered from the village pulpit by Mr. Writ, the lawyer. After dark the "sports of the night" begin with rockets, pinwheels, firecrackers, and serpents, all climaxed by a special event, "The Fun of Fire," during which the audacious young men of the village shoot homemade roman candles into the air and at one another. The effect, Cooper writes, his caustic tone giving way before a surge of appreciation on the part of his women characters, "was singularly beautiful," both charming and refreshing. As we shall see later, the Declaration of Independence figures more seriously in Cooper's *Wyandotté* when the national beginning, massive in power and implication, takes devastating precedence over the kind of individual beginning so common on the frontier.[86]

Three entries from the diary of Isaac Mickle of Camden, New Jersey, bring a personal and youthful perspective to bear on the public festivities I have been examining. In 1840, seventeen-year old

Isaac (later a lawyer and editor) noted the holiday in the inflated language of many orations: "*4 July, Saturday. Columbia's Birthday*"— honoring "a deed whose grandeur the capture of an hundred Troys would not measure."[87] On July 4, 1842, he held his own celebration before the public events began: "This morning I arose at the usual hour, about eight o'clock, and after breakfast went into my room tuned up my violin, and played *Hail Columbia, Yankee Doodle* and *The Star Spangled Banner*" (2:298). Two years later, his role in holiday festivities expanded (with mixed results) when he joined a group of German immigrants in Malaga as one of the invited speakers, heard the Declaration read in English and in German, and delivered "just such a speech I guess nobody ever heard before, and I doubt if ever any body will want to again." On his way home Mickle stopped at a party where he listened to "songs in five languages, and then they got me a violin and I played them a few jigs and reels." "Mortified," however, because he had made "such a speech," he finally went to bed "heartily tired with The Fourth" (2:457).

Mickle's practice of making the age of the nation part of his Fourth of July diary entries is a standard feature of Independence Day orations and official government documents, significant in all cases because it designates Independence Day as a point at which time began over again. Both the Articles of Confederation and the Constitution date the work of the signers in the year of the nation as well as in the year of the Lord. In the "Gettysburg Address," Abraham Lincoln not only reaches back to 1776 with his "fourscore and seven years" but doubles the aura of beginning with the metaphor of a nation "conceived" in liberty. Walt Whitman, who lived his last years on Mickle Street in Camden, likewise uses 1776 as the point of reckoning in "A Boston Ballad": "I, forty years old the Eighty-third Year of the States." In a variety of ways July 4, 1776, became a privileged occasion, a date from which one could measure both the extent and the quality of American history.

Despite differences of tone and substance, as we have seen, Fourth of July orations sought to recapture the possibilities inherent in the nation's beginning. With few exceptions they played a major role in festivities that became annual rituals of reenactment, secular versions of what Mircea Eliade terms the myth of the eternal return. As they sought to partake of and revivify the prestige of a unique national event, they projected it both as heroic and sacred—as a surpassing gesture of liberty, as the fulfillment of biblical prophecy, as a day "linked with the birth-day of the Saviour." Isaac Mickle's observation that Americans might quarrel on the third of July or on the fifth but that harmony reigned on the Fourth suggests how the mood of this commemorative day might recapture what was perceived as an original unity. Eliade argues convincingly that the most significant period of a society's past is its beginning, the time of magic and myth.[88] That this should be so is not surprising. For, as the evidence leads us to see, any act of beginning imitates or echoes, however feebly, the power and purity of genesis. Thus the attraction of beginnings—and the fascination of cosmology. Thus the appeal of a national beginning both proximate and accessible by means of which Americans, forever unworthy in their history, might renew their promise year after year.

Beginning by Nation *Why?*

ironic   concession (form of agreement)

An Enduring Habit   In response to a story that lamented the
inadequate telephone service in Squaw Gap, North Dakota, William L. Guy, then governor of the state, wrote a letter to *The Wall Street Journal* on January 7, 1972. Many
things a New Yorker might take for granted, he acknowledged, are lacking in Squaw Gap. Rather than "miles of
abandoned tenement houses," one finds vistas of "buttes
and ridges." Rather than an "oversized" telephone directory, one consults a book "that doesn't even have a yellow
page." Compared to New York, Governor Guy admitted
in his most sweeping concession, Squaw Gap has virtually
"nothing": "It has no crime, no air pollution, no water pollution, no noise pollution, no racial tension, no civil dis-
turbance, no congested highways, no congested airways."

*lack of
negatives
makes ur
good*

In thus speaking up for the honor of Squaw Gap, Governor Guy strikes a note that runs deep into American
history, beyond the familiar debate between village and
city, to a time when Americans adopted a similar posture
toward Europe as a way of asserting a sense of pride in
their new nation. The early expressions of this well-known
attitude were straightforward and ubiquitous, cautionary
and conventionally moral in tone. "Shun the lures / Of

Europe," wrote Timothy Dwight in his idyllic poem "Greenfield Hill" in 1794. "Be constantly awake" against the "insidious wiles of foreign influence" said George Washington in his memorable Farewell Address in 1796. In *The Contrast* (1787), Royall Tyler warned of the dangers of foreign, and specifically British, manners as he set the virtues of the American hero, Colonel Manly, against the vices of the Anglicized fop, Billy Dimple. A half-century later, Emerson expressed a similar attitude in a letter to Margaret Fuller, bemoaning the superficiality of nearby Cambridge society and adding that "our reverence for Cambridge which is only a part of our reverence for London must be transferred across the Allegany ridge." Emerson looked to the American West for purgation and replenishment: "If I had a pocketfull of money, I think I should go down the Ohio & up & down the Mississippi by way of antidote to what small remains of Orientalism—(so endemic in these parts)—there may still be in me, to cast out, I mean, the passion for Europe by the passion for America."[1]

My interest in Governor Guy's remarks, however, is less in their substance than in their rhetorical stance. By praising Squaw Gap for what it does not have, Governor Guy uses a mode of expression that has long been a national habit. Traditionally, Americans have found a series of compelling negatives the surest way of defining themselves and their nation. Crèvecoeur, for example, prepares for his celebrated definition of the American in *Letters from an American Farmer* (1782) by making a distinction between Old World and New in terms that became virtually a refrain in the years after the American Revolution: "here," he writes, "are no aristocratical families, no courts, no kings, no bishops, no ecclesiastical dominion, no invisible power giving to the few a very visible one; no great manufacturers employing thousands, no great refinements of luxury." The maverick Thomas Cooper, later president of the College of South Carolina, explained in 1794 that he and other Englishmen came to America because it had "no tythes nor game laws. . . . no men of great rank, nor many of great riches." "Nor" do the rich have oppressive power, "nor" are the streets filled with beggars. And Noah Webster, convinced that the United States was superior to Asia, Africa, Arabia, South America, and Rome, used an aggressive rhetoric to contrast the new country and Europe in 1793: "Here are no beggarly monks and fryars, no princely ecclesiastes and titled mendicants, no spies watch and betray the unsuspecting citizen, no

tyrant with his train of hounds, bastards and mistresses" empties
the treasury of the nation.[2] Such statements mark the difference
between an old world and a new by enumerating what is missing in
the new. Their manner is dismissive, abruptly so; for their intent is
to celebrate the absence of old-world constraint and authority by
staging a revolutionary festival of their own.

Although lists of this sort demonstrate a tendency (perhaps a
need) to negate Europe in order to identify and possess America,
they take form and impulse from early European conceptions of the
New World. The letters of Amerigo Vespucci (some based on experience, some apparently not) provide an example of how negatives
helped to convey to European readers a sense of what had been discovered. Extremely popular with a population hungry for information about the new lands, these letters describe such things as herbs
and fruits, local customs and sexual practices, in fascinating detail.
An authenticated letter of 1502 adds the following significant passage: the inhabitants, Vespucci writes, have "no religious belief, but
live according to the dictates of nature alone. They know nothing
of the immortality of the soul; they have no private property . . .
they have no boundaries of kingdom or province; they obey no king
or lord . . . they have no laws," and no master.[3]

By using negatives to characterize beliefs and customs in a land
not yet named, Vespucci adopts a manner of speaking that became
a formula in Europe before it evolved into an American habit.
Montaigne uses similar language when he praises the natural purity of the world "we have just discovered." He wishes he could tell
Plato of this place in which "there is no sort of traffic, no knowledge of letters, no science of numbers, no name for a magistrate or
for political superiority, no custom of servitude, no riches or poverty, no contracts, no successions, no partitions, no occupations but
leisure ones, no care for any but common kinship, no clothes, no
agriculture, no metal, no use of wine or wheat."[4] By way of John
Florio's translation of Montaigne, these same negatives found their
way into the different context of Gonzalo's speech about governing
the island with no name in *The Tempest*: "Had I plantation of this
isle," Gonzalo says,

> no kind of traffic
> Would I admit; no name of magistrate;

Letters should not be known; riches, poverty,
And use of service, none; contract, succession,
Bourn, bound of land, tilth, vineyard, none;
No use of metal, corn or wine, or oil;
No occupation . . .
No sovereignty . . .   (II,i, 148–56)

As Edmundo O'Gorman demonstrates, Europeans "invented" America—named it the New World, accommodated the staggering implications of that idea by endowing it with features of paradise, and projected a pent-up desire for freedom and space (and I would say possibility) upon it.[5] Endowed with simplicity and a fundamental purity, it was necessarily a negative invention. Bernard W. Sheehan observes the logic by means of which the myth of paradise generated much negative description: whereas imperfection, injustice, and disorder, came to be identified with "the complex of attachments and historical accretions that made up society," perfection came to signify "a societal void" occupied (somehow and theoretically) by primitive peoples who were said to be innocent of history.[6] Such peoples were thus indentured to the terms of European dialogue by a condescending nostalgia built in to the very concept of primitivism.

The negatives I am examining, however, came from a new and vital perspective, from colonists and from citizens of the United States who used the myth of paradise and more visceral contrasts to establish their own quite civilized identity as a nation unencumbered and therefore blessed with opportunity. At an early point, the experience of crossing the Atlantic dramatized to would-be colonists what it was to move from something to nothing, even as it demanded a radical re-cognition of the self.[7] Later, from a retrospective point of view, the purgation involved in such a crossing could be celebrated as a happy first step in making citizens for the New World. The most extravagant of the American negative catalogues, that of Mr. Evelyn in Sylvester Judd's *Margaret: A Tale of the Real and the Ideal* (1845), comes acrobatically out of such an assumption—with a regional bias thrown in for good measure. New England, Mr. Evelyn tells the young Margaret, is an "unencumbered region," which has advantages over "all other nations." When Margaret replies, in the manner of a rustic Orphan Annie, "Thoughts are coming upon me plenty as blackberries, and the more the better," her mentor proceeds with his homily. Pleased that much of "the Old World on its passage to the New was lost over- board," he asserts that "our ancestors were very considerably cleansed by the dashing waters of the Atlantic." Then follows his account of all that is missing from the soil of New England. Select- ed parts will serve to suggest its overblown manner as well as its serious import:

> We have no monarchical supremacy, no hereditary preroga- tives, no patent nobility, no Kings . . . . There are no fairies in our meadows, and no elves to spirit away our children. Our wells are drugged by no saint, and of St. Winifred we have never heard. . . . We have no resorts for pilgrims, no shrines for the devout, no summits looking into Paradise. We have no traditions, legends, fables, and scarcely a history. Our galleries are no cenotaphic burial grounds of ages past; we have no Haddon Hall or Raby Castle Kitchen; no chapels or abbeys, no broken arches or castled crags. . . . All these things our fathers left behind in England, or they were brushed away by contact with the thick, spiny forests of America. Our atmos- phere is transparent, unoccupied, empty from the bottom of our wells to the zenith, and throughout the entire horizontal plane. It has no superstitious inhabitancy, no darkening prevalence, no vague magistry, no Manichean bisection.

"New ENGLAND!" Mr. Evelyn adds on a personal note, "my birthplace, my chosen pilgrimage, I love it."[8]

Mr. Evelyn's intent at this point in *Margaret* is to instruct his pupil in matters of an American faith; accordingly, he rejoices in the absence of theological drama and religious practices that mediate between the individual and God. His controlling metaphors are those of cleansing, of things being brushed away—his tone that of a joyous iconoclast. He negates out of a preference for simplicity of belief, each declaration canceling European fullness in favor of an American emptiness. Although his monumental series of negatives does not improve the quality of *Margaret*, it does result in a vision of harmony that takes the eventual form of a Down-East utopian community.

To be sure of what they were, Americans thus converted a Euro- pean tradition to their own use and proclaimed (with developing conviction) what they were not. Fundamental and enduring, the carefully nourished image of the American Adam was made most compelling by the use of negative terms: a new paradise may flourish in the burgeoning nation, wrote Philip Freneau in "The Rising Glory of America" (1772),

> by no second Adam lost,
> No dangerous tree with deadly fruit shall grow,
> No tempting serpent to allure the soul
> From native innocence.[9]

The incisive rhetoric that promised Adam and paradise could be adapted to a variety of purposes—personal as well as national. To express a sense of his individuality, Thoreau invokes studied (almost Biblical) negative cadences in a journal entry in 1841: "When I meet a person unlike me, I find myself *wholly* in the unlikeness. In what I am unlike others, in that I am."[10]

A writer in *The North American Review* in 1818 (no doubt expressing the surge of nationalism following the War of 1812) found negatives the ready vehicle for chauvinistic strutting: "No people," he concludes after a standard portrayal of European institutions, have ever had such advantages; "we are favoured beyond all example." Using the same rhetorical strategy, a critic in the *American Quarterly Review* in 1827 described the democratic possibilities of American poetry (with contrasting echoes in this case from Gray's "Elegy"): although the country has as yet "no *national* poet," no one whose genius can vie with that of Homer or Milton, it "permits no talents to be inactive. . . . No 'village Hamden' can here be defrauded of his rightful fame; no Milton permitted to remain mute and inglorious."[11] And Marianne Moore (in her poem "England," more than a century later) paraded a remarkable series of negatives to contrast the cultured voice of England—"criterion of suitability and convenience"—with the voices of a land

> where there are no proofreaders, no silkworms, no digressions;
> the wild man's land; grassless, linksless, languageless country in
> which letters are written

not in Spanish, not in Greek, not in Latin, not in shorthand, but in plain American which cats and dogs can read![12]

Whether the occasion evoked a strident nationalism or an intense definition of the self, *uniqueness* was the issue. And a sense of *uniqueness* was best served, best asserted, best protected, by negation.

Beginning by Negation

Not all negatives, of course, were designed to feed the national ego. As students of American literature will recall, a number of nineteenth-century writers used familiar rhetorical patterns to lament the absence of legend and antiquity. In *Notions of the Americans* (1828), James Fenimore Cooper complained of a general "poverty of materials" confronting the American writer—with "no annals for the historian, no follies . . . for the satirist; no manners for the dramatist; no obscure fictions for the writer of romance; no gross and hardy offenses against decorum for the moralist; nor any of the rich artificial auxiliaries of poetry." Margaret Fuller took up what came to be a refrain when she recorded her impressions of an exhibition of Washington Allston's painting in 1840. "Our religion is that of the understanding," she wrote; "we have no old established faith, no hereditary romance, no such stuff as Catholicism, Chivalry afforded." Horatio Greenough, commenting on American architecture, used the same kind of language to make the same kind of point: "as Americans we have no childhood, no half-fabulous, legendary wealth, no misty, cloud-enveloped background." And Nathaniel Hawthorne, in the preface to *The Marble Faun* (1860), noted the difficulty of writing about a country with "no shadow, no antiquity, no mystery, no picturesque and gloomy wrong."[13]

The famous catalogue in which Henry James evoked the New England of Hawthorne's day has a different thrust and spirit. In the manner of Washington Irving or Greenough, James points out that the United States lacked ruins and thatched cottages. But the focus of his virtuoso list of negatives is on what he calls the "items of high civilization," the very things that Crèvecoeur, Noah Webster, and others had singled out as happily absent from the texture of American life. With condescending humor, James sketches a social scene that had "No sovereign, no court . . . no aristocracy, no church . . . no palaces, no castles," and ends with an indulgent flourish—"no Epsom nor Ascot!" The number of "absent things" in Hawthorne's America, he concludes, would probably appall an English or French imagination.[14] Written from the perspective of his own imagination, James's list (put together, as he admits, with "a little ingenuity") mocks a society from which such "things" were missing even as it demonstrates his conception of what a civilized writer needed for his art.

George S. Hillard's address to the New England Society in 1851 ("The Past and the Future") puts these various observations into helpful perspective by detailing the advantages and disadvantages of having the earliest periods of American history so clearly defined. Replete with a wistful sense of superiority, his assessment echoes the substance of words written more than fifty years before by American historians who welcomed the opportunity to fix a beginning, even as it recognizes the manner in which writers expressed concern about the possibilities of romantic art in the new nation. "The origin of our country," Hillard says,

> lies in the open daylight of history. We cannot go back to that morning twilight of tradition, from which poetry draws so many of its themes and so much of its inspiration. Such forms as Arthur and the Cid, in whom the real and the fanciful meet and blend . . . have no place upon our soil. The simple dignity of men like Carver, and Brewster, and Winthrop, can borrow no attractions from the hues of romance. If we lose something so far as imagination is concerned, by the nearness and distinctness of the settlement of the country, we gain much upon the side of truth.[15]

Few Americans in the nineteenth century would quarrel with Hillard's preference for the "daylight of history" over the "twilight of tradition." Even Nathaniel Hawthorne adds in his preface to *The Marble Faun* that a fortunate prosperity "in broad and simple daylight" prevails in his native land. *Daylight* was the American medium: as a commentator in the *Edinburgh Review* wrote in 1829, "No ghost . . . was ever seen in North America. They do not walk in broad day; and the night of ignorance and superstition which favours their appearance, was long past" before the United States came into being.[16]

Although the use of negative rhetoric flourished under many banners in the nineteenth century, the time-honored device of occupatio (so familiar in the work of Chaucer and Spenser) was seldom employed by American writers—doubtless because its sportive use of negatives assumes substance rather than absence. Washington Irving provides a rare instance of this strategy of telling by pretending not to tell at an early point in the *History of New-York*. Because it is Beginning by Negation apparent that "the country *has been discovered*," Diedrich Knickerbocker refuses to discuss the various arguments about who found it. He will not inquire "whether America was first discovered by a wandering vessel of that celebrated Phoenician fleet which, according to Heredotus, circumnavigated Africa; or by that Carthaginian expedition which Pliny, the naturalist, informs us, discovered the Canary Islands; or whether it was settled by a temporary colony from Tyre, as hinted by Aristotle and Seneca."[17] Nor, as I noted earlier, will he look into the claims that it was discovered by Chinese or by Norwegians. With cosmopolitan assurance and comic skill the youthful Irving makes occupatio a part of Knickerbocker's bumbling idiom and shapes it knowingly to the purposes of burlesque.

D. H. Lawrence observes that "people in America have always been shouting about the things they are not." Hyperbolic, more than a little preachy in its context, and unconcerned to fathom the meaning of American negations, the remark nonetheless moves to an essential truth about the new nation (to which, Lawrence observes, people have come "to get away from everything they are and have been").[18] Together with the flurry of celebratory negatives, formulaic catalogues of lament reinforce the sense of what was (happily) missing in the United States and thus constitute another way of juxtaposing the reality of the New World with that of the Old. Together, too, they point to an imaginative awareness of absence that has characterized American literature in surprising and enduring ways.[19] As we shall see, one encounters negation in various kinds of writing, literary and theological, political and commercial. It is a protean mode of discourse, sustained by a common structure, generated by impulses that are frequently iconoclastic and utopian. And it functioned in American hands as a way of stripping away to possibility so that one could measure the power of an original world.

Utopias and Flash-Utopias   What is common to most of the American negatives I have cited is not simply a formula for self-congratulation but an impulse to proclaim the absence of old-world institutions and practices so that the new nation might celebrate a genuine point of beginning—with its attendant hope and promise for the future. Concomitant with the manifest effort to fix a beginning *in* history, in other words, was a profound disposition (deriving ultimately, as we shall see, from the structure of neoplatonic thought) to define a beginning *outside* history—to begin by negating. The typical American lists are not, it should be noted, attempts to describe a perfect society; they differ in instructive and significant ways from the negations traditionally used to fashion literary utopias (notably in their celebration of the status quo). As Richard Helgerson points out, there is a provocative relationship between negatives and the idea of perfect societies in the English Renaissance, inhering in the capacity of negation "to annihilate as well as to create."[20] It is an observation that is helpful to remember in distinguishing between negative structures that project entire communities and those that proclaim more narrowly the absence of specific phenomena.

To bring this distinction into sharp focus, let us recall how negation functions in literary utopias—among them utopias imagined by some American writers—then consider the implications of the negative lists so prevalent in the United States. At the end of book 9 of Plato's *Republic*, Adimantus says that the ideal state described by Socrates could never be realized on earth. That fact, recognized and accepted, is a negation endemic to the idea of perfect societies; they are conceived (though not always presented) as projections of something that does not exist on earth but nonetheless challenges human beings to confront earthly imperfection. Thomas More's *Utopia* (1516) is a subtle case in point. With baffling charm, More goes out of his way to claim a reality that he repeatedly undercuts. The narrative, as readers know, begins its movement as the reflections of Raphael Hythloday, who supposedly sailed with Amerigo Vespucci, left the voyage to explore on his own, and lived five years in Utopia. It is Hythloday who describes Utopia from his experiences and observations. As many scholars have suggested, however, the presence of the author More as distinguished from the interlocutor More hangs puckishly over the unfolding story. The name Hythloday, for example, signifies nonsense-peddler; the Achorians are from no-place (*a* plus *chora*: without place); the river Anyder means a waterless river. Such etymological negations, verbal play at once making and unmaking (or creating and annihilating) identity, acknowledge the non-existence of places even as Hythloday talks rationally about them. That Thomas More links Hythloday with Vespucci rather than with Christopher Columbus sets up another smiling ambiguity; for Vespucci, as we have seen, had acquired an early reputation as a man who compromised the truth to court an audience throughout Europe. More germane to the nature of social organization in Utopia is the absence of money and private property. Betokening their importance in our imperfect world, these things are conventionally negated by visions of perfect societies in favor of a tranquil communism. "My dear More," explains Hythloday in the face of the character More's skepticism about motivation and authority in such a society, "to tell you what I really think, as long as you have private property, and as long as cash money is the measure of all things, it is really not possible for a nation to be governed justly or happily."[21] So little do the Utopians think of gold, Hythloday tells us, that they make it into chamberpots.

The pattern of life in Utopia features sameness and order (and suggests how closely a utopia can resemble an anti-utopia). There are fifty-four cities, all the same except for minor differences caused by geography; all houses are three stories high; every city has four hospitals on its outskirts. All Utopians wear white in church; they must get permission to travel from one city to another; and their days are rigidly ordered into periods for work, for leisure, and for rest. "So you see," says Hythloday, launching into a negative list after explaining the communal nature of this budgeted life, "there is no chance to loaf or kill time, no pretext for evading work; no taverns, or alehouses, or brothels; no chances for corruption; no hiding places; no spots for secret meetings" (49). There is, in other words, no privacy: "they live in full view of all." At this point More thus employs language that looks familiar with its repetitive negations; but the difference between negatives that create (in Helgerson's use of the term) and those that celebrate is manifest. In the first instance, the effort is to make something that constitutes a suppositional and better world—in the second to rejoice because of a situation already present. Even with the cross-currents of meaning in *Utopia*, one can see that negatives create this model community by abstracting, by setting out a blueprint, by making lines straight and angles predictable, by eliminating or reducing spontaneity and freedom. As J. C. Davis observes, the

Utopians "have accepted a discipline which is totalitarian in its scope and denial of human individuality."[22] In keeping with the emotionless nature of "that new world," as Hythloday calls it, five years in Utopia have left More's traveler with no friends or enemies or personal ties—nothing that would invade the geometrical balance of his description (30). If Plato's Republic conforms (as Socrates says) to an ideal pattern, More's Utopia embodies a theoretical one; Hythloday's descriptions extend to matters of administration and economics, hedonism and euthanasia, because of the demands of theory to complete the configurations it has begun. What individualizes a story in which individualism has no place are the lurking ironies of tone and substance generated by the interplay of language, character, and authorial stance.

Most later utopias stand related by influence or analogy to features of More's classic work (and we have all made free with its title). The Jewish merchant in Francis Bacon's *New Atlantis* (1626) alludes to Utopia as a feigned kingdom and says that the Atlantans object to the naked viewing of bodies that is part of Utopian courtship; but he goes through a similar explanation of Atlantan mores. The symmetrical patterns of Tommaso Campanellas's *City of the Sun* (1602), fervid transformations of monastic regimen and a proclivity for logic, resemble in many ways the uniform features of *Utopia*. And as Robert Fishman demonstrates, various plans for ideal cities—including those for Filarete's Sforzinda in the fifteenth century, for Claude-Nicolas Ledoux's Chaux in the late eighteenth and early nineteenth, and for Le Corbusier's *ville radieuse* in the twentieth—emphasize the need for purity of line, and central (even controlling) authority as they strive to envision a transforming sense of order in communal life.[23] Emerson's observation that "*right* originally meant *straight*" (in the "Language" chapter of *Nature*) finds geometric application in the designs of these cities and takes applied form in such a different venture as Robert Owen's New Harmony community, with its right-angled streets and moral quadrilaterals (for living and working), both supposedly conducive to a socialist life of rectitude. The effort, whether historical, linguistic, or archetypal, is to capture (and impose) an original harmony, to re-order a world that has lost its wholeness.

Modified by nineteenth-century concerns and expectations, both Edward Bellamy's *Looking Backward* (1888) and William Dean Howells's *A Traveller from Altruria* (1894) project societies in which money and private property are considered to be root causes of evil. From the vantage point of the year 2000 in Boston, Bellamy's protagonist tells us that there are no wars, no politicians, no lawyers, and no prisons; along with competition, these are things of the past. The nation has become "the sole capitalist and landowner"; benign and thorough (albeit with what Fishman calls "a strong authoritarian bias"), it "guarantees the nurture, education, and comfortable maintenance of every citizen from the cradle to the grave."[24] And just as the assortment of goods in every store is precisely the same, so an efficient standardization prevails throughout the society. At the conceptual center of *Altruria* is a contrast between altruism and self-interest. What is altruistic, or Altrurian, leads to social harmony; what is self-serving promotes discord. So different is Altruria from the world in which we live that one must negate prior experience to visualize it at all: "you will have to cast out of your minds all images of civilization with which your experience has filled them," cautions Aristides Homos, who has read the *New Atlantis* as well as the *Utopia* and believes that the citizens of his country have heaven on earth.[25] As all hypothetical societies must if they are to sustain their unlikeness, Altruria shuns commerce with the outside world. Howells sets his ideal society obscurely in the Aegean Sea, and the otherwise considerate Homos extends no invitations to visit. But locating Altruria (or Utopia or New Atlantis) is not of course the point: the provocative advice of Homos is not to go to Altruria but to let Altruria come to you. Howells hints at the possibility of realizing Altruria internally, though he leaves the necessary "Evolution" indefinitely in the future; after observing life in the United States, Homos writes in "Letters of an Altrurian Traveller" that "America is like a belated Altruria, tardily repeating in the nineteenth century the errors which we committed in the tenth."[26]

By the imaginary year 1940 in Charlotte Perkins Gilman's *Moving the Mountain* (1911), the United States has become a serene and socialist society, "a baby Utopia," as Gilman says in her Preface, "a little one that can grow." John Robertson, Gilman's protagonist, awakens suddenly, after a thirty-year lapse of memory, into a gardenlike and affluent New York. Everything in Gilman's urban setting, as Polly Wynn Allen points out, is clean and unpolluted—the air, the water, the factories, the modes of transportation; moreover, "all New Yorkers are healthy, sensibly dressed, cultured . . . happy."[27]

What brought about this ideal and sanitized environment was a radical change in the attitudes and assumptions of the people, who came, simply and profoundly, to understand the possibilities of life. There is, John Robertson learns, no "poverty—no labor problem—no color problem—no sex problem—almost no disease [and] practically no fires . . . no graft—no adulteration of goods—no malpractice—no crime."[28]

Although women have been in the forefront of what amounts to an accelerated evolution of the spirit, the result is a society neither feminist nor "masculist," but socialist and humanist. From the perspective of most readers, it is also harshly authoritarian. For the cost of cleaning up (and perfecting) a sloppy world dramatizes once again the kinship of utopian ends and totalitarian means. To maintain their model society, this government of the people insists on a "standard of citizenship": those who fail to meet the standard can be (and have been) "mercifully" executed by the state, which not only has the authority to compel men with venereal disease to register with the "Department of Eugenics" but to "amputate" such unpromising citizens as "perverts," "idiots," and "hopeless degenerates" from what Gary Scharnhorst aptly terms "the body politic."[29] As a fictive extension of Gilman's sociological study *The Man-Made World; or, Our Androcentric Culture* (also 1911), *Moving the Mountain* seeks to enact a deeply felt ideology of economic and social parity among human beings. If the effort results in a bland and tedious narrative, it likewise presents (as Allen observes) "a starkly racist utopia with sternly repressive tendencies."[30]

Four years later, Gilman's better-known (and decidedly more interesting) *Herland* offered a utopia comprised entirely of women. Into a mountain land long ago sealed from the world by volcanic eruptions come three men, adeptly characterized by Gilman to reflect the imperfections of our society by their reactions to a true community. Centrally important is the narrator Vandyck Jennings, qualified by temperament and by sociological training to appreciate the marvels of Herland. The other two men, stereotypical as they are, pump vitality into the tale: Jeff Margrave, who idealizes women "in the best Southern style"; and Terry Nicholson, macho male to the core, who divides women into two categories—"those he wanted and those he didn't."[31]

With his "old-fashioned notion of women as clinging vines," Margrave is ill-equipped to understand the self-sufficient citizens of Herland (though he defers to them in courtly fashion), just as Nicholson has no way of coping with the communal spirit of "Maland" (as he calls it) and balks at attending "a dame school" to discover its history and tradition (21, 32). It is from Jennings that we learn how war and natural cataclysm eradicated the men of this remote world and left a group of "harem-bred" women to fend for themselves—how, some time later, "the miracle happened" and one woman bore a child, "a direct gift from the gods"—how, as the years passed, "this wonder-woman" bore five children, all girls, each of whom, in turn, bore five daughters of her own (always beginning at the age of twenty-five). Thus, by the ongoing magic of fives and twenty-fives, pentasymmetry superseding the decasymmetry of the outside world, Herland was populated with "New Women" who had never known men. "There you have the start of Herland!" exclaims Jennings: "One family, all descended" from a single mother, who lived to see her one hundred and twenty-five parthenogenetic great-granddaughters come into the world, who died fulfilled, joyous in the knowledge that "she alone had founded a new race" (57)! For two thousand years no men have entered the land.

The Edenesque qualities of Herland are understated but unequivocal. From the outset Jennings reports that it is a well-tended and "enormous garden," with an ambience that gives him "a very early feeling" (11, 19). To summarize the happy condition of these "ultra-women," he resorts to sustained negative strategies and to one succinct list that not only echoes American words from another century but uses the pluperfect to encompass an entire history: "they had had no wars. They had had no kings, and no priests, and no aristocracies." Perhaps most surprising to the male visitors, these women prospered "not by competition, but by united action" (60).

Gilman's ability to use a utopian vision to generate fresh perspectives about women and Western society is the most fundamental achievement in *Herland*. As Jennings comes to see, these women, "inheriting only from women, had eliminated . . . so much of what we had always thought essentially feminine." He agrees with Nicholson that they are "strikingly deficient in what we call 'femininity,' " then wonders if what men call feminine charms "are not feminine at all, but mere reflected masculinity—developed to please us because they had to please us, and in no way essential" to true womanhood (58–59). It is a challenging perception that Jennings comes to, all the more compelling because he does not sacrifice his regard for his two companions or his citizenship in the world to which he will return (thanks to Gilman's artistic restraint), alert to its warts and blemishes rather than disgusted by its social malevolence.

Far different in form and function, virtually an explosive version of the typical American catalogues, is a series of negatives from the pen of the Anglo-American William Cobbett. In the United States, Cobbett wrote in his *Weekly Political Register* in 1818, every laborer has "plenty to eat and drink! Think of *that!*" And one "never" sees "the hang-dog face of a tax-gatherer. Think of *that!* No Alien Acts here. . . . No packed juries of tenants. No crosses. No Bolton Fletchers. No hangings and rippings up. No Castleses and Olivers. No Stewarts and Perries. No Cannings, Liverpools, Castlereaghs, Eldens, Ellenboroughs or Sid-mouths. . . . No Squeaking Wynns. No Wilberforces. Think of *that!* No Wilberforces!"[32] In this caustic scenario, the irascible Cobbett creates a highly personal and on-the-spot utopia by recognizing the absence of and simultaneously negating the so-called "tools of the borough-mongers" whom he scorned. Cobbett's reputation for volatility and the escalating *joie d'écrire* of his attack obviously temper the annihilating threat of his language. Such an outburst is what one (doubtless even Wilberforce) would expect from this perennially embattled journalist, who had more than once directed his ire at Americans. More importantly for the purposes of the distinction I am making, Cobbett has no need to recommend a course of action or to describe another place in order to express his individualized utopian vision. Quite the contrary: he exults in the status quo. The politicians he names are simply and fortunately absent from the place in which he happens to be. In the momentary flow of these highly focused negatives, the United States exists—clearly and emphatically—in its lack of specific British politicians. With the use of generic rather than personal targets, Herman Melville gives paradise a similar rhetorical existence in *Typee* (1846) and brings us once again to see a relation between negatives and beginnings that does not obtain in classic literary utopias. In *Typee*, the perspective of Melville's narrator generates a contrast between Western civilization and a primitive society rather than between America and Europe or America and Nowhere. After his leg heals, Tommo relaxes into his Marquesan surroundings; in a series of buoyant negative terms, he tells us that the Typee valley had "none of those thousand sources of irritation that the ingenuity of civilized man has created to mar his own felicity. There were no foreclosures of mortgages, no protested notes, no bills payable, no debts of honor"—"no poor relations" or "destitute widows" or "debtors' prisons . . . or to sum up all in one word—no Money! That 'root of all evil' was not to be found in the valley."[33] At this point in his adventures, Tommo rejoices in what the Typees lack. The simple irony of his stance is that he writes as a "civilized man" for the benefit of civilized readers and in telling about a very different society manages to satirize the civilization to which he and his readers belong.

Although it is cultural rather than personal in its thrust, Melville's negative list functions much like Cobbett's. Rather than outlining a program for social perfection in the traditional utopian manner, Tommo points out what is missing in the Typee valley. What he negates or annihilates is a selection of woes that vouchsafes (once again) the truth of the Biblical injunction, "money is the root of all evil" (I Tim. 6:10). By inference, Tommo also negates time: such things as foreclosures of mortgages, bills payable, and debtors' prisons exist because money has not been repaid in due time. It also takes time to produce the inequities that turn human beings into beggars and poor relations. In the flow of his negations, the Typees come to exist as a primitive tribe without money or a Western sense of time: for what Tommo has produced is a kind of flash-utopia brought into simplified focus by the capacity of negatives to celebrate and to satirize. Given his involvement with and effect on the Typees (totally different from Hythloday's impersonal life in Utopia), Tommo could neither recommend a voyage to the Marquesas as a cure for social ills nor envision the possibility of internalizing the local spirit. But he does give us a momentary glimpse of the myth of prelapsarian innocence, a beginning point of enduring appeal.

Just as there is more to life in the United States than Cobbett's negatives signify, so Typee society has a greater complexity (both cultural and ethical) than Tommo's list implies —especially with Tommo in their midst. If Cobbett's statement excludes such things as factionalism, slavery, and Indian warfare for the purposes of his fragmented utopian vision, Tommo's negative list achieves its focus by screening off the specter of cannibalism, his attachment to Fayaway, and the fact that the Typees are fighting among themselves at the time of his departure. "The not-relation," Josiah Royce points out in an incisive essay on negation, "is one of the simplest and most fundamental relations known to the human mind," crucial to the human sense of order. Royce puts the matter succinctly: "Without negation no order." Moreover, he continues, to describe by means of negation leads one to speak "in a more or less deliberately limited universe of discourse."[34] This last formulation is both significant and helpful to the distinction I am making here: the societies projected by More and Bacon, Bellamy and Howells, do introduce order—rationally and methodically—inside restricted fields of vision. Moreover, each reaches out, in Royce's words, to give the illusion of a "universe," strategically "limited"; each contains the blueprint of a country or city carefully organized to eliminate inefficiency and the unpredictability of spontaneous expression; each locates its vision of perfection elsewhere—in geography or in time. What I am calling flash-utopias, on the other hand, are restricted to the point of fragmentation. They substitute passion for rationality, intensity for breadth. Selecting extremely limited worlds of discourse held together only by negative association, they celebrate the immediate, the here-and-now, by focusing our attention on what is absent—theological complexity in Mr. Evelyn's speech to Margaret, royal privilege in Thomas Cooper's treatise on immigration, political lackeyism in William Cobbett's exulting diatribe.[35] Never do they take a general and balanced view of society or of the individual, not even in *Typee*, where Tommo's detailed account of such things as food, religion, and tatooing serves the resolution of Melville's narrative by fostering a tension between the attractions of lotusland and a longing for home. Rather, flash-utopias exist in and through their decisive grasp of what Royce calls "the not-relation"; they are not-places rather than blueprints. With an almost festive insistence, they establish the absence of institutions and complexities that have taken social form over long periods of time. In doing so, they make a sense of beginning proximate and vital.

Negative Structures   To appreciate more fully the implications of negatives in American society and to understand the forms they took in literature, it is instructive to consider their analogous function in three widely disparate modes of expression—those of mystical theology, revolutionary politics, and contemporary advertising.

For, in provocative ways, American negatives constitute a secular version of the body of apophatic theology by means of which cer- tain medieval thinkers formulated their insistent ideas of a Prime Cause. In powerful ways, they take on aggressive life and energize the arguments of American Revolutionary propaganda. And in pragmatic ways, they become a resource for the language of adver- tising and show us how formulas that have served a society since its inception can be manipulated for commercial use. To explore this diversity, to appreciate the persistent effect of rhetorical negation in both serious and comic manifestations, is to understand that it is not simply a habit (though its use is habitual) and even less a theme (though it may shape thematic concerns). With roots that go back to an austere, iconoclastic Neoplatonism, it is, I believe, a *structure*, part of the way Americans look at (and present) themselves and their actions in (and to) the world.

Writing under the pseudonym Ancilla in *The Following Feet* (1957), an American Episcopalian describes a personal religious experience that occurred in St. Sebalduskirche in Germany. Sudden-ly, he writes, he "*saw*" renunciation and moved away from the per-spective offered by his own consciousness. At that point something happened that "I can only use negatives" to explain. "I saw nothing, not even a light. I heard nothing, no voice, no music, nothing. Noth-ing touched me. Nor was I conscious of any Being, visible or invisi-ble. But suddenly, simply, silently, I was not there. And I was there. It lasted for a moment, yet it was eternal, since there was no time."[36]

This contemporary account of a mystical experience follows the contours of the *via negativa* defined by mystics from various cen-turies and various cultures. Richard of St. Victor's study of ecstacy in *Benjamin Major*, for example, describes a systematic process of renunciation as the condition of experiencing divine rapture—a suspension of the bodily senses, a forgetting of the external world, and, finally, a transcending of intellectual processes as one enters what he calls "the Cloud of Unknowing." Similarly, to know the Divine Abyss envisioned by John Tauler one must come by way of solitude to a changeless and timeless ground "so desert and bare, that no thought has ever entered there."[37] In entering the Abyss one leaves behind the limiting awareness of self and becomes imbued with a pure sense of the eternal. One cannot, of course, sus-tain such an experience; it takes place only at the instant in which the finite meets the infinite.

Evelyn Underhill notes that the language of mysticism is drawn to images of boundless spaces, vast seas, and barren deserts to explain the experience of emptiness and darkness that is the condition of becoming one with the Origin, the Prime Cause, the being of God. This is more, she believes, than a matter of convention or imitation; it is something that comes from straining language to its limits in an attempt to describe what is not by definition describable. With a grasp of the mystical tradition that has made her study useful after a century, Underhill says that to a sense of the inconceivable difference between the finite and the infinite, which usually goes "with an instinctive taste for Neoplatonism" and an "iconoclastic distrust of personal imagery, we owe all negative descriptions of supreme Reality."[38] Negations based on the premise of inexpressible difference certainly inform the *via negativa* as it is formulated by many writers—although an indulgence in imagery frequently adds a lushness to accounts of the mystical process. But the burden of negative or apophatic theology (as I see it for my purposes) was neither to recount a religious experience nor to lay out the recipe for one; it was, explicitly, to deny or strip away the attributes of God, to reach back to a condition of purity and simplicity, to Being as it was in the beginning.

Of particular importance in establishing the rhetorical patterns of negative theology was the student of mysticism we have come to call pseudo-Dionysius—the "fountain-head of Christian mysticism," according to William James.[39] By the best evidence a Syrian monk who lived in the latter part of the fifth century, this writer left ten letters and four analytical treatises in which he articulated a mysticism thoroughly imbued with the Neoplatonism of Proclus. Because he made himself known as Dionysius and mentioned persons who lived in the first century after Christ, he managed to convey the impression that he was Dionysius the Areopagite. As a consequence, his work acquired great authority as that of the convert of St. Paul. With few exceptions, scholars accepted it as such until the seventeenth century.

Brief yet profoundly influential, the *Mystical Theology* of pseudo-Dionysius petitions the "Supernal Triad" to lead our minds to the "incomprehensible" summit of "mystical Lore" where the "pure . . . immutable mysteries of theology" outshine "all brilliance with the intensity of their Darkness." Throughout, the presentation features the language of paradox (including such conceits as "dazzling obscurity" and "invisible fairness") and ambiguity (the word *bril-liance* suggesting both our experience with light and our intellectu-al capacity); the effort is to baffle normal human ways of knowing as the condition of penetrating to "pure" and "immutable myster-ies." Indeed, pseudo-Dionysius says bluntly that no one who remains "attached to the objects of human thought" can "describe the transcendental First Cause." Combining negation and paradox, he states that only by "unceasing and absolute renunciation," by "pure and entire self-abnegation" may a person "be borne on high . . . into the superessential Radiance of the Divine Darkness."[40]

Each of the final two chapters of *Mystical Theology* (there are five, and they total only fifteen pages) is made up of a single long sentence sustained by negatives. The sentence comprising chapter 4 argues that the *"pre-eminent Cause"* of all things exists without *being* any of those things:

> We therefore maintain that the universal and transcendent Cause of all things is neither without being nor without life, nor without reason or intelligence; nor is He a body, nor has He form or shape. . . . Nor has He any localized, visible or tan-gible existence; He is not sensible or perceptible; nor is He subject to any disorder or inordination. . . . He needs no light; He suffers no change, corruption, division, privation or flux; none of these things can either be identified with or attrib-uted unto Him. (15; my italics)

The remarkable sentence in chapter 5 extends the negative method and thereby escalates the writer's attack on the *attributes* of the Prime Cause. I cite representative parts of it:

> Again, ascending yet higher, we maintain that He is neither soul nor intellect; nor has He imagination, opinion, reason or understanding; nor can He be expressed or conceived. . . nei-ther has He power nor is power, nor is light; neither does He live nor is He life; neither is He essence, nor eternity nor time; nor is He science nor truth, nor kingship, nor wisdom; nor godhead nor goodness; nor is He spirit according to our understanding, nor filiation, nor paternity; nor anything else

known to us . . . neither can the reason attain to Him, nor name Him, nor know Him; neither is He darkness nor light; nor the false nor the true; nor can any affirmation or negation be applied to Him . . . inasmuch as the all-perfect and unique Cause of all things transcends all affirmation, and the simple pre-eminence of His absolute nature is outside of every negation—free from every limitation and beyond them all.   (16)

As the opening of the single sentence in chapter 4 demonstrates, pseudo-Dionysius goes out of his way to make statements in a negative way. Rather than saying that the transcendent Cause has being, life, reason, and intelligence, he runs around his forehand, as it were, so that he can formulate his idea in a "neither-nor" construction. Moreover, from the extreme perspective of chapter 5 ("ascending yet higher"), he contradicts these assertions in emphatic negative terms: the "unique Cause" does not "live" nor has He "understanding," although, it is interesting to note, "He" does have gender. Indeed, most of the statements in this second catalogue are astonishing when one considers the conventional language of Christian invocation. To deny that the Source of All Being is light and truth, or a king and a father, is to counter (quite deliberately) modes of piety and worship that developed in the early centuries of the Church. To assert that the preeminent Cause of all things is neither "godhead" nor "spirit" could be puzzling even to a student of theology. One must remember, however, that pseudo-Dionysius is negating things attributed to an Infinite Being by finite minds. Since human reason cannot comprehend the existence of a Supreme Being, we must conclude that such a Being has no "power" or "kingship" according to our ways of understanding (which are by nature limited). Even more significantly: because It exists beyond all human categories—once again, products of our understanding—the Supreme Being must be described as neither hot nor cold, neither darkness nor light, neither false nor true. Pseudo-Dionysius sets up a series of disjunctions in this climactic chapter of his *Mystical Theology*—forms of what came to be the Ramist logic so important to Puritan thinkers—then insists that none of them applies because the unique Cause is "outside" both affirmation and negation.[41] In this and other treatises he frequently uses terms such as *superessence* and *superbeing* to convey a sense, however faint, of a Being that surpasses all limitation.[42] To transcend, we see from his

work, is to negate; and to negate is to cancel attributes that stand
between the individual human being and the Source of All Being.
In a very different context, John Donne writes (in "Elegy XIX"),

> If that be simply perfectest
> Which can by no way be exprest
> But *Negatives*, my love is so.
> To All, which all love, I say no.
> If any who deciphers best,
>   What we know not, our selves, can know,
> Let him teach mee that nothing.

The poem, of course, is "Negative Love." The subject changes dras-
tically and the tone is sportive, but the way to the "simply per-
fectest" remains the same. And it remained dramatically the same
when Dennis Martinez of the Montreal Expos spoke of the experience of pitching a perfect game against the Los Angeles Dodgers
on July 28, 1991—twenty-seven batters faced, twenty-seven
retired: "I was blank," Martinez told reporters. "There was nothing
in my mind. I had no words to say. I could only cry. I didn't know
how to express myself. I didn't know how to respond to this kind of
game."[43] In the face of perfection, the professional athlete, the poet,
and the mystic share a common vocabulary.

Under the influence of pseudo-Dionysius, John Scotus Eriugena and Meister Eckhart later argued that to predicate anything of
God is an error; for, no matter one's intention, any predication limits the idea of an infinite being. Born in Ireland in the ninth century, Eriugena traveled to Paris before 850 and eventually became
highly important in transmitting Neoplatonic ideas to the mysticism of the later middle ages.[44] Paradoxically, he did not know the
work of Proclus, Plotinus, Philo, or even Plato at first hand. His
Neoplatonism came primarily from Origen, Gregory of Nyassa,
and (very directly) from pseudo-Dionysius. In 860 Eriugena was
commissioned by Charles the Bald to translate the work of pseudo-
Dionysius from Greek to Latin. Because his theological framework
was Latin and Augustinian, his study of pseudo-Dionysius became
crucial to his thinking: he believed he was bringing the subapostolic
authority of Dionysius the Areopagite to the support of Augustine's

teaching. His exploration of the resources of apophatic theology extended even the decided negative bias of pseudo-Dionysius.

Eriugena adapted the idea of a transcendent Cause of all Being from pseudo-Dionysius. In his view, it is possible to speak of this Prime Cause positively or negatively. Positive statements, however, are metaphorical, whereas negative statements are literal. Thus, if we say that God is Light or that God is Wisdom, we speak metaphorically. But as we have seen in the *Mystical Theology* of pseudo-Dionysius, God transcends light as we know light and wisdom as we know wisdom. Metaphorical statements are therefore valid only in a partial way and are of a lower order than are literal statements; they belong to an idiom of attribution that is reductive and limiting. To say that the Prime Cause is not Light or not Wisdom, on the other hand, is to speak literally; and although such statements might seem to be mere exercises in language, in reality they serve the significant purpose of canceling divine attributes predicated by human beings. Frequently, Eriugena says that God is more-than-good or more-than-eternal or borrows from pseudo-Dionysius the prefix *super*, so that the Infinite Cause becomes Superessence or even Superbeing (a term that suggests the negations involved in the making of pop culture superheroes). In his great work of spiritual anthropology, *Of the Division of Nature*, Eriugena wonders if such usage is positive or negative—or if it might combine both modes in a single statement. His conclusion is that the function of such terms as *more than* or *super* is to negate the finite reality we know; although they lack conventional negatives, they are (as we see repeatedly in the work of Edgar Allan Poe) rhetorical strategies to achieve transcendence.

Along with Eriugena, Meister Eckhart considered pseudo-Dionysius to have the authority of a disciple of St. Paul. Thomas Aquinas's approving commentary on the supposed Areopagite gave his work added importance in Eckhart's eyes. Following the example of pseudo-Dionysius, Eckhart holds that, no matter the piety of one's intention, to predicate anything of God is an error, an attempt to limit an infinite being. Hence, once again, the only valid statements that can be made of the Supreme Being are negative. Occasionally, it is true, Eckhart speaks of God in analogical terms. And in his vernacular sermons, as opposed to his more formal Latin treatises, he sometimes extends the idea of analogy to metaphors that portray the immanence of God in his creation. "All created things are God's speech," he says in one sermon; "The being of a stone speaks and manifests the same as does my mouth about God."[45]

Expressions of this kind, few as they are, have led some scholars to applaud what they see as a cataphatic or affirmative aspect of Eckhart's theology.[46] But Eckhart can hardly be turned into a medieval romantic: a negative thrust is dominant and startling in his work, and it is especially noticeable in his indictment of images. When Paul rose from the ground, Eckhart writes in one sermon, he saw nothing; therefore, he saw God. (One could hardly put the matter more emphatically.) In another sermon, Eckhart says to his auditors (a group of nuns who no doubt yearned for the comforts of a less austere faith), "If you visualize anything or if anything enters your mind, that is not God. . . . To speak about God in any simile is to speak of him in an impure mode. But whoever speaks of God through nothingness speaks of him to the point."[47] Again, he refers to "the illuminated Dionysius" who puts God beyond all being by using the terms *superbeing, superlife, superlight*. Eckhart's fundamental ideas are set forth with a rigorous clarity. "All things are created from nothing," he writes; "therefore their true origin is nothing." If you would come near God, he counsels, "Keep yourselves unencumbered and bare."[48] Stripped of a dependence on images, one becomes naked and pure, capable of being "translated" into the being of God, where, Reiner Schürmann explains, "all things are reinstated in their primitive fullness. There they 'are' what they were before being created."[49]

Bareness, unencumberedness, and purity are thus achieved by a process of continuous negation or subtraction that culminates in "the nothingness of origin." As the central body of apophatic theology demonstrates, the so-called Divine attributes are swept away by the insistent negatives of mystically inclined thinkers who would prefer to seek God in an original unity or emptiness than in a maze of anthropomorphic metaphors. If no attributions had ever been made about God, there would have been no need for apophatic theology; if no monarchies and ecclesiastical hierarchies had ever developed, there would have been no occasion for the kind of American negatives I have been adducing.

There is, of course, a noteworthy difference in perspective and purpose (and not just of subject matter) between these theological negations and those that mark the absence of Old World institutions in the United States: whereas one seeks to arrive at a pristine sense of an Original Being, the other celebrates a purified condition already existing; whereas one is aggressive and revolutionary, the other is appreciative and postrevolutionary. Pseudo-Dionysius cancels out terms that would domesticate the Prime Cause; Mr. Evelyn in *Margaret* rejoices that because much of the Old World was "lost overboard" on the way to the New, the American "atmosphere is transparent, unoccupied, empty," devoid of saints and shrines, kings and castles. So well established was the appreciative response that Shelley (who had "an extraordinary predilection for the negative," according to Timothy Webb) could pick up the refrain in "A Philosophical View of Reform" (1820) and praise the United States for having "no king . . . no hereditary oligarchy; no established church . . . ; no false representation."[50] In *Prometheus Unbound* (1820), moreover, Shelley adapts fundamental apophatic assumptions to his dramatic purposes. The poem culminates not only with a visionary journey from age to youth to childhood but with a process of reverse evolution by means of which the earth is "unwithered" and discrete forms of life are resolved into a common origin.[51] Whatever the context, epic or stridently comic, negative structures continue to work their magic: when the bachelor protagonist (Burt Reynolds) in the film *Paternity* (1984) wonders if he is missing something in life, an amazed friend reassures him by saying, "You've got everything—no wife, no children, no house, no mortgage." Henry David Thoreau could hardly have put it better.

But American negatives could likewise take on an aggressive stance and show revolutionary fervor (political rather than theological)—out of faith in a kind of primal equity. Perhaps the classic example is Thomas Paine's *Common Sense* (1776), which incorporates into its argument the same negating logic that is characteristic of apophatic theology. Admittedly, Paine reaches for any evidence he can use in his immensely popular essay: the distance between England and America becomes proof that heaven never meant one to rule the other; the relative size of England and America demonstrates the same point, since nature never makes a satellite larger than its planet. Much earlier in his pamphlet, however, Paine advances the line of reasoning that provides its basic structure. Since all men were "originally equals in the order of creation," he writes, "the equality could only be destroyed by some subsequent circumstance." The principal destructive circumstance is the growth of monarchy, an institution both idolatrous and disastrous. Coming at the matter in a different way, Paine tells us that "in the early ages of the World according to the Scripture chronology there were no Kings; the consequence of which was there were no wars; it is the pride of Kings which throws mankind into confusion." In the third of "The Forester's Letters," written in response to William Smith's attacks on *Common Sense*, Paine returns to his fundamental idea that monarchy has subverted the harmony of creation: "If the history of the creation and the history of kings be compared together the result will be this—that God hath made a world, and kings have robbed him of it."[52] To eliminate monarchy, a "subsequent circumstance" of the worst kind, would thus be to restore an aspect of God's original world. The author of *The Cloud of Unknowing* says with dismay that some people "would fashion a God according to their own fancy, and dress him in rich clothes and set him on a throne."[53] It is an image that pseudo-Dionysius and Thomas Paine would topple in concert, each for his own purifying reasons.

By negating the institution that has destroyed the harmony of the original world, Paine sets the conditions for his famous pronouncement in *Common Sense*, "We have it in our power to begin the world over again." Equally important though less well known are the following two sentences: "A situation, similar to the present, hath not appeared since the days of Noah until now. The birthday of a new world is at hand." As the argument of his famous pamphlet makes clear, Paine saw this birthday or beginning as immanent in the events taking place around him—six months before the signing of the Declaration of Independence. His confidence derives from the sense of potential endemic to beginnings, his ebullience from his proximity to a momentous event. The progression of ideas in Paine's statement is significant. First comes the assertion of an ability to begin the world not ex nihilo but "over again." No matter the depth of his commitment to revolution, Paine does not and could not claim that absolute creation was in the offing. Rather, he turns to the compelling and frequently used model of a beginning offered by Noah and the Flood: just as Noah emerged from a catastrophe that sent waters over the earth and allowed for a momentous new start, so the American colonies have the opportunity to erase the nefarious things of the past and start again. It is, indeed, a rare opportunity. After almost three hundred years, the New World will sponsor the birth of "a new world." Paine's view is prospective and confident: he is locating a radical beginning in the immediate future.

The strategy of negating problems to attain a sense of a promising new world can be put in the service of any program. In other words, anybody can play the game—and since the structure itself is morally neutral, dependent on the player, there are no built-in rules or restraints. Direct and brutal, frightening in its cool contemplation of an unspoken genocide, the racist argument of *Nojoque; A Question for a Continent* (1867) by Hinton Rowan Helper concludes after 474 pages that "No new golden age, no general jubilee, no Eden-like millennium, no prolonged period of uninterrupted peace and joy" will come to North America "until in the total absence of all the swarthy and inferior races of men."[54] This negative catalogue obviously functions in a different way than do those of Sylvester Judd or Cobbett or Crèvecoeur, who, as makers of flash-utopias, rejoice in the status quo. Helper's strategy is to adapt to his own purpose the form of argument basic to Thomas Paine's *Common Sense*: whereas Paine calls for the elimination of kings, Helper looks forward to the absence of "inferior races." With the Revolution as part of our history, we make Paine a hero; with the holocaust a part of our experience, we shudder at Helper. The negatives in *Nojoque* begin with the obvious and increasingly ominous title, spell out in detail the problems caused by "inferior" human beings, and end with a vision of white supremacy that depends on the "total absence" of entire races—the "negro," the "Indian," and the "bi-colored hybrid."[55] Helper makes it clear that to find the joy of an "Eden-like millennium" the nation must get rid of these troublesome people. If stripping away is essential to his vision of peace and harmony, absence remains the final consideration—not so much *what* in this case as *who*.

With its continuous need to find formulas that make products seem appealing, the antipodal world of modern advertising has adopted the use of negative rhetoric in ways that can complement our sense of its traditional function. A land investment company in Florida promotes the glories of San Salvadore, an island with no extremes of weather, no traffic jams, no capital gains tax, no inheritance tax, no real estate taxes, and no income taxes, "personal or corporate."[56] The Nova Cookware company boasts of a product with "No stick,

No scrape, No scour, No scrub." In some cases, of course, the message is more complex. On July 24, 1971, the *New Yorker* carried an advertisement for Swissair that offered a disconcerting commercial reprise on Tommo's description of his surroundings in *Typee*. Visit Zurich, reads the text of the advertisement, "a city with no slums, no strikes, no poverty, no unemployment, no raucous noise, no cliques of malcontents." Unlike *Typee*, with its playful primitivism (or the early negative catalogues with their comfortable—for us— contrast between New World and Old), this invitation uses negatives, with chilling precision, to relocate paradise in a European city—appropriately Swiss and therefore clean. What is negated are not traffic jams, inclement weather, and a host of taxes, but the symptoms of urban unrest in contemporary America. What remains is a generalized sense of peace and quiet, a haven from stress, a commercially fashioned flash-utopia that has a curious resemblance to Squaw Gap, North Dakota, in the details of its negative existence. Unlike Squaw Gap, of course, Zurich has a telephone directory with many yellow pages, a sure sign of business, banks, and private property.

Out of our avid concern for the purity of what we eat and drink comes advertising of a different sort, amusingly similar to the polemic of apophatic theology. For a number of years known as the Uncola, Seven-Up appeared before television audiences in 1983 as a beverage with "No caffeine, no artificial flavors, no artificial colors. No wonder," concluded the spokesman, "Seven-Up has a clear, refreshing, unspoiled taste." In September, 1993, an advertisement in the *USAir Magazine* praised the Charleston weight loss program for having "no amphetamines, no drugs of any kind, no pills, no powders, no chalky-tasting drinks, no ketosis, no bad breath odor" (19). Even more elaborate in its claim to primacy is the series of Perrier advertisements published in the *New Yorker* in 1983. Perrier, we read, is the "Earth's first soft drink. Not manufactured, but created by the earth when it was new." Perrier *remains* "clear, pure and sparkling, and minus all those additives that civilization has invented. There's no sugar. No artificial sweetener. No calories. There's no caffeine, no coloring. And Perrier is recommended for salt-free diets, as well."[57]

Seven-Up has an "unspoiled" taste. The Charleston program is "wholesome." Perrier is "pure." The atmosphere of New England is "transparent." A person must be "unencumbered and bare" to come near God. One basic function of negating, as I suggested earlier, is to strip away phenomena—"additives" in the Perrier advertisement, "attributes" in apophatic theology, "subsequent circumstances" in *Common Sense*—that have been produced in time, be they artificial flavors, elves, monarchies, or images of the Unique Cause, and thereby arrive at the concept of an original, uncompromised reality—an ontological beginning for some, a societal beginning for others, a point of generative power for all. We negate, in other words, to cancel out what others have done to limit or compromise our world. The impulse to strip away itself transcends cultures and centuries: it proceeds from a cast of mind common in a Western tradition to the early Neoplatonists and to mystics of various periods, to Puritans, Quakers, Anabaptists, and the Cambridge Platonists—all of whom saw grievous need to negate—and manifests itself in American society primarily as a way of celebrating the existence of a nation at ever-renewable points of beginning, untrammeled by the constricting institutions of an older world.

Confrontations with Nothing   Quite obviously, not all negative rhetoric celebrates the idea of a beginning and a fresh start. Although the process of stripping away may remain the same, in some instances the consequences turn out to be radically different. Depending on what is negated, or—perhaps more accurately—on how the negating is accomplished, the effect may be one of comedy, terror, or the ambiguity of a situation yet to be resolved. When Mark Twain observes in *Roughing It* (1872) that Mono Lake has "no fish . . . no frogs, no snakes, no polliwogs—nothing, in fact, that goes to make life desirable," the boyish naming of things that are absent converts Nothing to comedy ("polliwogs" is the master stroke) even as it characterizes the bleakness of that alkaline lake.[58] In *Pierre*, on the contrary, Melville constructs a scenario of terror when he moves beyond the perceptions of his protagonist to generalize about the quest for truth and substance in the world:

> Ten million things were as yet uncovered to Pierre. The old mummy lies buried in cloth on cloth; it takes time to unwrap this Egyptian king. Yet now, forsooth, because Pierre began to see through the first superficiality of the world, he fondly weens he has come to the unlayered substance. But, as far as

any geologist has yet gone down into the world, it is found to consist of nothing but surface stratified on surface. To its axis, the world being nothing but superinduced superficies. By vast pains we mine into the pyramid; by horrible gropings we come to the central room; with joy we espy the sarcophagus; but we lift the lid—and no body is there!—appallingly vacant as vast is the soul of man.[5]

As the passage suggests, Pierre's innocence stands no chance against the brooding omniscience of the narrator.

In works as different as Willa Cather's *My Ántonia* (1918) and William Bradford's *Of Plymouth Plantation* (begun around 1630), the initial recognition of blankness and absence is accompanied by feelings of wonder if not dismay. Cather's narrator, Jim Burden, recalls his first impressions of the Nebraska prairie in stark terms: he feels that he is being "erased," "blotted out," taken "over the edge" of the world, "outside man's jurisdiction." As he rides out to his grandparents' home at night, he peers over the side of the wagon and sees nothing at all, "no fences, no creeks or trees, no hills or fields. If there was a road, I could not make it out in the faint starlight. There was nothing but land: not a country at all, but the material out of which countries are made."[60] The task of Cather's narrative is to participate in an original kind of shaping, to fashion a country from material almost threatening in its lack of form, to bring the prairie within the "jurisdiction" of her narrator's imagination so that the reader may look out *and* back with Jim Burden and recognize the pattern of a beginning.

The incipient fear in Jim Burden's first account of the prairie is heightened by Mr. Shimerda's suicide even as it is modulated by the nostalgia of his narrative voice. The teller of Cather's tale is, after all, remembering experiences that cohere in the bountiful figure of Ántonia. William Bradford has no such luxury. After recounting the difficulties of the voyage in *Of Plymouth Plantation*, Bradford pauses to consider the situation of the Pilgrims at the time of their landing in 1620. Fatigued and beset with cares, he remembers, the company "had no friends to welcome them nor inns to entertain or refresh their weather beaten bodies; no houses or much less towns to repair to, to seek for succor"—no "Pisgah" to afford them a view of "a more godly country."[61] Bradford's voice conveys the sense of civilized human beings facing "a hideous and desolate wilderness," a place totally beyond the range of their experience. Let us recall that Bradford had already negated the law of his native country in the name of a higher law and then, in a literal sense, seceded. What he describes is what remained after he had stripped away the world he knew (including the hardships and securities of Holland) and suffered the death of his wife by accident or suicide even before she left the *Mayflower*: an alien land, with no inns or towns or friends and not even a Mount Pisgah to provide a vision of the future. From our perspective, Bradford's statement in *Of Plymouth Plantation* affords an early and dramatic example of beginning by negation. In December of 1620, however, this courageous Pilgrim might not have been sure. For the recognition of nothing (as we see in *Pierre)* is a perilous business.

Such a recognition is precisely the business of "Bartleby the Scrivener" (1853) and "The Beast in the Jungle" (1903), stories that court terror and enigma by making the confrontation of nothing a subject in itself. In "The Beast in the Jungle," John Marcher falls victim to a self-nourished principle of transcendence. He does nothing until nothing becomes his fate. Out of a belief that he faces a unique destiny, Marcher abstains from human commitment because no imaginable choice seems sufficiently high and rare to set him apart from others. Over the course of his life he searches (and waits) for something "more than" (as Scotus Eriguena might say), and by the annihilating glare of his search cancels out the world around him. His recognition of his life as nothingness—success in devastating guise—precipitates the spring of the beast and Marcher's futile embrace of May Bartram's grave. In concluding his tale with a burst of clarifying action, Henry James manages a quality of explanation that Melville does not vouchsafe in "Bartleby the Scrivener." Whereas James puts us on the inside, Melville keeps us at a distance. In "Bartleby," we look at a protagonist who provides no story through the eyes of an engaging narrator determined to tell a story even though "no materials exist" to help him. Accordingly, Bartleby comes to exist in roles that serve the prudent consciousness of the narrator—first (literally) as scrivener and reluctant proofreader, then (thoroughly abstracted) as an object of pity and a cross to bear. Because "nothing is ascertainable" about him, we know little of what Bartleby thinks.[62] That he prefers not to have contingent (assigned) existence, however, is central to Melville's fictional meditation. For in this story Melville adheres to the dualism characteristic of his work and distinguishes between existential and social being. Stripped of roles by his repeated "I would prefer not to," Bartleby exists, purely and simply, screened off conveniently from those in the lawyer/narrator's office, blocked in visually by the blank wall outside his window, shut away permanently from the larger community by his confinement in the Tombs. His death in prison signals Melville's dismay with the fate of pure existence, naked humanity, in a society agreeably dedicated to business and profit.

Three years before, in the "The Whiteness of the Whale" chapter in *Moby-Dick*, Melville had addressed the enigma of noncategorical being with a carnival burst of negation. To convey a sense of what the white whale was "at times" to him, Ishmael constructs near the outset of that chapter a sentence of more than four hundred and fifty words, carefully sustained by a series of concessions. His effort is to encompass and move beyond traditional associations of *white* into what Paul Brodtkorb, Jr. terms an ontological realm of signification.[63] Ishmael's repetitive "though, though, though" phrases generate a mounting rhythm of wonder and expectation, at once dismissing the world of experience and straining the capacity of language to apprehend a reality that presents no categories for interpretation, no way of being processed by the human mind. Paradoxically but predictably, Ishmael fulfills the structural logic of his sentence by moving beyond logic: "yet for all these accumulated associations, with whatever is sweet, and honorable, and sublime, there yet lurks an elusive something in the innermost idea of this hue, which strikes more of panic to the soul than that redness which affrights in blood."[64]

The pattern of Ishmael's sentence is the pattern of the chapter: throughout, increasing clusters of phenomena are stripped away to suggest an underlying, indefinable, and horrific presence. As Brodtkorb observes, Ishmael overwhelms us with the reflections of someone "trying to think the unthinkable."[65] With an élan in the face of apprehension that Melville could no longer call upon in *Pierre* and "Bartleby," this narrator proceeds by negation, blending assumptions of Kantian metaphysics and the paradoxical conceits of apophatic theology into a rhetorical tour de force. Determined to pierce through the world of phenomena to a noumenal presence (or to convey a "dim, random" sense of that presence), Ishmael speaks of "a dumb blankness, full of meaning," of "the visible absence of color," of "heartless voids" and "nameless things." Mixed with the parade of negatives is a conviction that the world of appearances masks a subtle "demonism," that although "in many of its aspects this visible world seems formed in love, the invisible spheres were formed in fright" (195). Thus the portentous quality of Ishmael's rhetorical questions and brooding allusions.

In the context of *Moby-Dick* "The Whiteness of the Whale" bears a mighty burden. For as Ishmael demonstrates at length, one can describe whales, measure whales, paint pictures of whales, "try" whales, mince whales, eat whales, use the skin of a whale's phallus for a coat—one can do all these empirical things and still not know Moby Dick. What the white whale is to Ahab, to Starbuck, to Stubb and other sailors, becomes clear in the progress of the narrative. But only in this chapter is Ishmael at pains to articulate his personal sense of the white whale. If light, he bids us consider finally, operated "without medium upon matter," all creation would be blank (195). Such blankness, eloquent in its representation of an unadorned universe, is what the whiteness of the whale epitomizes to him.

Despite the radical differences of their fictional situations, Ishmael's metaphysical inquiries are similar in progression to John Marcher's systematic cancellation of experience in "The Beast in the Jungle": whereas Marcher cancels specific life choices, Ishmael cancels phenomena in his effort to disclose a reality other than what we know, reality as we do *not* experience it, reality that simply *is*, without historical association or interpretive handles. Marcher's fate is to meet his fate, clearly and definitively. Ishmael's fortune is to glimpse the unbearable awe-fulness of being "at times" and thereby survive to tell the tale. His contemplations on the whiteness of the whale are potentially as crippling as Pip's encounter with the "strange shapes of the unwarped primal world" during the cabin boy's plunge into the shoreless Pacific (414). To pierce through the world of phenomena to a perception of ontological being requires a vision unrelenting in the severity of its negation. To lose oneself in the infinite, as Pip did, is to undergo the ultimate negation of self, to see "God's foot upon the treadle of the loom" (414).

Despite the capacity of narrative to evoke a sense of awe and peril by courting the infinite, the primary purpose of negative strategies in American writing, as we have seen, has been to celebrate a cleansed world and to voice optimism for the future. If such reflexive confidence seems difficult to sustain in the late twentieth century, it is still possible to invoke the formula in a context of the times. Tentative and even wistful, a meditation on beginnings offered by the *New York Times* on the first day of 1991 bids us look hopefully to the year ahead. "One night last week," the lead editorial begins,

> winter's first snow fell on New York, and the city woke to a new world. An icy Eden it was, the roads not yet ribboned by car treads, the sidewalks unscarred by footsteps, the trees glazed. Later in the day there'd be holes in the blanket, and urine stains and streaks of soot; and the trees would have shaken off their shining coat. But not at dawn. At dawn on that chill morning, New York, hushed and unsullied, promised perfection.
>
> So does a New Year. Three hundred and sixty-five days lie ahead, each one a blank, beautiful page. No turned-down corners, no coffee stains, no scribbles. These pages are pristine, and there's no way to know what will appear on them eventually. No way at all.

What we have in these paragraphs is a touching evocation of a beginning that sets the "first snow" of the winter against the background of conventional New Year considerations, that nourishes hope even while acknowledging the ephemeral nature of an untarnished world. The rhetorical strategies for conceptualizing the pristine remain the same as they were for Paine, for pseudo-Dionysius, or for Mr. Evelyn in *Margaret*: the first snow of the winter (whiteness now a blanket of purity rather than a mystifying presence) creates "a new world," an "Eden" characterized by "unscarred" sidewalks, by a city "unsullied"; the day, moreover, epitomizes the year, its pages stretching ahead, with "No turned-down corners, no coffee stains, no scribbles." In this scenario "blank" is "beautiful," and New York "at dawn" promises perfection.

But the bombast and vaulting assurance of earlier American centuries no longer informs this postmodern list of negatives. After acclaiming the promise of perfection, the editorial quickly acknowledges the later realities (the "subsequent circumstances") of the day as inevitable, first by noting streets "not yet ribboned" with tire marks, then by mentioning "urine stains and streaks of soot"—stern emblems of urban life. The moment of stillness and purity is temporary, presocial, unsupported by ritual that could cast it, atemporally, in a sacred frame. For this new world—demonstrably secular, recognizably ours—is destined to replicate the scarred world of yesterday; this Eden is fated to succumb to experience. Yet the moment, fleeting as it is, generates an up-beat perspective; amid metaphors of gambling and optimism and the observation that "everyone's hopeful on New Year's Day," the editorial concludes with the words, "this year, maybe, the jackpot." Hope might not be eternal but it is perennial, even when figured as (or reduced to) "another roll of the dice, another pull on the one-armed bandit." And it is made possible by language that negates the corrosive atmosphere of the present in the interest of possessing a sense of beginning—no matter how transitory.

2

Part
Two

3

The Negative Character in American Fiction

One of the most persistent manifestations of the tendency I have been describing can be found in fictional characters who enact the negative principle, whose function it is to measure the world in which we live by the worlds in which they are unable to live. The most carefully delineated of these characters—among them Natty Bumppo and Huckleberry Finn in the nineteenth century, and Isaac McCaslin and Randle Patrick McMurphy in the twentieth—exist in narratives that virtually recapitulate the experience of America. And appropriately so: for such characters, amplified by the resonant figure of a nonwhite partner/mentor, tend to play the role of original (unattached, even revolutionary) American in a socially insistent environment and thus to precipitate by collision or contrast the constricting torrent of our history.[1] Out of differences in the narratives come variations in the role. Marilynne Robinson's *Housekeeping* (1981) crosses gender lines with quiet but unrelenting authority in its portrayal of the "unredeemed transient," Sylvie. Jerzy Kosinski's *Being There* (1970) forgoes the frontier ethos that sustained earlier negative figures to present Chauncey Gardiner, modern man as tabula rasa. All such characters, however, no matter their age, gender, or location in time, are defined by the personal and social ties they lack or, in some cases, which they strive to cancel from their lives—as does Isaac McCaslin in *Go Down, Moses* (1942). All are products of negative conceptions that display identity in unlikeness. Moreover, none of them has any idea of founding a better society, despite the insistent hopes of well-meaning critics that they should do so. Their function (and I repeat to make the point clear) is to show us the world in which we live—and the beginning ethos we have forgone—by showing us the worlds in which they are unable to live. Three lines from one of Whitman's Inscriptions to *Leaves of Grass*, the title of which the poet changed from "Originators" to "Creators" to "Beginners," capture the essence of the negative character as a kind of resident alien in society:

> How dear and dreadful they are to the earth,
> . . . .
> How people respond to them, yet know them not,
> How there is something relentless in their fate at all times.[2]

James Fenimore Cooper's figure of Natty Bumppo stands as the classic example of a negative character in American literature. In *The Pathfinder* (1840) Natty says that he is a man with "neither daughter, nor sister, nor mother, nor kith nor kin, nor anything but the Delawares to love" and thus describes himself by stipulating the personal and civilizing ties which he lacks.[3] The focus on female relatives in Natty's list suggests how unequivocally women were equated with society in his (and Cooper's) mind. At an earlier point in the same novel Cooper defines Natty Bumppo as "a sort of type of what Adam might have been supposed to be before the fall, though certainly not without sin" (*Path*, 134). Clumsy, halting, and anomalous, the definition nonetheless presents us with a figure whom Cooper takes care to wed to the wilderness and not to society. What remains after the stripping away in Natty's list of negatives and Cooper's definition is a character whom Cooper refuses to implicate in an encroaching and fallen world.

Far apart in time and temperament is the figure of McMurphy in Ken Kesey's *One Flew Over the Cuckoo's Nest* (1962). Yet there is a genetic similarity linking the two characters: as the narrator, Chief Bromden, tells us, McMurphy is radically different from the other patients on the Big Nurse's ward because he has "No wife wanting new linoleum. No relatives pulling at him with watery old eyes. No one to *care* about, which is what makes him free enough to be a good con man."[4] Again, a sense of unlikeness impinges on a world of sameness; again, a negative rhetoric stipulates the absence of social and personal ties. What remains in this case is energy, the sudden release of outrageous energy into a starched and tyrannical fictional world.

I cite the brief negative catalogues pertaining to Natty Bumppo and McMurphy in order to come with the most explicit evidence to the kind of imaginative conception that gives them fictional existence. How such characters function, how—that is to say—Cooper, Kesey, and other writers involve them in narrative, is a direct result of this conception. In these two instances, the extreme difference in fictional ambience (and the protagonists' deportment) suggests both the diverse use to which negative characters may be put and the radical alignment of their fates. To accent considerations of difference and of similarity, I shall proceed by juxtaposition and conceptual pairing in the discussion that follows; I shall examine first the world of Natty Bumppo and that of McMurphy, then the strategies of disassociation practiced (or attempted) by Isaac McCaslin and Huckleberry Finn, and finally (recognizing the cultural evolution of a type) the advent of the woman and the possibilities of satire in contemporary figurations of the negative character.

From the Forest to the Looney Bin: Natty Bumppo and Randle Patrick McMurphy

Not until he brought Natty Bumppo back to life in *The Pathfinder* and *The Deerslayer* (1841) did Cooper feature him as what James Grossman calls "one of the great negative characters of literature."[5] Signs of a developing negative conception, however, accumulate throughout the earlier Leatherstocking Tales. In *The Prairie* (1827), for example, Natty tells Ishmael Bush that he has "no regular abode" and adds conventional metaphors of disengagement to a self-portrait drawn for Hard-Heart: "I have never been father or brother. The Wacondah . . . never tied my heart to house or field, by the cords with which the men of my race are bound to their lodges."

Again, during his elaborate death scene, Natty announces that he is "without kith or kin in the wide world!"[6] In *The Last of the Mohicans* (1826), he explains to Chingachgook that because he has "no kin, and . . . like you, no people," he is free to share the memory of Uncas.[7] And in *The Pioneers* (1823) he faces the most troublesome (and instructive) situation of all—that of an incipient negative character detained by loyalty in a region that has become inimicable to his temperament.

In *The Pioneers* Cooper introduces a Natty Bumppo who is bound by a prior obligation. He must remain near Templeton because of his acknowledged duty to Major Effingham. Never again does he come into a narrative so encumbered, so bound to a place that is being transformed by time. Quite obviously, Templeton is not authoritarian in the manner of Kesey's hospital in *One Flew Over the Cuckoo's Nest*. The presiding figure of Judge Temple seeks to temper the extravagance of the settlers in a community still striving for social equilibrium; Oliver Effingham and Elizabeth Temple embody a legitimate promise for the future. Because of his allegiance to an earlier world, however, Natty Bumppo becomes an anachronism in this novel, the futile antagonist of a progress to which Cooper is committed. Elizabeth Temple puts the matter bluntly: even "were we so silly as to wish such a thing," she says to an assenting Oliver, it would not be possible to "convert these clearings and farms again into hunting-grounds, as the Leather-stocking would wish to see them."[8] Inevitably, as one trapped in a linear movement of time, Natty Bumppo feels constraints. Inevitably, developing social forms operate to imprison him. The spectacle of Natty in jail and in the stocks epitomizes the position of the negative character (no matter how virtuous) in society (no matter how benign). For the social conception and the negative conception are antithetical in nature; neither can accommodate the other.

As part of Cooper's effort to treat American themes and materials in his work, *The Pioneers* takes its form from the insistent movement of American history. If the underlying model is the inevitable thrust of settlement, however, the relation of public and private worlds shifts in important ways that suggest the priorities of Cooper's imagination. The famous last sentence of *The Pioneers*—"He had gone far towards the setting sun,—the foremost in that band of pioneers, who are opening the way for the march of the nation

across the continent"—absolutely forsakes Natty Bumppo's attitude toward events in the interest of a communal point of view.
When Cooper invokes the grand drama in terms of which the action of the novel takes its fullest public meaning, Natty's departure is given a national function quite at odds with his motive for leaving Templeton. The conclusion of *The Pioneers*, of course, depends on more than the final sentence, no matter its lofty perspective. Flimsy in conception and awkward in presentation, the Edwards-Effingham subplot nonetheless manages to resolve highly charged issues in the novel. Once the secret of Natty Bumppo's hut stands revealed in the person of Major Effingham, Judge Temple can demonstrate the responsibility with which he has discharged his trust. The marriage of Oliver Effingham and Elizabeth Temple unites the legitimate heir to the estate and the daughter of him who developed it. If Oliver (as Thomas Philbrick observes) is likewise "the inheritor of the Indians' moral claim to the land," Elizabeth (as Cooper makes clear) is the bearer of culture to a new settlement.[9] Both characters, moreover, have had a special friendship with Natty Bumppo, something not possible for Judge Temple as the authority figure of the growing settlement. The death of Major Effingham marks the end of the old order and the responsible advent of the new: after a troubled interim period, civilization has come into the hands of its best representatives.

Although the resolution of problems in *The Pioneers* comes with the rush attendant upon disclosures of secrets and identities, one cannot deny its consolidating promise nor overlook the powerful rhythms of death and renewal that Cooper brings to the assistance of his formulas. Philbrick is perceptive in noting the mood of benediction in the final chapter of the novel, the feeling that a large movement of history has concluded and "a fresh beginning" can now be made.[10] At this early point in Cooper's career we see a tendency to resolve issues with a sense of beginning. We see, too, that this kind of resolution, societal in focus, perforce excludes Natty Bumppo. By means of a surprising enlargement of perspective, however, Cooper manages to assign Natty a function crucial to a nation that will bring future Templetons into being.

All of this is very neat. And yet Cooper in *The Pioneers* has already conceived a Natty Bumppo who stands against Templeton and the heralded march of the nation because of an orientation toward beginnings far different from that envisioned by society.

Natty may be an anachronism to those who are settling the village. But he is also a character who has seen this world from a perspective prior to history. In a memorable scene in chapter 26 he remembers that in his youth the area around what is now Templeton was "a second paradise"; filled with reminiscence, he then tells Oliver of one of his favorite spots on earth, a ridge high in the Catskills to which he would climb in his younger days, and his association with beginnings suddenly takes its most radical form. Indeed, as Natty recollects the setting, the ingredients of an elemental creation story come into somewhat incongruous focus. Mountains "blue as a piece of clear sky" balance clouds on their tops; the "High-peak and the Round-top . . . lay back like a father and a mother among their children"; and the ridge itself juts out over a river almost a thousand feet below. When Oliver asks what he saw from the ridge, Natty replies, "Creation . . . all creation, lad." Cooper, of course, has no way (and no intention) of sustaining such a primal vision. Images of turmoil, of venality and excess, quickly modify the scene. Natty could see not only the highlands of the river from his ridge but General Vaughan's troops burning the town of Esopus (near Kingston) during the Revolutionary War. Thus he beheld a vast panorama of creation and the events that corrupted it, "all that God had done, or man could do, far as the eye could reach" (*Pi*: 292–93).

Equally close to Natty's heart is a stream that has been "playing among the hills since He made the world, and not a dozen white men have ever laid eyes on it." In his judgment, it is "the best piece of work that I've met with in the woods; and none know how often the hand of God is seen in the wilderness, but them that rove it for a man's life" (*Pi*: 294). To say that Natty Bumppo belongs to a preagrarian world would be to understate the case. He is a character whose vision is associated with creation, whose experience reaches back to a world unmediated by history. His motive for leaving Templeton is to realign himself with beginnings—which in the Leatherstocking Tales characteristically take the form of an unspoiled wilderness. As he explains to Oliver and Elizabeth, "The meanest of God's creaters be made for some use, and I'm formed for the wilderness; if ye love me, let me go where my soul craves to be ag'in!" (*Pi*: 454).

Even at this point in a Leatherstocking series not yet conceived, Natty Bumppo's wilderness is preeminently temporal. Natty goes to find, "ag'in," a *time* no longer furnished by the *place* in which he has lived for many years. Cooper's sense of the American frontier (which is to say, ours), superimposes itself on this temporal quest so that although Natty says nothing whatsoever about direction, we know that he must go "towards the setting sun." If *West* signifies future for the nation and for Cooper's public voice, *wilderness* signifies early for Natty and for the conception that brought Natty into being. One can measure the total embrace of the Leatherstocking Tales by means of this distinction between West and wilderness—one geographical, which moves in consonance with the flow of American history and culminates in *The Prairie*, and one temporal, which reaches back to an earlier world and culminates in *The Deerslayer*. Although Cooper is reluctant to send Natty Bumppo westward without a role that serves society, he has already presented a character who yearns for the values of an original world. Ultimately, he would give that character both Lake Otsego (the setting of *The Pioneers*) and the wilderness in the final novel of the series.

In *The Pioneers*, *The Last of the Mohicans*, and *The Prairie*, the evidence of Natty Bumppo's negative status comes exclusively from his own dialogue. The point is worth noting, for one of the distinguishing features of the final two Leatherstocking tales is that Cooper adds his narrative voice to the making of Natty's negative portrait. If Natty describes himself as without daughter, sister, or mother in *The Pathfinder*, it is the narrator who defines him as an Adamic figure. If a disappointed Natty tells Mabel Dunham that he "shall return to the wilderness and my Maker," it is the narrator who tells us that Natty forced himself to leave "as one snaps a strong and obstinate cord" (*Path*: 460). And if the youngest Natty of all rejoices at the sight of a pristine forest with "not a tree disturbed even by red-skin hand . . . but everything left in the ordering of the Lord," it is the narrator who observes that "it was the air of deep repose, the solitudes that spoke of scenes and forests untouched by the hands of man, the reign of nature, in a word, that gave so much pure delight to one of his habits and turn of mind."[11] Cooper, in other words, joins forces with the resurrected Natty Bumppo, adopts—and even enlarges—his perspective, and presents him authorially as a character who functions by negation.

Cooper's emphasis on the uplifting virtues of nature in *The Pathfinder* and *The Deerslayer* becomes a significant part of a developing negative strategy. Uniquely affiliated with the wilderness,

Natty Bumppo partakes of its original coherence and innocence—
so much so that as James E. Swearingen and Joanne Cutting-Gray
suggest he embodies in *The Pathfinder* a "temporal boundary" that
projects atemporality and "situates us at the birth of America" with
a fresh perspective on its "origin and character." In the final two
novels of the series, John F. Lynen finds, "the landscape creates"
the protagonist, "just as he, in turn, interprets it."[12] What one
should bear in mind in adopting these perceptions is that Cooper's
landscapes augment the creation of character and our sense of an
original world by means of a traditional use of negative rhetoric.
"Far as the eye could reach," writes Cooper in *The Pathfinder*,
"nothing but the forest was visible, not even a solitary sign of civilization breaking in upon the uniform and grand magnificence of
nature" (*Path*: 289). The appeal of Glimmerglass in *The Deerslayer*
comes from the surrounding "forest grandeur": "the hand of man
had never yet defaced, or deformed any part of this native scene"
in which the "unbroken verdure" accentuates "the mirror-like surface of the lake" (*D*: 36). Blake Nevius has reminded us of the
problems encountered by early nineteenth-century writers who
sought to portray the American wilderness with such negative
terms as *boundlessness* and *interminableness*. As Nevius demonstrates, Cooper had acquired by 1840 a "visual discipline" that
allowed him to make varied use of scenic material.[13] Still, he often
describes by negation in *The Pathfinder* and *The Deerslayer*. He
tells us repeatedly what the wilderness is by telling us what it is
not. He evokes (in *The Deerslayer*) a sense of timelessness, of a pristine "world by itself," by rhetorically canceling out the signs of civilization (*D*: 149). And he thereby fashions a setting that validates
the identity of a negative character who knew long before that he
was "formed for the wilderness."

It took five novels to establish Natty Bumppo as the classic negative character. And the writer who thought of calling the final
Leatherstocking tale "Judith and Esther, or, the Girls of the Glimmerglass" could not have been fully aware of the implications of his
work.[14] Nonetheless, during the course of these novels Cooper
manages to create the prototype of the character who takes form
from a negative impulse. No matter their different situations, all
such characters (including Kesey's McMurphy and Robinson's
Sylvie) experience society as a constricting force. The tone may
vary—as when Huckleberry Finn in *Tom Sawyer* is not only "intro-

duced" into society but "dragged" and "hurled" into it—but the
metaphors remain tellingly the same: what Natty Bumppo refers to
as "cords" and "ties" become for Huckleberry Finn "bars and shackles" that bind him "hand and foot." Even the daily routine of a community thwarts the natural habits of the negative character. "I eat
when hungry and drink when a-dry; and ye keep stated hours and
rules," Natty Bumppo says to Oliver and Elizabeth toward the end
of *The Pioneers* (*Pi*: 454). Similarly, Huckleberry Finn tells Tom
Sawyer that "the widow eats by a bell; she goes to bed by a bell—
everything's so awful reg'lar a body can't stand it." To Tom's rejoin-
der that "everybody does that way," Huck replies (quite accurately),
"I ain't everybody, and I can't *stand* it. It's awful to be tied up so."[15]

In chapter 3 of *The Prairie*, a momentarily wistful Natty Bumppo tells Paul Hover that if he could choose his "time and place
again" he would speak for "twenty and the wilderness!" (*Pr*: 32).
Wishing against the grain of time, Cooper's aged trapper longs for
youth and an unspoiled setting, while the narrative moves inex-
orably toward the solemn spectacle of his death. From start to fin-
ish *The Prairie* is valedictory in tone. Cooper's statement that "this
book closes the career of Leather-stocking" expresses his own feeling of having completed an imaginative venture by taking it in the
only direction it could go—toward fulfillment in death (*Pr*: 6). Perhaps because of this the novel honors Natty Bumppo as few literary works do their protagonists. So thoroughly does a quality of res-
ignation pervade Natty's thoughts and actions that he virtually
becomes his vision of all he has seen—a character who exists in the
exalted form of moral perspective. That Cooper's allegiance to society still generates an ambivalence toward this character, however,
can be seen in Duncan Middleton's ultimately qualified praise of
Natty, recited as part of a family tradition handed down from Duncan Heyward (from *The Last of the Mohicans*): uniting the best of
the civilized and natural worlds, Middleton is pleased to say,
Leatherstocking is a man "of sterling worth," endowed with the
judgment to distinguish good from evil, yet unable to attain his
"proper elevation and importance" because he has lived "in the forest" (*Pr*: 114). Such is society's best articulated view of Natty
Bumppo—laudatory, concessive to a point, but finally insistent on
its own priorities. Yet Cooper transcends the terms of this estimate
in *The Prairie* by incorporating Natty's moral perspective into his
own public vision. Edwin Fussell maintains that in this novel Natty

Bumppo "*is* the West."[16] The logic of this assertion leads us to see a portentous intersection of personal and cultural crises in Natty's elaborate death scene. With *The Prairie* as our evidence, we may say that Cooper demurs from the cherished assumption of the inexhaustibility of the American frontier. At the culminating point of Abiram White's execution, Cooper's setting becomes an eloquent metaphor of desolation, leafless and without vegetation, a barren land over which "the rushing of the wind sounded like the whisperings of the dead" (*Pr.* 362). It is a West not simply exhaustible but exhausted, marked with ancient evil. A short time later, as he assimilates the glory of an autumn sunset, Natty Bumppo carries Cooper's West with him into a death that is at once transfiguring and prophetic.

Resigned to his unlikeness in this novel, Natty explains to Mahtoree that he migrated to the prairie "to escape the wasteful temper of my people" (*Pr.* 213) and exempts himself from Le Balafré's charge of white cupidity by saying, very honestly, that he has never wanted "more ground than the Lord has intended each man to fill"—that is, the ground on which he stands (*Pr.* 314). By the time of *The Prairie*, Natty has been defined as a landless man who has avoided the practices of a grasping society because of his dedication to an original world. And when in *The Deerslayer* Cooper grants him a purified setting drawn to the specifications of "twenty and the wilderness," Natty is free to enact what became the essential reverie of the negative character—the freedom of a pre-adult life.

As many critics have pointed out, Natty Bumppo regresses psychologically in the final two novels of the Leatherstocking series.[17] Reflecting on his romantic misadventure in *The Pathfinder*, Natty admits that he has made a mistake in aspiring to Mabel Dunham's hand and has suffered as a result, almost as if he has had to come to self-knowledge by painful indirection. It is no wonder that he suffers from confusion: Cooper's uncertain handling of details—especially those concerning Natty's age—suggests an authorial problem in taking a resurrected character back to the wilderness. Never too precise about the age of this essentially presocial character, Cooper provides muddled and conflicting information in *The Pathfinder*. During his first conversation with Mabel, to take but one example, Natty says that Sergeant Dunham is "thirty years my senior" (*Path:* 37). Later, however, the Sergeant replies affirmatively when asked if Natty is not "within ten or twelve years" as old as he (*Path:* 310).

From a potential suitor whom Mabel's father has regarded "as a sort of son," Natty thus moves closer in age to his longtime friend until—with the death of the Sergeant—his role becomes that of designated husband and surrogate father (*Path*: 92). It is an uncomfortable, indeed, impossible role, and Natty goes through emotional throes because of it. Once Mabel marries Jasper Western, this father figure can step aside, painfully, if according to form. From the time Sergeant Dunham first speaks of a marriage between Natty and Mabel, however, Natty becomes a regressive figure. Because of his clear conscience, the Sergeant believes, Natty will remain "a mere boy all his life" (*Path*: 132). Cooper's narrator portrays his mind as "almost infantine in its simplicity" and compares him to Adam before the fall (as we have seen) to suggest his instinctive innocence (*Path*: 278). And Mabel, after refusing Natty's proposal of marriage, comforts him by saying that he will dream again of hunting, of deer, "and of the beaver you have taken" (*Path*: 275). Happiness for Natty, as Cooper makes clear, consists in being a little boy again, free from the threatening promise of sexuality. The necessity for such regression balances its cost: childhood affords the ultimate protection against marriage. Since women are the bearers of culture in Cooper's fiction, since they provide what Nina Baym calls "the nexus of social interaction," to marry would be to form a bond with society.[18] In making Natty a father figure, Cooper resolves the emotional situation of his novel in a socially convenient manner. In making him childlike, Cooper prepares him to return "to the wilderness and [his] Maker," to a beginning world proximate to creation.

The consensus is that Natty Bumppo weds the wilderness at the end of *The Pathfinder* and that the wilderness is, in Joel Porte's paraphrase of Melville, "a Paradise for bachelors only."[19] Provocatively discussed by critics of different persuasions, the friendship of Natty and Chingachgook takes on a new vitality in the final two novels of the Leatherstocking series, not simply as a substitute for women but as a means of sustaining a negative conception to which Cooper is now committed. Cooper seems deliberately to pair his two characters in these novels. When Natty, in *The Pathfinder*, says that Chingachgook "has no children to delight with his trophies, no tribe to honor by his deeds," that he is "a lone man" who "stands true to his training and his gifts," he could well be looking into a mirror (or a pond) and describing a "red" version of himself (*Path*: 79). As they come into *The Deerslayer*, neither Natty nor Chingachgook has yet slain a human being; and Glimmerglass (somewhat surprisingly for men who have been tromping around upstate New York) is the first lake either has seen. Out of this pairing, as I have observed elsewhere, comes a developing strategy of doubling Natty's consciousness to include that of Chingachgook—so that innocence is at once protected and heightened by experience it does not, objectively, have.[20] The classic example can be seen in Natty's story of discovering six sleeping Mingos, told in response to Charles Cap's question about temptation in *The Pathfinder*. "What an opportunity that would have been for the Sarpent," muses Natty the storyteller, aware that Chingachgook would have claimed lives and scalps in an instant. So imminent was the Chingachgook-in-Natty that the occasion was "a desperate trial" (the "hardest" temptation of his life) to one who could neither scalp nor kill sleeping enemies, even in wartime. Shortly after Natty's later and allowable ambush dispatched five of the six, Chingachgook appeared with the five Mingo scalps at his belt, "hanging where they ought to be." "So, you see," Natty concludes, "nothing was lost by doing right, either in the way of honor or in that of profit" (*Path*: 435–36).

This intriguing little story not only illustrates the idea of racial *gifts*. It also suggests a dependence on Chingachgook as an agent who allows Natty to practice a morality of abstention and then take an almost Franklinesque satisfaction that "nothing was lost" by resisting temptation. By attributing to Natty Bumppo the consciousness but not the act of savage experience, Cooper makes the solitary Serpent serve the interests of the solitary Adam. And he leaves a legacy to future negative characters who would need a friend from beyond the ranges of society to help chart the course of their asocial experience.

From its opening pages *The Pathfinder* dedicates itself to the uplifting virtues of sublimity. Working within eighteenth-century and romantic conventions, Cooper extols the vastness of the forest and of Lake Ontario and makes a response to nature an index to moral character more explicitly than ever before. What Natty Bumppo knew in *The Pioneers* now receives official narrative sanction: the wilderness is the work of the Creator, capable of nourishing the noblest qualities of man. Cooper carries his value-generating aesthetics into the cameo setting of *The Deerslayer* with maximum effect. Whereas Thomas Hutter and Hurry Harry witness the brilliance of a sunrise "without experiencing any of that calm delight which the spectacle is wont to bring when the thoughts are just, and the aspirations pure," Natty Bumppo is overcome with awe at the sight of the woods and of Lake Glimmerglass (*D*: 324). "He loved the woods," Cooper writes, "for their freshness, their sublime solitudes . . . and the impress that they everywhere bore of the divine hand of their creator" (*D*: 278). In his youngest form, Leatherstocking is not so much a philosopher as a "poet" of the wilderness (*D*: 46).

The special feature of the setting of *The Deerslayer* is its freshness and isolation. Cooper brings us to a microcosm of a continent that "existed apart . . . without an origin that the annals of man can reach," and bids us discover America for ourselves (*D*: 149). Although he places his story in the 1740s, the ambience of the novel yields a controlling sense of timelessness: protected spatially and temporally, as H. Daniel Peck demonstrates perceptively, the world of *The Deerslayer* "suggests a time *before* history."[21] Repeatedly, as we have seen, Cooper speaks of a wilderness "untouched by the hands of man," and the tone of his narrative voice continues to be indistinguishable from that of Natty Bumppo. Chingachgook's statement—"This is the country of the Manitou!"—confirms the sense of the immanence of the Creator in the setting (*D*: 428). It is, indeed, an early world, intact in its original harmony, admirably suited to Natty's temporal needs.

What critics of *The Deerslayer* dispute is the extent to which the action of the novel compromises the figure of Leatherstocking as part of the setting. Peck believes that Cooper contains the violence, that "the full force of history is never allowed to break in."[22] Such an assessment allows one to see the ending as a moment of relative stasis or cessation of movement that includes—indeed, features—Natty Bumppo. Thus, as Peck argues both in *A World by Itself* and in his later introduction to the World's Classics edition of *The Deerslayer*, we have at the conclusion a sense of temporal immobility, a "commitment to a vision of permanence."[23] From the perspective of a different idiom, Edwin Fussell finds that *The Deerslayer* ends with the image of a transcendent Natty Bumppo "on the frontiers of heaven." And Joel Porte argues that by leaving Natty "shining forever in eternal youth," Cooper attempts "to mingle his hero with the universe, in order to profess his profound belief that a sinless existence passed in communion with the American forest would confer immortality." We may take the demurral of John P. McWilliams, Jr., to represent the opposing view. Stressing the corrosive moral effect of the scalp laws, the carnage wrought by the soldiers' bayonets, and the pragmatic innocence of Natty Bumppo, McWilliams concludes that "by entering Eden, man corrupts it." With its "dark ending," *The Deerslayer* closes the Leatherstocking series "because it has in effect killed the hero whose life it is initiating."[24]

I come to the evidence by way of my interest in beginnings. As we have seen, Cooper takes care to make the setting of *The Deerslayer* an embodiment of creation and thus a radical beginning world. Additionally, he provides episodes that constitute personal beginnings for Natty Bumppo. Natty's initial response to Glimmerglass tallies in both ways, embellishing the pristine image of the lake even as it establishes a *first* in his life. The ritualized contest in which Natty kills his first Indian (and receives the name "Hawkeye" from his dying foe) evokes an important soliloquy from the youthful victor: "Well, this is my first battle with a human mortal, though it's not likely to be the last. I have fou't most of the creatur's of the forest . . . but this is the beginning with the redskins" (D: 126). Additionally, as the narrator reports, the scene in which the vengeful Hurons admire the composure of the captured Deerslayer "may be said to have been the commencement of the great and terrible reputation" that Leatherstocking came to have among Indian tribes (D: 291).

Beginnings such as these (generated by the model of an individual life) imply a later development, a movement through time, not only validated by novels previously written but already underway in *The Deerslayer*. Natty Bumppo's killing of three more Hurons, for example, validates his feeling that the victory over le Loup Cervier was "the beginning with the redskins." And in the final pages of the novel Cooper offsets the tranquility of his changeless wilderness with a mood at once nostalgic and expectant. Along with Chingachgook and Uncas, Natty Bumppo returns to Glimmerglass "on the eve of another, and still more important war." Offering a reprise on his subtitle, Cooper tells us that this had been the region of the "First War-path" for Natty and Chingachgook, that it recalled "scenes of tenderness" and "hours of triumph." They leave with "melancholy feelings," but they leave with a purpose—taking their way to the Mohawk "to rush into new adventures, as stirring and as remarkable as those which had attended their opening career on this lovely lake" (*D*: 546–47). In this novel of *firsts*, Cooper greets an already well-known Leatherstocking at the beginning of a turbulent and preachy career; the logic of such a beginning invokes a sense of forward motion rather than of stasis.

Out of a concern to see the figure of Natty Bumppo emerging from the author's consciousness, we tend to read the Leatherstocking tales in the order of their composition.[25] It is well to remember, however, that Cooper consistently spoke of the sequence in terms of Natty's advancing age. Even when there were three novels in the series, he advised his publisher that "the order" should be "Mohicans, Pioneers, and Prairie" because Natty Bumppo "makes debut, properly, in the Mohicans." While at work on *The Deerslayer*, he promoted it as first "in the order of the books." He was, in other words, consciously writing the last novel of the series as the first novel of the series—"to fill up," as he said, Natty's "history."[26] And thus, in what should probably be seen as an effort to have it both ways, Cooper strove in the context of his timeless setting to anticipate details already recorded in previous novels (supplying the genesis of the name "Hawkeye," for example, alluding to Natty's service under Major Effingham) and to provide a suitable introduction to a well-defined life. With that introduction completed, he points Natty forward in time with a sense of graduating development: in the present war Natty's fame has already "spread far and near," and, as we have seen, a "still more important war" lies ahead (*D*: 545).

For a socially embattled Cooper, *The Deerslayer* enacts the desire to imagine the world over again, to possess the promise not simply of childhood but of childhood dreams. Conceived long before as a character associated with creation, Natty Bumppo is the appropriate vehicle for a symbolic journey home. It is a beguiling alliance, that between Natty and an original wilderness, and the more one contemplates it the more one wants it to be permanent. But radical beginnings in American fiction are primarily narrative strategies, accessible as points of reference and departure. As isolated moments, they are for leaving, for pushing off into the swirl of human events. Emerson (as we shall see in chapter 5) may speak in compelling metaphor for the possibility of eternal youth; Thoreau may bid us wake to each day as if it were the first of our lives. But Cooper, as a writer of narrative, uses beginnings differently. In *The*

Deerslayer he makes no effort to eternalize the youthful image of
Natty Bumppo. Quite the opposite: Cooper's radical beginning,
carefully nurtured, becomes a strategy for portraying the personal
beginnings of a life. And nothing accentuates narrative movement
more surely than a set of anticipatory *firsts* guaranteed by a life
already lived. One should not forget the text: at the end of *The
Deerslayer*, Natty Bumppo is ready to go to war, not to the frontiers
of heaven.

In the final chapter of the novel, Natty tells Judith Hutter that
"this very spot would be all creation to me, could this war be fairly
over once; and the settlers kept at a distance" (*D*: 541). From his
ridge in the Catskills, we recall from *The Pioneers*, Natty had once
commanded a vision of "all creation." Glimmerglass now becomes a
potential distillation of that vision, an emblem reaching back to a
world prior to history. That Natty mentions settlers in his remark
to Judith suggests that he has prophetically carried his later experience back to the beginning with him. And this in turn confirms the
perception that Cooper has in *The Deerslayer* reached backward in
time only to lean forward in expectation: the final, and youngest,
Natty Bumppo can define the realities—war and settlement—that
would forever keep him from abiding with "all creation." With
apocalyptic generosity, Walt Whitman once said that Natty Bumppo "is from everlasting to everlasting."[27] So, in narrative range, are
the Leatherstocking tales. For the conclusion of the series marks a
celebratory beginning that prefigures the death, already inscribed,
of a negative character who has long yearned for "twenty and the
wilderness."

Unlike Natty Bumppo, McMurphy has but one life to give to his
fiction. And *Cuckoo's Nest* moves with lyric intensity to dispose of
him in sacrificial victory. For Kesey introduces us to a negative
character who is about to *care*: McMurphy may enter the novel with
no wife and no watery-eyed relatives encumbering him, but toward
the end of his six weeks on the ward he deliberately ties himself to
the shrunken men around him, taking on himself the burden of
their struggle for wholeness and integrity. Not that the transition
from self-propelling freedom to responsibility for others takes place
overnight. We are treated in the first half of the novel to the engaging and aggressively adolescent spectacle of McMurphy challenging every restriction to his unbridled spirit, then—after he learns

that he has been committed to the institution and will be released
only on the recommendation of Miss Ratched—to his sobering
decision to play her game her way for himself. But when McMurphy finally reaches out to help fellow patients who are in the hospital only because they fear the outside world, he commits himself—and thereby surrenders the negative qualities that originally
defined him as a character.

Given the total conception of *Cuckoo's Nest*, there is no way to
sustain the negative impulse that brought the primitive force of
McMurphy into existence. To account for the protagonist's prior
independence, Chief Bromden surmises that he has had to keep on
the move in a twentieth-century America increasingly regulated by
the Combine. Maybe because he grew up "wild all over the country," the Chief says, he was never subjected to schooling or, in his
later and "lightfooted," days, to social adjustment (89). Mobility is
clearly a necessary condition of McMurphy's unencumbered status,
a contemporary substitute for the sense of space that sustained the
earlier Leatherstocking, ambivalent because of its tendency to
nourish the attributes of the confidence man that McMurphy has
in abundance. In the tightly controlled world of the hospital,
mobility faces an ultimate threat.

The specific makeup of the Combine remains vague in *Cuckoo's
Nest*, as indeed it must, since the word *combine* is not simply a syn-
onym for *organization* but Chief Bromden's protean metaphor for
all that mechanizes, threshes, and levels—for all that reduces
human beings to products.[28] In this sense, the term contributes
powerfully to the dramatic coherence of the novel. The Ward, the
Chief says, employing the logic of the metaphor, "is a factory for the
Combine. It's for fixing up mistakes made in the neighborhoods
and in the schools and in the churches" (38). As a freewheeling and
"moving target," McMurphy is worse than a mistake; having somehow slipped through or around the machinery of the Combine
whole and entire, he needs *fixing* rather than "fixing up." He is not,
of course, an easy victim. His aversion to regimen is deep (befitting
what Bruce Carnes calls a "primary" character), and it transcends
conventional allegiance: having earned a Distinguished Service
Cross in Korea for leading an escape from a Communist prison
camp, McMurphy later received a dishonorable discharge for
insubordination. With the authority of experience, he twice compares Miss Ratched's modes of tyranny with those of the prison

camp.[29] When this unbridled and original human being swaggers onto the ward for the first time, brash, boisterous, his heels ringing off the floor "like horseshoes," he commands the astonished attention of patients long debilitated by a diet of weakness and fear. Chief Bromden hears him before he sees him—and he "sounds big." McMurphy enters laughing; it is the first genuine laughter the Chief has heard "in years" (10–11).

Laughter, we come to understand, is crucial to McMurphy's identity as a character. When McMurphy abruptly stops laughing, Chief Bromden observes, the "laughing sound hovers around him, the way sound hovers around a big bell just quit ringing—it's in his eyes, in the way he smiles and swaggers, in the way he talks." Moreover, because laughter in this narrative takes the form of expanding circles, sound waves, that become liquid by metaphorical association, it becomes a powerful antidote to the narrow discipline of the Ward. McMurphy's first laugh, for example, is "free and loud and it comes out of his wide grinning mouth and spreads in rings bigger and bigger till it's lapping against the walls all over the ward" (11). Similarly, during the hectic moment on the fishing trip when Candy's breast is bruised and bleeding and the Chief's thumb smarts red from the line, McMurphy again laughs—"because he knows you have to laugh at the things that hurt you" or the world will run "you plumb crazy." This time the laughter is contagious: "swelling the men bigger and bigger," it rang out on "the water in ever-widening circles, farther and farther, until it crashed up on beaches all over the coast, on beaches all over all coasts, in wave after wave after wave" (238). If liquidity signifies expansiveness and freedom, glass symbolizes its frozen and brittle opposite. Thus, when McMurphy runs his hand through the window of the nurses' station in feigned unawareness of its presence, "The glass came apart like water splashing." (190). And when the Chief throws the control panel through screen and window at the end of the narrative, "The glass splashed out in the moon like a bright cold water baptizing the sleeping earth"—a final sacramental image of rebirth (310).

Throughout *Cuckoo's Nest* there is a sense of something lost—spontaneity, early happiness, a capacity for joy. All such things belong to a forgotten world of freedom until they are resuscitated by McMurphy, the negatively conceived character who embodies, insists upon, and finally supplies in caricature what the original world contained. On occasion, the language of the novel encourages us to see him as a roughneck Christ figure: "Anointest my head with conductant," he asks at shock-therapy time; "Do I get a crown of thorns?" (270). And as the fishing trip gets underway, the Chief observes that "McMurphy led the twelve of us toward the ocean" (227). Quite apart from such allusions, however, the fishing trip is the climactic event of the novel: it is the occasion during which the patients achieve a vibrant sense of community and the point after which the protagonist's career as a negative character loses its momentum. Tied now to the other patients, gradually drained of the force he once possessed in abundance, McMurphy is virtually diffused among his comrades. "He doled out his life," Chief Bromden says with oracular precision, "for us to live" (245).

Kesey fashions his protagonist from a melange of stereotypes, among them the fast-talking gambler, the brawling Irishman, the "cowboy out of the TV set walking down the middle of the street to meet a dare" (189). Both lightning and thunder are metaphorically associated with his actions, and as a dynamic new character in Chief Bromden's "cartoon world" (31) the early McMurphy is "a giant come out of the sky to save us from the Combine" (255). Moreover, in *Cuckoo's Nest* Kesey has adapted to his purposes distinctive characteristics of the frontier braggart as well as those of the confidence man. If McMurphy inherits something of Simon Suggs's idea that "It's good to be shifty in a new country," he is the full beneficiary of the rhetoric of extravagance that energized the work of Southwestern humorists in the nineteenth century.

Paul Zweig reminds us of the persistence of "ritual boasting" over the centuries, in one form that of the epic hero, in another that of the American backwoodsman.[30] Such a tradition, significant and undeniable, links the proud language of Beowulf with the grandiose rhetoric of Muhammad Ali. And in the hyperbolic language of many frontier characters in nineteenth-century American writing—among them Robert Montgomery Bird's Roaring Ralph Stackpole and Mark Twain's Child of Calamity—it takes on a lusty, comic dimension. "Here am I, Ralph Stackpole the Screamer, that can whip all Kentucky, white, black, mixed, and Injun," announces Bird's extravagant character, horse thief and fearless combatant, buffoon and Mississippi alligator. The verbal sparring of the Child of Calamity and Big Bob in the raftsman passage of *Life on the Mississippi* displays most of the conventions established by the brag-

101

The
Negative
Character
in
American
Fiction

gart, whose frequent cowardice and ineptness brings a touch of the mock-heroic to the comedy of his situation. Bob claims to be "the original iron-jawed, brass-mounted, copper-bellied corpse-maker from the wilds of Arkansaw . . . Stand back," he bellows, "and give me room according to my strength!" The Child takes a different tack, warning his auditors not to look directly at him: "Smoked glass, here, for all! Don't attempt to look at me with the naked eye, gentlemen! . . . I scratch my head with the lightning and purr myself to sleep with the thunder . . . ! I put my hand on the sun's face and make it night in the earth. . . . Contemplate me through leather— *don't* use the naked eye."[31]

Although McMurphy is neither inept nor cowardly, his language has affinities with this kind of joyous boasting. Immediately after his arrival he announces with a grin that he is the new bull goose loony. And as he prepares for his patently doomed effort to lift the control panel, he spits in his hands, slaps them together, and proclaims to the wondering men around him, "Okay, stand outa the way. Sometimes when I go to exertin' myself I use up all the air nearby and grown men faint from suffocation. Stand back. There's liable to be crackin' cement and flying steel. Get the women and kids someplace safe. Stand back" (120). But when an attendant at the gas station calls McMurphy a bull-thrower after hearing his claim that he killed a man in the ring, McMurphy's response, concessive yet deliberate in manner, takes us to the man behind the words: " 'Now I didn't say that bull-throwing wasn't also one of my abilities, did I? But I want you to look here.' He put his hands up in the guy's face, real close, turning them over slowly, palm and knuckle. 'You ever see a man get his poor old meathooks so pitiful chewed up from just throwin' the *bull*? Did you, Hank?' " (225). In this instance, the record of combat rather than the rhetoric of prowess results in respect for the patients who are en route to the fishing expedition.

Chief Bromden regards McMurphy's hands as "a road map of his travels up and down the West" (23). Scarred, callused, and tattooed, they are the "color of raw meat" (80). Yet this man with carbon under his fingernails can also paint on paper that has "no lines or numbers anywhere" and write letters "in a beautiful flowing hand." On one occasion he is visibly "upset and worried" over a letter he receives (153). Kesey tells us nothing further about McMurphy's ties to someone somewhere in the world, and it is possible that he inserts such anomalous details only so that Chief Bromden (himself surprised) can say that McMurphy's appearance does not rule his life anymore than does the Combine. A more characteristic use of his literacy can be seen in McMurphy's mirror-writing prank: having put some "strange writing that looked like a foreign alphabet" on a slip of paper, he sticks it under a toilet bowl rim with a wad of gum. When Miss Ratched uses her mirror to scan the underside of the rim for cleanliness, "she gave a short gasp at what she read reflected and dropped her mirror in the toilet"—another instance of glass yielding to water.

103

The
Negative
Character
in
American
Fiction

From a hospital record read aloud by Nurse Ratched we learn that McMurphy is thirty-five years old and has never been married. Cleared of a charge of statutory rape because his sexual partner would not testify, he objects to Miss Ratched's insinuation of guilt with boastful protestations of helplessness. The girl said she was seventeen, he recalls; eventually she became so demanding that "I took to sewing my pants shut." He had to leave town because she was wearing him out, he explains to Doctor Spivey: she "got to where she was tripping me and beating me to the floor." Both the Doctor and the patients manage smiles at these sallies, but in these days before McMurphy's presence is fully registered on the Ward they are careful not to "come right out and laugh" (43). Once he understands the plight of the patients, however, McMurphy's ability to transpose the bravado of the boast to tall tales of sexuality involving others becomes crucial to his function in the novel. The ward has acquired a story-teller, the traditional opponent of authoritarian rule.

With the florid irony that masks his hopelessness, Harding explains to McMurphy that the patients are "victims of a matriarchy" (61). If Nurse Ratched has unquestioned control, other female characters in the novel are cast in supporting postures of tyranny. Harding's wife is a stereotyped bitch whose remarks are guaranteed to make Harding fall back on defenses she scorns. In a different way, Billy Bibbit's mother is a debilitating force in her son's life. And Chief Bromden, too, knows of female dominance. His Indian father took his white wife's name when they married and suffered a diminishment of self ever after. The father fought the Combine, which of itself would make him smaller, "till my mother made him too little to fight anymore and he gave up" (208). The white reduced the Indian; the female reduced the male. The Chief has only to think of his parents to know the legacy of his people.

Only McMurphy, the epitome of unharnessed energy and unvarnished maleness, stands outside such domination. And thus he and the Big Nurse come to be opposed in every way. As Barry H. Leeds points out, "the polarity between the mechanical sterility of Big Nurse and the fertile animality of McMurphy" permeates the narrative.[32] He is the rowdy, she the manufacturer of docility; he is the gambler, she the designer of rules. More than anything else, of course, he is the stud who would make the patients big, she the "ball-cutter" who would make them little. After hearing Harding's admission that every patient on the Ward lives in fear of losing "his whambam," McMurphy's command of hyperbole and macho therapeutic instincts issue forth in vignettes that delight his fellow patients (65). Clowning at breakfast to make the assembled men laugh, McMurphy turns to the shy Billy Bibbit with a sudden question about the "two twitches" they once picked up in Seattle. To a surprised audience he continues: "We'd never have brought it off" except that the women had

> heard tell of Billy Bibbit. Billy "Club" Bibbit, he was known as in them days. Those girls were about to take off when one looked at him and says, "Are you *the* renowned Billy 'Club' Bibbit? Of the famous fourteen inches?" And Billy ducked his head and blushed—like he's doin' now—and we were a shoo-in. And I remember, when we got them up to the hotel, there was this woman's voice from over near Billy's bed, says, "Mister Bibbit, I'm disappointed in you; I heard that you had four—four—for goodness *sakes!*"　　　　　　(98–99)

As puerile as it is, the story makes the blushing Billy Bibbit grin with pleasure.

With profit as his ultimate motive, McMurphy puts together one of his tales for the private benefit of the shrunken Chief Bromden. Throughout the novel, as one might expect, his force is registered most dramatically in the responses of the narrator. Upon first shaking McMurphy's hand, the Chief reports that his own hand began "swelling up out there on my stick of an arm, like he was transmitting his own blood into it. It rang with blood and power" (24). After the fishing trip the Chief attributes his rekindled optimism to the fact that "McMurphy was teaching me" (243). Before

the fishing trip, however, McMurphy offers to make Chief Bromden "big" again, to restore him to full size (so that he can bet on the
Chief's ability to lift the control panel). In a "rollicking auctioneer's
voice" he dreams out a vision drawn to epic proportions:

> *There* you'll be. It's the Big Chief Bromden, cuttin' down the
> boulevard—men, women, and kids rockin' back on their heels
> to peer up at him: "Well well well, what giant's this *here*, takin'
> ten feet at a step and duckin' for telephone wires?" Comes
> stompin' through town, stops just long enough for virgins, the
> rest of you twitches might's well not even line up 'less you got
> tits like muskmelons, nice strong white legs long enough to
> lock around his mighty back, and a little cup of poozle warm
> and juicy and sweet as butter an' honey.   (211–12)

In the quiet dark McMurphy continues, "spinning his tale" about
beautiful young girls running after the Chief: "I tell you, I tell you,"
he concludes, embellishing the Chief's powers of conquest with his
own former boast, "you'll have women trippin' you and beatin' you
to the floor." As he walks away to sign his friend up for the fishing
trip, he peels the covers off Bromden's bed with a sweep of his arm,
leaving him prostrate and naked. "Haw," McMurphy laughs;
"What'd I tell ya? You growed a half a foot already" (212).

Invariably, the appearance of a figure like McMurphy signals an
influx of vitality into the routine of an established fictional setting.
Let us note by way of example the curious similarities between
McMurphy and Maxim Petrovich Chaly, a minor character in
Alexander Solzhenitsyn's *Cancer Ward* (1968). On a somber day in
a hospital in eastern Russia, an "energetic-looking man walked
briskly and healthily" into a ward filled with listless and dispirited
patients. "He didn't really enter the ward," Solzhenitsyn writes, "he
burst into it" as if there were "a guard of honor drawn up in ranks
to greet him."[33] When he senses the malaise of the men in the
room, this new man stops short and whistles. In precisely the same
situation, McMurphy challenges the patients by saying, "Damn,
what a sorry-looking outfit. You boys don't look so crazy to me"
(*CN*: 17). Chaly does the same "in a voice of energetic reproach":
"Hey, boys, you're a lot of dopes, aren't you? Have your feet shriv-
eled up or something?" Shortly afterward, he pulls out a pack of

cards and invites his neighbors to play whist or twenty-one or poker. Because of his buoyant mood, some of the patients think he may not be ill; but Chaly has cancer of the stomach—which he treats outwardly with disdain and inwardly with vodka, a cure, as he says, "for all illnesses" (*CW*: 321).

Although the medical authorities in Solzhenitsyn's hospital are pleasant and helpful, the men on the ward live with a sense of doom; their languid talk of politics gives small respite from their preoccupation with illness and disease. Thus, Chaly's entrance, like that of McMurphy, excites varying degrees of wonder. To his drinking and card playing he adds the motto, "A woman a day keeps the doctor away" (*CW*: 310). When one supposed wife arrives with food and drink, and later another, Chaly announces to general laughter that women are all alike and that it does no harm to please them: "Kitchen maid or Lady Muck / They're all the same, they like a fuck" (*CW*: 319). Chaly, "the artful dodger," as Solzhenitsyn terms him, is also something of a con man in the contemporary Soviet Union. To the astonishment of some patients and the disapproval of others, he tells of smuggling tomatoes by bribing the guard at the railroad station and the conductor on the train. His manner is jaunty, his perspective that of a man who assumes that one must cut corners to get by in the world.

Whereas McMurphy can dominate *Cuckoo's Nest*, the central issues of *Cancer Ward*—survival rather than sacrificial triumph, accommodation rather than self-assertion—relegate Chaly to a minor role. He is only a thought at the end of the narrative when Oleg Kostoglotov, the protagonist, sees people carrying baskets to a waiting train and wonders if (like Chaly) they are smuggling vegetables "to make up for mistakes in the supply system" (*CW*: 533). But there is a more fundamental difference between the two novels and thus between these two characters. With grim realism, Solzhenitsyn shapes a complex portrait of post-Stalinist Russia, out of which comes the question that haunts Kostoglotov near the end of the novel: "A man dies from a tumor, so how can a country survive with growths like labor camps and exiles?" (*CW*: 523). Chaly's bright interlude brings only a momentary vitality to this world. His crude jokes exemplify a kind of locker-room humor that presents women as sexual objects—but not as enemies to be feared. Kesey, on the other hand, fashions a narrative that emphasizes by caricature the increasing standardization of American society. In this simpler and more fervid fictional world, Kesey's women are also given the role of sexual objects. The distinguishing feature of *Cuckoo's Nest*, however, is that they are seen as creatures of malevolence who tyrannize men.

107

The
Negative
Character
in
American
Fiction

In his excellent study of the confidence man in American literature, Gary Lindberg examines the traditional opposition between the confidence man and women. Because the confidence man requires flexibility of scene together with a succession of audiences that have faith in him, and women represent stability and social convention, the one typically sees the other as an inhibiting force to fool or exploit and then leave behind.[34] This certainly seems to be the case with Chaly, who regards the world as his oyster and has no serious thoughts (pro or con) about women. But McMurphy can no longer solve his problems by leaving town; he now confronts a woman and a set of circumstances that he cannot avoid. At times he generalizes on the situation, on society. After identifying the Big Nurse as a ball-cutter, for example, he goes on to say that he has seen a thousand like her across the country, "old and young, men and women," people who try to make you weak so you will "follow their rules" (58). In this speech gender is irrelevant; McMurphy warns against an insidious kind of human being who strikes him as all too common. Later, however, he associates women, power, and an inability to laugh in the manner of a veteran confidence man: "When you lose your laugh," he announces to the timorous men around him, "you lose your *footing*. A man go around lettin' a woman whup him down till he can't laugh anymore, and he loses one of the biggest edges he's got on his side. First thing you know he'll begin to think she's tougher than he is" (68). The healthy combination of laughter and freedom confronts its nemesis in the suffocating combination of women and power.

McMurphy's efforts to profit from the good he is doing make him (in Lindberg's words) less than a "self-abnegating hero."[35] But McMurphy has, of course, never claimed to be a hero of any kind. When Nurse Ratched wonders if any of the patients would call McMurphy a saint or a martyr, no one raises a hand. As Harding observes, their resident confidence man would "take it as a direct effrontery to his craft" to have "simon-pure motives" attributed to his actions (254). Of his craft McMurphy has made no secret. Chief Bromden reports on the way he manipulates the patients during a blackjack session, even to the point of spelling out his formula for success: "The secret of being a top-notch con man is being able to know what the mark *wants*, and how to make him feel he's getting it." Having won "pyramid" stakes of cigarettes, he finally lets the others win them back, shaking his head at their skill, complaining that he would be "leery of playing against such sharpies for real money tomorrow." And every man acts out his assigned part, raking in cigarettes with a "smirk on his face like he's the toughest gambler on the whole Mississippi" (78–9).

After his bruising fight with the orderlies, fought to protect George Sorenson, there are no further questions about McMurphy's motives. And during his final march to the Big Nurse's office it is the collective need of his "forty masters" that drives him forward, as it had made him "wink and grin and laugh and go on with his act long after his humor had been parched dry between two electrodes" (304–5). Overwhelmed finally by doctors, supervisors, and nurses after his assault on Miss Ratched, McMurphy appears "for a second upside down" before his face is smothered by white uniforms. In that instant "he let himself cry out: A sound of cornered-animal fear and hate and surrender and defiance, that if you ever trailed coon or cougar or lynx is like the last sound the treed and shot and falling animal makes as the dogs get him, when he finally doesn't care any more about anything but himself and his dying" (305). In this sentence, worthy of Faulkner in its allegiance to momentum, Chief Bromden records the elemental and savage cry that is the protagonist's final sound. With his confidence guise stripped away, McMurphy's primal nature surges to the fore—solitary, alien, and profoundly negative.

Kesey has introduced a negative character, plunged him into a world of intensified experience, and shown us that he combats a general diminution of self at the necessary expense of his original status—and thus of his life. Since it is the abiding function of such a character to measure rather than to recast society, McMurphy's victory is neither literal or final. In the terms offered by this fable, it is a matter of legacy. Having taken McMurphy's life into his own, the Chief is the direct recipient of that legacy. He embodies McMurphy's vision of "the Big Chief Bromden, cuttin' down the boulevard," as he escapes from the hospital, taking "huge strides," floating "a long ways" between steps: "I felt like I was flying. Free." And when he gets a ride with "a Mexican guy going north with a truckload of sheep," the lingering presence of McMurphy is obvious: the Chief tells the curious driver "such a good story about me being a professional wrestler the syndicate had tried to lock up in a nuthouse that he stopped real quick and gave me a leather jacket to cover my greens and loaned me ten bucks to eat on" (310–11). McMurphy has empowered Chief Bromden, has surrendered his spirit to a native American whose living (and loving) tribute is the text we read. With all his adolescent posturing and moral ambiguity, McMurphy stands as a powerful example of the form and the fate of a modern negative character.

Compounded Difficulties:
Huckleberry Finn and Isaac McCaslin

In diverse and instructive ways, Huckleberry Finn and Isaac McCaslin are beset by the worlds that surround them—Huck by the strictures of a society he needs but necessarily refuses to join, Isaac by the configurations of a history he seeks to disown. Again it is important to understand how these characters relate to and take their identity from a total fictional context—from the forces and assumptions that give each narrative its specific form. Of the two, be it said, only Huck emerges as a negative character, a "benign, defensive trickster," as Warwick Wadlington properly calls him, fundamentally separate from the world he visits and therefore capable at the end of signaling a decision to "light out" from those who seek to transform him into one of their own.[36] Isaac McCaslin, on the other hand, enters the interwoven world of *Go Down, Moses* (1942) encumbered, oppressed by a heritage he refuses to acknowledge. If the cartoonlike simplicity of *Cuckoo's Nest* yields a protagonist who makes his life complex, the baroque complexity of Faulkner's novel presents a character who seeks to make his life simple. Yet what Isaac McCaslin longs for is not what the forces of the novel devise for him: his efforts to cast off the burdens of history dramatize both the predatory nature of the past and the cost of his principled and unavailing innocence.

Central to the plot of *Go Down, Moses* is Isaac McCaslin's refusal to accept his inheritance, the estate bequeathed by his grandfather, Lucius Quintus Carothers McCaslin. From his reading of the ledgers in the plantation commissary, Ike (in 1885, at the age of eighteen) comes into the knowledge that his grandfather not only owned slaves and had a child by a slave-mistress but that he later committed incest with his own slave child—an act that drove the mother to suicide. The callous disregard of human beings made possible by the institution of slavery is the "general wrong" to which Ike refers; what his grandfather did is the specific evil of which he wants no part. Because it is tainted, he will not (at the age of twenty-one) accept his patrimony.

Only once in *Go Down, Moses* does Isaac McCaslin succumb to the pressures that would have him assume his family inheritance. Arguing in terms of a moral absolute that equates ownership and original sin, he rejects the idea that he has repudiated the inheritance because, as he says, "It was never mine to repudiate."[37] But Ike does marry, and the consequences of that (mis)alliance subject him to the constraints of social priorities in a no-doubt rare moment of passion. For it is his wife, intent on possessing "The farm. Our farm. Your farm," who coerces a promise that Ike's extravagant dialogue with McCaslin Edmonds could never extract (362). Faulkner's scene implicates sexuality and the eternal Eve with the desire for property; what the pressures of inheriting cannot bring to pass, the woman will. Ike hears "the bell ring for supper," locks the door and undresses at his wife's command, sees her nakedness as "the composite of all woman-flesh" since the creation of man, feels the pressure of her fingers tugging at his wrist ("as though hand and arm were a piece of wire cable with one looped end") while he says "No . . . I wont. I cant. Never," until he surrenders to desire with "Yes" and the thought that "*We were all born lost*" (313–14). Following the amazing theological drama of this encounter—profound in implication, comic in manner—Ike becomes "unwidowered but without a wife" (281). Twenty years later he is a widower in fact, forever lacking the son he had apparently talked to his wife about before his passionate encounter, "uncle to half a county and father to no one" (3).

With immense sweep, *Go Down, Moses* engages the turbulent issues of American history, alludes to the discovery of an "already tainted" promise in the new world, and appropriates the story of our first parents' dispossession from Eden to its thematic purpose. Faulkner's aggressive negative language attains its greatest intensity in "The Bear." When Isaac McCaslin finds Fonsiba's cabin, for example, rain is reducing it "to a nameless and valueless rubble of dissolution in that roadless and even pathless waste of unfenced fallow and wilderness jungle—no barn, no stable, not so much as a hen-coop: just a log cabin built by hand and no clever hand either" (277). Predictably, there is no fire on the stove; predictably, too, out of a succession of negations come Fonsiba's only words—"I'm free" (280). Slender words, these, sadly overwhelmed from an economic perspective by Fonsiba's surroundings, yet simple and unadorned in their proclamation of an original condition, a point of being that is noncommodified, prior to such things as outbuildings, fences, and a domestic "fire on the stove."

It is by means of relentless negations that Faulkner evokes the "anachronism" of the bear in *Go Down, Moses* and fashions the wilderness that will be Ike's "mistress and his wife" (193, 326).[38] But the wilderness—threatened long before by "the axes of the choppers," as Natty Bumppo remembers in *The Prairie*—is the doomed victim of accelerated progress in this novel: Ike has seen it retreat "year by year before the onslaught of axe and saw and log-lines and then dynamite and tractor plows" (354). Having outlived Old Ben and Sam Fathers, he incorporates their spirit into his feeling that he and the wilderness are coeval. He has no Glimmerglass to enrich a life after death. But he does have similarities with the figure who came into existence at the age of seventy in *The Pioneers*, wished for "twenty and the wilderness" when he was past eighty in *The Prairie*, and finally took on youth and a natural innocence in *The Deerslayer*. "Born old," as Faulkner writes, Isaac McCaslin becomes "steadily younger and younger until" (nearing eighty) "he had acquired something of a young boy's high and selfless innocence" (106). And Faulkner grants Ike a corollary vision of himself and the wilderness "running out together, not toward oblivion, nothingness, but into a dimension free of both time and space" in which all the hunters he has known can move "again among the shades of tall unaxed trees and sightless brakes where the wild strong immortal game ran forever before the tireless belling immortal hounds, falling and rising phoenix-like to the soundless guns" (354). It is a harmless hunting ground that Ike envisions, sport made eternal by the extravagant use of negative rhetoric. In such a paradise, he would surely be entitled to echo Fonsiba's words, "I'm free."

What Ike does say, of course, is "Sam Fathers set me free" (300). For it is the half-Indian and half-Negro Sam Fathers who schools Isaac McCaslin in the ways of the wilderness and makes his renunciation of the world not only possible but spiritually inevitable. The negative and hence asocial (or presocial) impulse in "The Bear" issues from the wilderness itself, emerges, shaped, in the colossal figure of Old Ben—"so long unwifed and childless as to have become its own ungendered progenitor" (210)—and passes mystically into the human form of Sam Fathers, who (like Chingachgook at the end of *The Last of the Mohicans*) *"had no children, no people, none of his blood anywhere above earth that he would ever meet again"* (215). It is from Sam, "his spirit's father," that Ike inherits the invincible purity of the wilderness that stands opposed to the rapacious legacy of Carothers McCaslin (326). Faulkner has conceived a character who struggles to be negative but who must witness the confining spectacle of a family history that remains in motion (as we learn in "Delta Autumn") and inevitably breeds new injustice out of the original wrong. By means of Ike's stance, Faulkner projects in high relief the agony of "a whole land in miniature," even as he poses (and pursues) the question of the fate of innocence in a fallen world (293).

Critical assessments of the role of Isaac McCaslin in *Go Down, Moses* have been remarkably if predictably dichotomous. Some early judgments credited Ike with a laudable integrity for spurning the wealth of a corrupt world, living humbly without coveting material possessions, and cultivating a private purity of existence. Contrary views depicted him as a loser who invokes an impossible "innocence" to escape responsibility and the difficulty of living in a fallen world. If R. W. B. Lewis (the most compelling of the early critics) could see Ike as "Christ-like," a transcendent saint who experiences an incarnation, David H. Stewart (reading the same text a decade later) could define this curious protagonist as one who achieves little but "cheap self-satisfaction."[39] Positions between these extremes censure Ike for not being more activist or point out that his rejection of the past is both admirable and futile. Because *Go Down, Moses* is what David Minter calls "a participatory reader's perfect text" (virtually demanding "interpretive activity" outside the boundaries of the novel), judgments about Ike's decision continue to be articulated with fresh conviction in scholarly journals and, with engaging fervor, in classroom discussions.[40]

What Eric J. Sundquist calls "the precarious form" of *Go Down, Moses* may have helped to develop the contours of this critical dialogue.[41] For the novel is not simply an assemblage of stories but a melange of fictional rhetorics, and one's sense of linguistic priority may well influence one's view of Isaac McCaslin. Quite apart from the various ludic, domestic, and tragic styles of the narrative, a compelling sacramental idiom surrounds the character of young Isaac in "The Old People" and "The Bear": he is baptized into the ritual of the hunt; he serves a "novitiate" in the woods; to be worthy of seeing Old Ben he must cast aside his gun (the instrument of aggression), then divest himself of compass and watch—thereby stepping outside the world of space and time. Yet the abundant metaphors that promote Ike's mystic consecration to the wilderness give way to a wry account of his self-approving decision to emulate the Nazarene by becoming a carpenter and, finally, in "Delta Autumn," to a brusque grammar of social realism: the melancholy lesson of that story is that an aged Ike is not only "outmoded" like the wilderness; he is, finally, encumbered by the racist attitudes of his time and place (343). Whether one faults Ike for copping out or faults society for its avarice may depend in part on one's response to the different languages of the novel.

Some matters in *Go Down, Moses*, of course, are established beyond debate: the conceptual unity of the novel assumes that all pasts, and not just that of the white southerner, are tainted— versions of original sin replicated throughout history. The Indian Ikkemotubbe, for example, is a native American version of Ike's grandfather, if anything more ruthless in his quest for power: after poisoning several puppies by way of warning, then murdering his cousin's eight-year old son to become king, Ikkemotubbe sells his own son, Sam Fathers, to Carothers McCaslin—along with his paramour and the slave to whom he has married her. As Ike's cousin Cass argues in their swirling conversation in the commissary, there is no such thing as an uncompromised past; one must do the best one can with what history has bequeathed to the present.

But that is precisely what Ike refuses to do as he spins his elaborate argument about ownership and the unspoiled condition of the earth as God created it. In effect, Ike's logic (in the mode of negations that strip away to a beginning) is this: in the beginning there was an original purity, with no such thing as ownership and thus no buying or selling of property. Now, however, the self-serving practice of ownership is sovereign—and it was made even more corrupt by regarding human beings as chattel. Rather than call for a revolution to eliminate ownership and restore the earth to its original state (in the manner of Thomas Paine, who, as we have seen, advocated the overthrow of kings to reclaim the world God had made), Ike renounces property on his own, aware that some citizens of Yoknapatawpha County consider him foolish and weak for doing so. On the first page of the novel we learn (before we know its full import) that

> in all his life [he] had owned but one object more than he could wear and carry in his pockets and his hands at one time, and this was the narrow iron cot and the stained lean mattress which he used camping in the woods for deer and bear or for fishing or simply because he loved the woods; who owned no property and never desired to since the earth was no man's but all men's, as light and air and weather were. (3)

Unable to translate the world back to a primal purity or to take his way to (or toward) a fresh geographical location, an aging Ike can only draw upon that youthful moment when he discarded compass and watch as the condition of seeing Old Ben and project it into a dream of himself and the wilderness vanishing into eternity, liberated forever from the demands of "time and space." It is a private dream that Ike harbors, an undefiled and undefilable substitute for the future, and it leaves him stranded in an innocence that has no impact on a present generated by the sins of the past. The full array of Faulkner's rhetorics of fiction in this "participatory" text implicates reader as well as character: what Ike wishes for (and necessarily lives against) in *Go Down, Moses* comes under the unremitting pressure of a world to which we all belong.

As Isaac McCaslin seeks to escape the burdens of the past, Huckleberry Finn seeks to evade the perils of the present. Transposed into Huck's idiom, metaphors of feeling constrained by society carry over from *Tom Sawyer* (1876) into *Huckleberry Finn* (1885) and persist throughout that narrative. The final episodes of the earlier novel not only "introduced" Huck into society, as I have noted, but "dragged him into it, hurled him into it—and his sufferings were almost more than he could bear." Working with figures of imprisonment so basic to defining the negative character, Twain adds that "whithersoever" Huck turned "the bars and shackles of civilization shut him in and bound him hand and foot." As this "unkempt, uncombed" fugitive from regimen explains to Tom Sawyer, "It's awful to be tied up so" (*TS*: 233–34).

Such tropes, at once whimsical and rich in implication, come from an entertaining narrator who manages the events of *Tom Sawyer* from a variety of intrusive perspectives, all of which depend on distance. What *Huckleberry Finn* gives us is something radically different—a sense of immediacy, a narrator virtually without perspective on matters that press him sorely. Huck, as narrator, does speak tellingly of society's constraints as he did in *Tom Sawyer*: his generalization about feeling "cramped up and smothery" in society corresponds to his earlier complaint that "It's awful to be tied up so."[42] In *Tom Sawyer*, however, an omniscient narrative voice subsumes Huck's remark into a larger and playful context. In *Huckleberry Finn*, on the other hand, Huck and his context are one; and the tenor of his words is serious during these latter "adventures" because society is not only smothery but threatening—to him as well as to others. William C. Spengemann observes that Huck's world "arises entirely out of his immediate experience." Thrust at him from the outside, bristling with "insoluble problems," experience for this narrator is both "unwelcome" and "unavoidable." Thus, according to Spengemann, Huck's passivity; thus, his ingenuous response to the difficulties society presses upon him.[43]

To observe the manner in which Huckleberry Finn comes into being as a negative character it is helpful to consider his evolving role in *Tom Sawyer*. Not until chapter six of that novel does Huck appear: by that time Tom has (during the course of a weekend) raided Aunt Polly's sugar bowl, vanquished the new boy in the village, figured out how to get the fence whitewashed, shown off to Becky Thatcher, and in Sunday school identified the first two disciples as David and Goliath. On his way to school on Monday morning, heavy-hearted at the prospect of "going into captivity and fetters again" even when a crowd of boys admires his ability to spit through the gap where he has lost a front tooth, Tom encounters Huck—who does "not have to go to school, or call anybody master, or obey anybody . . . nobody forbade him to fight . . . he never had to wash, nor put on clean clothes. . . . In a word, everything that goes to make life precious that boy had" (*TS*: 71, 74). Before the two boys have exchanged a word in the novel, Huck thus emerges as the embodiment of Tom's desire for freedom.

Throughout *Tom Sawyer*, Huckleberry Finn defers to Tom on matters of literacy and organized role-playing—on such things as devising a blood oath or planning a pirate raid. For this is Tom's novel: its primary conception radiates out from the central character, society's ultimate darling; Tom has the answers, and other characters exist in terms of their relationships to him. At one extreme is Sid Sawyer (Tom's half-brother), who, as Forrest Robinson remarks, threatens the "boyhood paradise" of the novel with his "kill-joy" manner and "serpentine malice."[44] At the other extreme is Huck, who (unconsciously) threatens the social economy of the novel with his asocial ways. Despite Tom's centrality, however, during this first meeting of the two boys Huck is anything but deferential: not only does his knowledge of superstitions equal Tom's but it is Huck who shows greater authority on a subject pertaining to nature. In the face of Tom's disdain for a small tick Huck has found in the woods, Huck says "I'm satisfied with it. It's a good enough tick for me." He then identifies it as "a pretty early tick . . . the first one I've seen this year," and when Tom offers to swap his tooth for this rarity, it is Huck who makes the decision to trade (*TS*: 77). Moreover, Tom seems fully aware of the power of Huck's reputation in the village; he virtually carries this "juvenile pariah" into the schoolroom with him when, ordered to account for his tardiness, he answers, "I STOPPED TO TALK WITH HUCKLEBERRY FINN" (*TS*: 78). He plays Huck's name, that is, as a trump card, knowing that the astounded schoolmaster will send him to the girl's side of the room, knowing, too, that he will have to take the one empty seat, next to Becky Thatcher. Tom has used his proximity to the socially anathematized Huckleberry Finn to gain proximity to the socially approved Becky Thatcher—with whom he later shares the climactic adventure of the novel while Huck languishes in the throes of a mysterious illness.

One of Mark Twain's original designs in *Tom Sawyer* was to have Pap Finn play the role eventually given to Muff Potter. No doubt because this bit of plotting would have required a personal reaction from Huck and given him (and Pap) what Paul Baender calls "inappropriate focal stature," the reprobate father was excised from the story. Another revision (in chapter 25) involved Huck's reaction when Tom announces he will "get married" (after buying a drum, a sword, a necktie, and a bull pup) if the two friends find buried treasure. Originally, Huck's disappoval was expressed in the present tense—"Look at Pap and my mother. Fight! Why they fight all the time." In the final version this became "they used to fight all the time. I remember, mighty well."[45] In each case the effect of the revision is to set Huck's parents at a distance, to establish conditions that make it possible for Huck to emerge as a negative character.

117

The
Negative
Character
in
American
Fiction

In *Tom Sawyer*, Huckleberry Finn is not so much a foil as a contingent character, dependent on Tom's presiding presence for his function, on Tom's initiatives for his actions. He may live, as he says, in hogsheads and dress in castoff clothes, but he exemplifies midnight, the woods, and freedom—a marginal world that Tom schemes to visit and strives to master before resuming his public (and prankish) life at home, in school, and in church. Huck's association with darkness and the forbidden leads Alan Henry Rose to the provocative observation that the fate of Huckleberry Finn is "strangely tied" to that of Injun Joe in this novel. While Joe is dying in the cave, he reminds us, Huck is ill, delirious, debilitated even after Tom's triumphant return. Rose argues convincingly that a vision of order and light prevails in the novel, and that it excludes both the asocial and the antisocial character. The "repressive movement" of *Tom Sawyer*, he believes, not only chokes off the "demonic energy" of Injun Joe but "simultaneously undercuts Huck Finn's vitality."[46] How much "lyrical energy" Huck brings to the novel I am not sure, although Rose makes a strong case for Huck's "fluidity" and his freedom from time and space. But in pointing to a bond, subtextual and enigmatic, between a negative character in-the-making and a malevolent nonwhite character, Rose prepares us to appreciate the open and intricate relation of Huck and a benevolent Jim in *Huckleberry Finn*.

In *Huckleberry Finn*, Huck is a character is his own right, validated by his idiom. Tom Sawyer is still present, not only at the beginning and end of the narrative but in portable form as a thought, a model whom Huck evokes for approbation or for help in adding "the fancy touches" to an adventure (*HF*: 29). As the various episodes unfold, however, an increasingly independent Huck is more vulnerable than ever before. For if the fact of his being a boy removes him from the encumbering threat of marriage, it likewise leaves him prey to the aggressive demands and confining kindnesses of the world around him. Between the regulations of Miss Watson and life with Pap one may not see much choice; initially, however, Huck prefers the latter because he can smoke and fish and because there are "no books nor study" (*HF*: 33). Only when Pap,

already a menace with his hickory stick, locks him in the cabin for days at a time is Huck driven to stage his own death—the ultimate act of negating a vulnerable social self. At this point he begins the

life of necessary disguises by means of which he can move in and out of social contexts, characteristically entering with an impromptu scenario of domestic tragedy that serves him as a means of survival and departing (usually posthaste) for the safety of the raft when the ongoing mayhem of society threatens to engulf him. At this point, too, Mark Twain introduces a runaway Jim and thus incorporates the issue of property into the nonwhite character who will accompany Huck on the trip down river.

While some of Huckleberry Finn's extemporized fictions are self-contained and directed at a specific audience, others depend on an auditor's contributions to make them effective—participatory authorship making for credible text. As Sarah Mary Williams, Huck tells Judith Loftus that his "mother's down sick, and out of money and everything, and I come to tell my uncle Abner Moore," an invented relative strategically placed in a real town ten miles away. Embarrassed and "sort of cornered" when he is exposed in his masquerade, Huck adopts Mrs. Loftus's compassionate (and melodramatic) notion that he is an abused "runaway 'prentice" and surrounds it with a blizzard of details: in this version of the truth he is George Peters, whose mother and father have died, who fled the cruel farmer to whom he was "bound," stealing some of "his daughter's old clothes," then traveling by night and sleeping by day (*HF*: 48, 52). The technique of the double lie, made possible by the gullible complicity of an auditor pleased at having seen through the initial falsehood, serves Huck well. What he learns at the Loftus household precipitates the journey downriver with Jim.

Other instances of Huck's improvised tales (all of which intensify the narrative thrust of the novel even as they screen him from society) include his encounter on the river with men seeking a runaway slave and his arrival at the Grangerford home. Once he tells his auditors that the man on the raft is white (the primary fiction) in the first of these episodes, Huck can proceed no further; he requires a response, some hint of an enabling scenario from which he can take his cue. Seizing an opportunity to introduce a version of his standard donnée into the developing drama, he says he needs help because his pap and mam and sister Mary Ann are sick on the raft; at this point (as he must) he allows the men gradually to project their fears onto the situation (*HF*: 77). The strategy of permitting, even enticing, an audience to scare itself with its own story works handsomely: the men donate forty dollars to a distressed family brought summarily into existence by Huck's groping outline and afflicted with smallpox as the participatory text takes form. It is the price of admission to a far more resonant drama than the spectator-authors could know. Huck has lied to save Jim, has acknowledged him as a father-figure, and has survived a struggle with his conscience. As we know, he splits the money with Jim—without whom there would have been no drama at all.

119

The
Negative
Character
in
American
Fiction

When challenged by the Grangerfords to explain his dripping-wet presence at their door, however, Huck spins an elaborate and self-contained tale of woe to an audience he must convince outright:

> They all asked me questions, and I told them how pap and me and all the family was living on a little farm down at the bottom of Arkansaw, and my sister Mary Ann run off and got married and never was heard of no more, and Bill went to hunt them and he warn't heard of no more, and Tom and Mort died, and then there warn't nobody but just me and pap left, and he was just trimmed down to nothing, on account of his troubles; so when he died I took what there was left, because the farm didn't belong to us, and started up the river, deck passage, and fell overboard; and that was how I come to be here. (*HF*: 84)

After hearing this account of tribulation and loss, the Grangerfords offer Huck a home "as long as I wanted it." One can understand why this family would treasure the memory of their daughter Emmeline.

Huck's fictions center on a self bereft of family; they are tales of death told to sustain life, melodramatic displacements of fact contrived to protect the boy behind the mask. Gary Lindberg calls *Huckleberry Finn* "one of the great shape-shifters in literature," and his kinship with such notable confidence men as the King and the Duke and Randle Patrick McMurphy cannot be overlooked.[47] But to see similarities is to be struck with differences: on the convincing surface Huck's tales are designed to fool an audience; their underlying motive, however, is typically self-effacement rather than self-aggrandizement, self-preservation rather than self-sacrifice, the welfare of others rather than personal profit.

Together on the raft Huck and Jim frequently enjoy the fragile luxury of an original world in which society vanishes into silence. As they float by St. Louis in the deep of the night, they see a wondrous display of light, but "there warn't a sound there; everybody was asleep" (*HF*: 56). On other occasions they sit on the sandy bottom of the river and witness the dawn of a new day: "not a sound, anywheres—perfectly still—just like the whole world was asleep" (except for "bull-frogs a-cluttering, maybe"). During these interludes of repose they listen "to the stillness" and go "naked, day and night" (when the "mosquitoes would let us"), a non-attire befitting their elemental condition (*HF*: 99–100). They talk "about all kinds of things" in an unobstructed universe: enacting the impulse to explain creation, for example, they speculate about whether the stars were made or "just happened"—their naïveté a comic substitute for the truly primitive. When Jim suggests that maybe the moon laid the stars, Huck finds the idea "reasonable" because he has "seen a frog lay most as many, so of course it could be done" (*HF*: 101). It is the accumulated memory of such occasions that brings Huck to tear up his note to Miss Watson: "I see Jim before me, all the time, in the day, and in the night-time, sometimes moonlight, sometimes storms, and we a-floating along, talking, and singing, and laughing" (*HF*: 179).

Huck's memories come to us in a language of incantation—not to be denied in its celebratory power—a language incompatible with ownership or social institutions. The cadences are those of a narrator who has relaxed into his own asocial identity and has no need, as himself, to invent personae or explain his presence. The society that enslaved Jim can make him a freed man. Stripped of society's perspective, however, Huck shares the raft with a man who is free because he exists. Unaware of the priority of his new and revolutionary perspective—unaware of his virtue, as James M. Cox and Michael Davitt Bell have put it—Huck pledges his allegiance to a primary world.[48] Two memorable statements bring the significance of the raft into vital focus. Following the Grangerford-Shepherdson episode: "We said there warn't no home like a raft, after all. Other places do seem so cramped up and smothery, but a raft don't. You feel mighty free and easy and comfortable on a raft" (*HF*: 99).

And after the brouhaha at the Wilkes farm: "it *did* seem so good to be free again and all by ourselves on the big river and nobody to bother us" (*HF*: 172). What is noteworthy in these passages is not simply the association of the raft and freedom but the phrases "We said," "all by ourselves," and "nobody to bother us." The raft, Huck's words tell us, is a home for two, not one, a place of mutual, not solitary, freedom. Which is to say that Huck needs not the raft but Jim-on-the-raft to compose a primary world as compelling as it is unsustainable.

Toni Morrison observes that "there is no way" in this novel "for Huck to mature into a moral human being *in America* without Jim."[49] To combine this observation with the conclusions of my analysis is to see that Huck, having experienced freedom with and because of Jim-on-the-raft, has no way to take up life in society, except as surrender. He is, as we know, overjoyed to be taken for Tom Sawyer (and thus delivered from a difficult situation) as he approaches the Phelps farm: "it was like being born again," he says, "I was so glad to find out who I was" (*HF*: 188). But it is both appropriate and portentous that he becomes Tom Sawyer at this point. For that is what he would have to become if he allowed society to adopt him.

Debate over Huck's decision to "light out for the territory ahead of the rest" will doubtless continue. Such major critics as Henry Nash Smith and Michael Davitt Bell have found it "unconvincing" and (from the perspective of Howellsian realism) *"irresponsible."*[50] From a broader perspective, Robert Penn Warren describes *Huckleberry Finn* as "the American un-success story" and with a provocative grouping of themes and characters includes Leatherstocking and Isaac McCaslin in the recurring "drama of the innocent outside of society."[51] An awareness of the negative structures in American writing, I believe, allows us to define such characters still more precisely, to understand their function in a significant context even as we distinguish among them. In that way, one sees Huckleberry Finn's final statement as a gesture, the final gesture of a character who functions in a tradition adapted to the purposes of this particular novel. Once again, the negative character has renounced society and made us see it anew. Once again, the negative conception proves difficult to sustain—all the more so since Huck is our narrator and there is no alternative perspective into which his voice can

121

The
Negative
Character
in
American
Fiction

be subsumed. But this chronically lonesome boy who seeks to evade experience does what he must at the end of *Adventures of Huckleberry Finn* when he signals a desire *not* to join society because he has "been there before." His home is with Jim-on-the-raft. It is we who live in the "cramped up and smothery places."

Variations on a Type   So long as the female character was conceptualized as the embodiment of social values, one could not present her by means of a rhetoric of negation. In the novels and tales we call Westerns, as Jane Tompkins has demonstrated with compelling (and entertaining) authority, language was the province of the woman. Whereas the male hero conventionally speaks a "minimalist" language or muses in a "not-language" equated with power, the woman opens up, describes such things as emotions and motives, and brings language into association with deportment, "religion, and culture."[52] If we take the developing love story in Owen Wister's *The Virginian* (1902) as a model, we may project a typical narrative in which untutored cowboy, courageous in temperament and barbarian in manners, meets school teacher who has come West from New England; gradually, after episodes in which she begins to respect his capacity for silence (at once masterful and imprisoning), she teaches him to respect her domain—education, the law, social institutions; she brings him, for better or worse, into an alliance with the rudiments of culture. Their predictable marriage signifies that she admires his masculinity and that he has wed society.[53]

Assumptions about the virtual identification of women and society were frequently tested if not directly challenged in nineteenth-century fiction. In what might be seen as the first step toward imagining a female negative character, the woman's emerging concern for a sense of *self* was frequently dramatized in terms of dependence and independence—with tragic as well as hopeful results. Already locked into a set of social interrelationships when we meet her, Edna Pontellier in Kate Chopin's *The Awakening* (1899) is frustrated by her life and victimized by her tendency to infatuation; her unavailing efforts at an ill-defined independence along with the collapse of her romantic dreams lead her to despair and suicide. Louisa May Alcott's *Work* (1873) presents a different set of possibilities. The novel opens with Christie Devon, on the eve of her twenty-first birthday, informing her Aunt Betsey that she wants to make her own "Declaration of Independence." The mobility of Christie's career over the next twenty years is manifest: in turn, she is a governess, an actress, a nurse, and a wife and mother; again on her own after her husband dies bravely in the Civil War, she becomes the center of a women's movement, "a loving league of sis- ters, old and young, black and white, rich and poor, each ready to do her part to hasten the coming of the happy end."[54] Christie is still a social creature, very much so; but she will point society and the society-in-her in what she sees as a necessary direction.

The figure of the tomboy offered a different way of presenting a female character without making her the stereotyped embodiment of social values. Alfred Habegger's survey of the tomboy "type" in the 1860s reveals a variety of prepubescent characters who are athletic, spunky, and witty—some with boy's names, including Jo in Alcott's *Little Women* (1868); Harvey in Anne Moncure Seemüller's *Opportunity* (1867); and others who cross-dress, among them Capitola Black from Mrs. E. D. E. N. Southworth's *The Hidden Hand: Capitola the Mad-Cap* (1859). If Mrs. Southworth wrote that novel, Habegger has reinvented it as a text for our time. Captivated (for good reason) with Capitola, he sees her as an urban, female version of Huckleberry Finn, "street-wise and self-sufficient." Capitola is an orphan in New York; to protect herself from the depredations of the world around her, she dons a cap and boy's clothes and in that disguise is able to sell newspapers. More important from my perspective, she exasperates a minister into banishing her not literally but by negation: "You have no reverence, no docility, no propriety," exclaims this pillar of society. Under threat of having her "indulgences" curtailed, Capitola replies, "The same fate that made me *desolate* made me *free!*"[55] Mischievous, funny, and intelligent, her freedom is a function of her age; she can be a nascent negative character because she is not yet a woman.

Grown-up but still youthful, the tomboy could become any one of a number of cross-dressing western characters, chief among them Calamity Jane, who makes her appearance in the first volume of Edward L. Wheeler's Deadwood Dick series in 1878 as "a trim boyish figure" with a "hand of creamy whiteness"; "This way, pilgrims," she whispers, as she ushers her friend Harris and the newcomer, Redburn, to safety. Unaware of her identity, Redburn sees her as a "strange youth,"

Of medium hight [sic] and symmetrically built; dressed in a carefully tanned costume of buckskin, the vest being fringed with the fur of the mink; wearing a jaunty Spanish sombrero; boots on the dainty feet of patent leather, with tops reaching to the knees; a face slightly sunburned, yet showing the traces of beauty that even excessive dissipation could not obliterate; eyes black and piercing; mouth firm, resolute, and devoid of sensual expression; hair of raven color and of remarkable length.

Harris later identifies her as Calamity Jane, who "can ride like the wind, shoot like a sharp-shooter, and swear like a trooper," a ubiquitous and mysterious friend who "is here, there and everywhere, seemingly all at one time." He objects strongly to Redburn's observation that Jane seems "debased," explaining to him (and to us) that "She was *ruined* . . . and set adrift upon the world, homeless and friendless; yet she has bravely fought her way through the storm. . . . True, she may not now have a heart; that was trampled upon, years ago, but her character has not suffered blemish since the day a foul wretch stole away her honor." Although few people know her name, "it is said that she comes of a Virginia City, Nevada, family of respectability and intelligence."[56]

In the final chapter of this brief tale of robberies, shoot-outs, and rescues, Deadwood Dick proposes marriage to Jane. "Haughtily, sternly," and (I might add) knowingly, the woman refuses: "I have had all the *man* I care for," she tells Dick, adding that they can be friends.[57] "Heroic" in her service to those in trouble, she remains an anomalous blend of stereotype and exception; conventionally "ruined" and bereft of family, she is light-hearted and daring in gun battles, determined never to marry, and possessed (somehow) of a good deal of property in Deadwood. "Calamity Jane is still in the hills," we read at the end of the tale. It is an appropriate gesture of freedom and farewell, a female version of "Heigh Ho, Silver, away!"; for if Jane is not presented by negation, she is nonetheless a character who is in society without, finally, being of it, public in her performances, private in her motives and withdrawals. She makes no commitments; she requires no closure.

In the spare and haunted story entitled "The Walking Woman" (1909), Mary Austin imagined a woman character remote in her mystery yet capable of defining the fundamental experiences of her life to a comprehending narrator. Negation is built into the form of "The Walking Woman," into its tone and style. The technique of the story is elliptical, the revelations fragmentary, divorced from social bearings both before and after the meeting of narrator and protagonist. The sentences that introduce the Walking Woman are appropriately severe in their focus on the unknown spaces in her life: "She was the Walking Woman, and no one knew her name." "She came and went, oftenest in a kind of muse of travel which the untrammeled space begets." "She had been set on her way by teamsters who lifted her out of white, hot desertness and put her down at the crossing of unnamed ways, days distant from anywhere. And through all this she passed unarmed and unoffended."[58] The narrator, who relates what she has heard with quiet confirmation, tells us that the Walking Woman had "lost her name. I am convinced that she never told it because she did not know it herself." That the woman is called Mrs. Walker contributes a kind of allegorical spookiness to the tale. That she had "short hair and a man's boots" is a double detail in the tradition of the mannish accoutrements of an unconventional woman.

At the center of Austin's tale is a recounting of three experiences that gave value to the wandering protagonist's life, the first of which—working together with a man—had come to her during a sand-storm "on the south slope of Tehachapi in a dateless spring" (93). The other two—loving together, and knowing the small mouth at the breast—followed from the first. The protagonist speaks of these things, touches the narrator's arm to confirm a sense of their import, then departs. And the final sentences of the story leave the interview isolated, without surrounding context: "she went as outliers do, without a hope expressed of another meeting and no word of good-bye. She was the Walking Woman. That was it. She had walked off all sense of society-made values, and, knowing the best when the best came to her, was able to take it" (97).

The paradox of Austin's story is that it presents an eccentric woman who is outside society—an obliquely known negative character—to specify the treasured experiences of a woman's life. "But look you," concludes a suddenly peremptory narrator as she turns to *her* audience, "It was the naked thing the Walking Woman grasped," not something "dressed or tricked out" or surrounded by proper "decorations" (97). What this negative character celebrates is human, not social. Disengaged from social contexts, moving beyond the realities of time and space, the Walking Woman in her peripatetic solitude tells us what has made her life complete. As the narrator sees, it was all she needed.

Compact in form and gothic in its evocation of desert vacancies, "The Walking Woman" exhibits the values of a negative character with clarity and precision. Far more extensive in narrative reach, Marilynne Robinson's *Housekeeping* (1981) incorporates a variety of story-telling modes in the course of shaping its far-reaching negative impulse. Once upon a time, we may say, there were three sisters—Molly, who went to China as a missionary; Helen, who drove her car (with determination) off a cliff and into a lake; and Sylvie, who became a hobo. The ensuing story, narrated by Helen's daughter Ruth, features the triumph of life over death, a "parturition" brought about by the unconscious power of Aunt Sylvie to undo order, regularity, and the quotidian things prized by society and by Ruth's older sister, Lucille. At stake is the fate of Ruth, herself.

The dialectic of *Housekeeping* first juxtaposes Sylvie (perennially unaware of her effect on others) and Lucille, then, after Lucille leaves Fingerbone forever, the same guileless Sylvie and the proper citizens of the town. While Lucille tries valiantly to provide "some seemly shape" to family life, Sylvie can offer nothing but shapelessness.[59] With feet "bare except for loafers," a "shapeless" raincoat, and the habits "of a transient," Sylvie is redolent of nature, not civilization. "Sometimes," Ruth reports, she came home from the lake (in which Ruth's mother had died) "with fish in her pockets"—symbols of life masked by evidence of sloppiness (136). Years before, Sylvie's disapproving mother had negated her domestically and legally by omitting her name from conversation "and from her will" (42). But Sylvie's negative characteristics prevail against both domestic and social institutions. With a marriage "of sufficient legal standing to have changed her name," she "simply" chooses "not to act married" (43). She has "no awareness of time," she is "neither patient nor impatient," and although she speaks of her loneliness (as does Huckleberry Finn), she never answers the telephone (165–66). She also teaches Ruth (effortlessly) that possessions are a burden—that "it is better to have nothing" (159).

The fundamental movement of Robinson's narrative is the liberation of Ruth from patterns of repression and self-destruction. Necessarily, the focus is on Sylvie—for changes in Ruth are part of an evolutionary process brought about by the attraction of Sylvie's life-affirming innocence (and quickened by Lucille's departure). It is through Ruth that we follow the contour of events that lead to a complementary doubling of the two characters, Sylvie the ingenuous facilitator, Ruth the cognizant articulator. At times Ruth's statements are metaphorical and rich in fecundity, at times straight-forward in their assessment of social implications. As they walk toward the fateful lake one winter morning, for example, Ruth follows Sylvie "as if I were her shadow, and moved after her only because she moved and not because I willed this pace. . . . I walked after Sylvie down the shore, all at peace, and at ease, and I thought, We are the same. She could as well be my mother. I crouched and slept in her very shape like an unborn child" (145).

But Ruth is also kind to the reader in her literal reports of what is happening. Sylvie, she says, "was an unredeemed transient, and she was making a transient of me" (177). And she is aware that society disapproves of Sylvie as her unofficial guardian; she admits candidly that the stalwart citizens of Fingerbone, including the wife of a probate judge and the sheriff, "had reason to feel that my social graces were eroding away, and that soon I would feel ill at ease in a cleanly house with glass in its windows—I would be lost to ordinary society." Immediately after making this realistic assessment, however, Ruth addresses a poignant and metasocial truth in an idiom of self-appraisal: "I would be a ghost, and their food would not answer to my hunger, and my hands could pass through their down quilts and tatted pillow covers and never feel them or find comfort in them. Like a soul released, I would find here only the images and simulacra of the things needed to sustain me" (183). The direction of Ruth's life is clear: not only does she agree with Sylvie that families should stay together (in a kind of negative domesticity), but she "like[s] to think we were almost a single person" (209).

Threatened finally with separation, Ruth and Sylvie burn their house, cross a hazardous railroad bridge over the lake, and allow the people of Fingerbone to think they have fallen and drowned. They have not exactly staged their deaths in the manner of Huckleberry Finn, but they take pleasure in reading a newspaper clipping with the headline, "LAKE CLAIMS TWO" (213). They are "drifters," Wandering Women who lead lives defined only by what they are not. The final paragraph of the novel suggests how thoroughly a principle of negation has pervaded Ruth's perspective on the world. After "many years," she imagines Lucille waiting for a friend in a restaurant in Boston (proper-town for proper-lady), "tastefully dressed, wearing, say, a tweed suit with an amber scarf at her throat to draw attention to the red in her darkening hair." And then come the virtuoso negatives in a passage I should like to quote in full:

> Sylvie and I do not flounce in through the door, smoothing the skirts of our oversized coats and combing our hair with the back of our fingers. We do not sit down at the table next to hers, and empty our pockets in a small damp heap in the middle of the table, and sort out the gum wrappers and ticket stubs, and add up the coins and dollar bills. . . . My mother, likewise, is not there, and my grandmother in her house slippers with her pigtail wagging, and my grandfather, with his hair combed flat against his brow, does not examine the menu with studious interest. We are nowhere in Boston. However Lucille may look, she will never find us there, or any trace or sign. We pause nowhere in Boston, even to admire a store window, and the perimeters of our wandering are nowhere. No one watching this woman smear her initials in the steam on her water glass with her first finger, or slip cellophane packets of oyster crackers into her handbag for the seagulls, could know how her thoughts are thronged by our absence, or know how she does not watch, does not listen, does not wait, does not hope, and always for me and Sylvie.
>
> (218–19)

Such is the nature of this negative life, not celebratory, not despondent, but resigned in its freedom.

Just as a negative rhetoric could be used to distinguish Squaw Gap from New York City, or to serve the purposes of mystical theology or advertising, so the negative conception of character, as we have seen, can be manifested in different forms. If *Housekeeping* inverts the ideas of domesticity and social stability so that a woman can be defined by negation, Jerzy Kosinski's *Being There* (1970) demonstrates how a negative character can serve the purposes of satire.

Concerned to establish the identity of Chance, the gardener, whose name is mistakenly taken to be Chauncey Gardiner, government officials in this short novel can find only that "he has never been in any legal trouble," that he "has never been hospitalized," that he "carries no insurance." As Chance rises to prominence, even the Russians can discover nothing about him: "he has no driver's licence," "no credit cards, no checks, no calling cards." Like all negative characters, he lacks normal family ties; in this extreme case there is "no record" of birth or parents or family. (The Russian code name for him is "Blank Page.") Chauncey Gardiner is pure poten- tiality, an empty innocent, of himself no-thing. Thus he can be pro- jected into any role. Because "It's clear what he isn't," as a political adviser to the President says, he comes to be seen as an excellent candidate for the vice-Presidency of the United States. "A man's past cripples him," says the adviser; Chauncey Gardiner is "our one chance."[60] In a bizarre and satiric way, the basic function of American negatives fulfills itself in the final sentence of the novel when Kosinski writes, "Not a thought lifted itself from Chance's brain. Peace filled his heart."

4

Telling the World
Over Again:
The Radical Dimension
of American Fiction

Appropriating a Beginning   To recall two examples of conspic-
uous confidence: Thomas Paine proclaims "We have it in
our power to begin the world over again"; John Quincy
Adams defines the signing of the Declaration of Independence as an event unprecedented in "the annals of the
human race." As we shall see in chapter 5, Thoreau—with
equal assurance—observes that an American is "advantageously nearer to the primitive and the ultimate condition
of man" than is an Englishman. And Emerson tells us that
the person "who has seen the rising moon break out of the
clouds at midnight has been present like an archangel at
the creation of light and of the world."[1] Despite their
rhetorical extravagance, none of these statements is merely
decorative. In each case the writer appropriates a point of
genesis that serves the purpose of his argument: with an
imminent sense of radical change, Paine projects a
euphoric vision of the future; with a prophetic sense of
national glory, Adams celebrates the anniversary of American independence; with a persistent sense of the original
purity of existence, Thoreau satirizes British pomp; and
with an assured sense of how nature mimes the absolute,
Emerson brings a domesticated Neoplatonism to his view

of history. The effect, characteristic of though by no means limit-

ed to American writing, is not only to magnify the importance of the subject at hand but to affirm a beginning world bright with possibility.

In narrative, the impulse to re-present the world takes the form of designs both synecdochic and metaphorical that establish centers of value and thereby *tell* the world over again. Classic texts such as the *Aeneid* and *Paradise Lost* fasten boldly on events that generate a perception of authority and consequence. Gabriel García Márquez's astonishing *One Hundred Years of Solitude* (1967) suggests how making a fictional world seem *early* can enhance the significance of setting and release the flow of narrative. Marquez constructs his deconstructive fable on the foundation of "a world . . . so recent that many things lack names." No one has yet died in the village of Macondo. Century-old discoveries are made afresh with fierce pride: emerging from days of wasting meditation, José Arcadio Buendía proclaims to his family, "The earth is round, like an orange"—after which his wife smashes his astrolabe to the floor. In each of these cases a beginning or congeries of beginning moments fulfills what Edward W. Said calls a "primordial need" to be certain of one's story—the prerequisite for structure and coherence.[2]

Out of a feeling that radical beginnings were accessible for narrative (and that the nation needed to have its story fashioned and refashioned) came the American habit of telling the world over again. Washington Irving's *History of New-York, from the Beginning of the World to the End of the Dutch Dynasty* (1809) stands as an excellent example of how readily the practice of appropriating a beginning took form: in the bumbling idiom of Diedrich Knickerbocker, Irving links creation, Noah, and Christopher Columbus to the city of New York by a parodic "chain of causation."[3] Works as different as Thomas Bangs Thorpe's "The Big Bear of Arkansas" (1841) and Owen Wister's *The Virginian* (1902) likewise invoke the idea of creation, the first by setting the tall tale in the "creation state of Arkansaw" and featuring "a creation bear" that could have licked Samson "in the twinkling of a dice box"; the second by juxtaposing the squalor of a raw Western town with the pristine atmosphere of "creation's first morning"—out of which "Noah and Adam might come straight from Genesis."[4] Jack London's *Before Adam* (1906) goes at the matter in a different way, presenting a dramatized version of evolution projected by the narrator's dreams of a remote ancestor, Big Tooth; what the novel cannot help but show is the labor of courting a beginning by means of prehuman responses. Recurrent references to Noah and the Flood in Marilynne Robinson's *Housekeeping* serve a more intricate (albeit tentative) function by echoing the suicide of the narrator's mother even as they promise renewed life for her and Sylvie. In its own way, each of these narratives establishes a relation between acknowledged beginning points and the story at hand. Each enhances the reach and resonance of its fiction by connecting it with a point proximate to genesis.

Repeatedly in the work of James Fenimore Cooper, Willa Cather, and William Faulkner, one finds narrative heightened in implication by the accoutrements of genesis or by the grandeur of elemental forces. Examples are plentiful—Natty Bumppo remembering the panorama of creation in *The Pioneers* (1823) and Mark Woolston witnessing creation in *The Crater* (1848); Tom Outland "breathing the sun" on the Blue Mesa in *The Professor's House* (1925) and Bishop Latour adjusting his refined expectations to a primal world in *Death Comes for the Archbishop* (1927); Quentin Compson in *Absalom, Absalom* (1936) visualizing Sutpen's Hundred being dragged out of "the soundless Nothing" and Isaac McCaslin in *Go Down, Moses* (1940) carrying the idea of ownership back to Eden in an attempt not to claim kin with original sin. Telling the world over again does not of itself guarantee work of high quality. But it does reveal a disposition to appropriate the power of radical beginnings for the purposes of narrative. And it suggests how relentlessly these three writers, thus empowered, could explore the national experience.

Cooper . . . and *The Crater* Out of his effort to incorporate the shaping power of beginnings into narrative come a number of Cooper novels, not only tales of settlement such as *Wyandotté* (1843) but those that reach to primal and mythic locations as the condition of their telling—among them *The Deerslayer* and *The Crater*.[5] It is to these three texts, and especially to *The Crater*, that I now turn.

Because it pits the overwhelming power of a national origin against personal endeavors that Cooper associates with genesis, *Wyandotté* offers a troubled instance of what can happen when one kind of beginning moment overtakes another. Cooper's narrative voice takes on a beguiling enthusiasm as it generalizes about the joys of "diving into a virgin forest, and commencing the labors of civilization." The pleasure of subsequent activities, we read, is hardly to be compared with these original feelings—which are akin to those of "creating . . . pregnant with anticipations and hopes."[6] Reifying the *original* from a different perspective in "Man the Reformer" (1841), Emerson comes to a similar conclusion: to avoid fatal compromise with the world of commerce, he says, there is nothing to do but "begin the world anew, as he does who puts the spade into the ground for food."[7] By means of tone and incident Cooper proceeds in *Wyandotté* to enhance the merit of Captain Willoughby's move into the wilderness. The Captain and his party travel into a world in which settlements, including Cooperstown, "did not exist, even in name" (*W*: 26). They drain a beaver pond (practical action that makes the labor of clearing unnecessary) and have sudden access to four hundred acres of postdiluvian farmland. Drawing on resources both biblical and local, Cooper thus sketches an unnamed world affiliated with creation and the flood; in that world Captain Willoughby will undertake his orderly labors.

But in *Wyandotté* Cooper cannot gainsay the force of the American Revolution, a "civil war" that divides families even as it promotes greed and social upheaval (*W*: 100). With a sure sense of an unfolding national drama that leaves no room for doubt and demurral, he introduces a copy of the Declaration of Independence into the novel, into the very hands of Captain Willoughby, who pronounces it "creditable" and "eloquently reasoned," although his conservative instincts give him no cause to celebrate the birth of the new nation (*W*: 177). From his caustic perspective in the 1840s Cooper broods over the document that brings life to the nation and ruin to the Captain. In *Home as Found* (1838), he had drawn an extended, primarily satiric, and yet comic portrait of an amateurish Fourth of July celebration. In *Wyandotté*, his manner is acerbic: the commemoration of national independence on the Fourth of July, he informs us editorially, has become an "all absorbing and all-*swallowing* jubilee," which overshadows every other holiday (*W*: 83). As a number of scholars have observed, the later Cooper projected much of his disappointment in American democracy into tales of the Revolution. Contentious and severe in its judgment, *Wyandotté* enacts this disappointment by closing out a personal world of possibility to which Cooper has a fundamental allegiance. In its place comes a national beginning defiled by its consequences.

135

Telling
the
World
Over
Again

In the work of nineteenth-century American painters, Angela Miller has pointed out, "space" became the "generalized expression of the American condition." Typically, artists favored the depiction of "natural" processes and "agrarian Edens" as they sought to invent a national landscape.[8] For writers, the fact of uninterrupted space similarly signaled the absence of conventional patterns of demarcation; since their medium was words, they turned characteristically to a language of negation to describe the American wilderness. In the work of William Gilmore Simms, Lydia Maria Child, Laura Ingalls Wilder, and others (including Cooper, Cather, and Faulkner), forests tend to be "trackless," expanses "limitless," and prairies "boundless" as the writers develop a reliance on and an ease with verbal strategies of representation. The language of negation finds eloquent manifestation in *The Deerslayer* where (as we have seen) it claims for narrative purposes an otherwise inaccessible point of beginning, a world without origins that "the annals of man can reach." My discussion of *The Deerslayer* in the previous chapter examines the manner in which the novel completes the career of Natty Bumppo at its inception. What I would like to stress here is that Cooper leaves this mythic setting intact even as he makes it the occasion for projecting Natty's achieved career. Perforce, a youthful Natty Bumppo must come into contact with this virginal world if we are to apprehend it. As the classic negative character, he can be trusted to validate its pristine harmony: "Not a tree," as he says, has been "disturbed even by red skin hand ... but every thing left in the ordering of the Lord."[9]

Cooper's reverence for the setting of *The Deerslayer* led him to make it indestructible, ultimately resistant to the ravages of time. When Natty, Chingachgook, and young Uncas visit Lake Glimmerglass fifteen years after the bloody denouement of the story, "all was unchanged." Nature has reasserted its primal mastery: "the season's rioted" in what is now Hutter's unroofed castle; "a few more gales and tempests, would sweep all into the lake, and blot the building from the face of that magnificent solitude"—leaving the setting, presumably, in its original negative condition.[10] This pattern of finding and leaving an *un*changed world, an aspect of what William P. Kelly calls the circular pattern of *The Deerslayer*, is unique in Cooper's work; in *The Pioneers*, *Wyandotté*, and other narratives, *leaving* takes place because of changes that mandate depar-

ture.[11] In the novels of Willa Cather, to look ahead for a moment, the method of telling the world over again is fundamentally different. Typically, Cather's locales change as the narrative moves from formlessness to form, from an apprehension of nothing to a perception of fullness and fruition—with a sensitized character measuring the quality of the transformation. Cooper in *The Deerslayer*, on the contrary, manages his materials as if he had visualized a painting, then superimposed a narrative moving (through time) across the same canvas.[12] While the narrative moves on, the painting heals and remains; in other terms, what man has wrought passes, what the Creator made continues. Such is the commanding presence of Cooper's idealized setting—existent from the beginning, found intact by Natty Bumppo, and in the process of reconstitution at the end.

Stark and meager at the beginning, the setting of *The Crater*, unlike that of *The Deerslayer*, comes into spectacular existence during the course of the narrative and disappears entirely at the end. As Wayne Franklin has observed, Cooper no doubt intended his story to serve "as a sermon on the text of the national ills"; in reaching admonitorily past local issues, however, it became a virtual "allegory of the whole American past."[13] Yet more than any work in the Cooper canon, this curious narrative presents a radical beginning in insistent form. As he presides over the birth of a world, Cooper lavishes detail both on his creation chapters and on the elemental toil that precedes them, telling *of* a beginning with evident pleasure, telling a later story of deterioration with evident disdain. The anomalies in *The Crater* are significant; and the most basic, involving the ownership of property, works at cross-purposes with Cooper's homiletic rhetoric. Yet Cooper manages to evoke a primal beginning with authority and assurance before the heavy-handedness sets in. If the subtext of *The Crater* is the bright promise of America that faded into history, Cooper's depiction of that promise is, by any critical standards, of high order.

After some conventional chapters in which the protagonist, Mark Woolston (born one year after the birth of the nation), secretly marries Bridget Yardly and then goes to sea, *The Crater* moves to a process of stripping down as the condition of reaching a beginning. A drunken captain, degenerating emblem of civilized authority, and a series of storms reduce the cast of characters to two, Mark Woolston and his loyal companion, Bob Betts. With ship intact after a night of peril, they find themselves at the center of a circle of breakers, unable to sail out, wondering how they got there safely.[14] Cooper stresses (in negatives both familiar and appropriate) the barrenness of the reef on which his two characters have landed. It has no plants, no shrubs, no trees—no vegetation whatsoever— and no fresh water.[15] As a reef of "purely volcanic origin," it is sim- ply a mass of hardened lava (59). Yet the "utter nakedness" of the reef, in conjunction with the dawn of a new day, inspires a feeling of proximity to creation, with rock and surf and atmosphere appearing as if they have come "fresh and renovated from the hands of the Creator." Determined "to make a good beginning" in this barren place to which Providence has led him, Mark Woolston sets aside Sabbath days as "holy times" sacred to the purposes of the Creator (49, 85).

Having reduced his cast of characters to two and put them on a naked rock, Cooper explains how Mark (of necessity) brings a nurturing world into existence; painstakingly, he makes a rudimentary kind of soil and exposes it to the air and water so that it might nourish seeds that are happily part of the ship's cargo. Unexpected help comes at one early point when rain brings food from above, "minute mucilaginous particles" that are "manna" for the animals carried on the ship (82). Mark and Bob use picks, axes, and a wheelbarrow from the ship to facilitate their work. Soon, a reef that had lain "for thousands of years in its nakedness," is "blest with fruitfulness." This beginning is elemental in nature, literally so: once Mark Woolston produces earth, the other three elements—air, water in the form of rain, and fire as rays from the sun—combine to bring new life into being. His happiness, Cooper notes (with the priority of values he acknowledged in *Wyandotté*), is of a special kind: "it far exceeded the joy" one might have in removing the danger of hunger at a time of peril, "for it resembled something of the character of a new creation" (101–102).

This first, carefully detailed section of *The Crater* obviously calls up echoes of *Robinson Crusoe*. Indeed, Cooper invites a comparison between the two novels when Bob Betts twice observes that they will have "to Robinson Crusoe it" on the reef and when Mark Woolston is "reminded of the goats of Crusoe" as he watches his goat frisk playfully in the afternoon sun (50, 65, 86). The similarities and differences are worth noting. Both protagonists are cast upon a lonely island. Both salvage tools from a ship that can no longer be sailed. Mark Woolston has plenty of clothing, water in casks, and (most surprising of all) materials for a second ship in the hold of the "embayed" *Rancocus*. Robinson Crusoe retrieves carpenter's stores from his foundered ship and quickly makes a chair and table; he likewise has a grindstone and flour, enabling him to bake bread. Unlike Mark Woolston, who does not drink or smoke, Robinson Crusoe treasures his rum, pipe, and tobacco. More importantly, each protagonist suffers through a violent illness and a terrifying earthquake, which bring him closer to God. And each is called "governor" (Crusoe with ironic purpose) toward the end of his adventures. These similarities and others suggest that Cooper made use of Defoe's classic tale to establish the texture and rhythm of his narrative.

Crusoe's single allusion to creation and his sole use of a negative list, however, reveal the differences between Defoe's concerns and those of Cooper—even in this early section of *The Crater*. After shooting at a bird Crusoe says, "I believe it was the first gun that had been fired there since the creation of the world."[16] The effect of the statement is to dramatize not the proximity of but the distance between Crusoe's civilization and creation. Crusoe is solitary, but he is a man of his time. When he later comes to see advantages as well as disadvantages to the island on which he lives, he couches his assessment in negative language: he is marooned in "a place where, as I had no society, which was my affliction on one hand, so I found no ravenous beasts, no furious wolves or tigers, to threaten my life; no venomous creatures or poisonous, which I might feed upon to my hurt; no savages to murder and devour me."[17] This interesting list of negatives, cast entirely in terms of fears of eating and being eaten, defines felicity as the absence of pain and misfortune. Rather than stripping items away and arriving at an original purity or harmony, however, Crusoe's negative list leads to a misleading sense of safety. Moreover, as it applauds the absence of tigers and venomous creatures and laments the lack of society, the rhetoric mirrors the division in Crusoe's mind. For in keeping with the back-and-forth narrative snaps in *Robinson Crusoe* (which lead Crusoe repeatedly toward and away from a new-found spirituality), devouring savages are precisely what he must fear.

Additional differences between *Robinson Crusoe* and *The Crater* are both prominent and abundant. Crusoe's time on the island— twenty-two years, two months, and nineteen days—itself signals a difference in conception between the two novels. Crusoe lives on his island for fifteen years before he sees the footprint of a cannibal. He meets Friday (a cannibal) only four years before his rescue. His later fight with a horde of wolves while en route from Lisbon to Paris, as well as his adventures in China and Russia (in volume 2 of his *Life*) and his particular kind of homily (in volume 3) have no counterpart in *The Crater*.

139

Telling
the
World
Over
Again

Rendered with Defoe's talent for quotidian detail, the account of Crusoe's day-to-day existence makes *The Life and Strange Adventures of Robinson Crusoe* a seductive model for any castaway story— as Bob Betts and Mark Woolston acknowledge. What takes *The Crater* beyond an account of the tactics of survival on a naked reef is that all of the early nurturing and Defoe-like chapters (accompanied by the stripping away of the social order) function as a rehearsal for the spectacular account of creation in chapters eleven and twelve. Put another way: creation, personal and domestic, issues into Creation, primal and extravagant, and becomes the generative center of the novel. Cooper works with care and purpose in this part of the narrative. For the idea of an underwater volcanic eruption and an earthquake thrusting up islands from below the ocean he apparently drew on Charles Lyell's *Principles of Geology*. Lyell's account of Graham's Island in the Mediterranean Sea, which emerged from under the surface in 1831 only to disappear in the same year, provides both detail and pattern for *The Crater*.[18] Dismissing Bob Betts from the scene during a violent storm, Cooper brings his sole remaining character into close proximity with the drama of creation. He describes the onset and the physical devastation of Mark Woolston's violent fever in graphic detail, even surpassing Defoe's meticulous account of Crusoe's illness. The fever becomes an avenue, purgative and rugged, to a new spiritual awareness for Mark. He is now "our solitary man," and the effects of his purgation and solitude lead him to spiritual awareness: "Cut off, as he was, from all communion with his kind; cast on what was, when he first knew it, literally a barren rock in the midst of the vast Pacific Ocean, Mark found himself . . . in much closer communion with his Creator, than he might have been in the haunts of the world" (139). Although he is deservedly not known for studies of the individual consciousness, Cooper has managed to introduce Mark

Woolston to the rigors of the *via negativa* common to mystics by a
skillful use of incident and metaphor. At this point Mark stands
prepared for a transcendent experience of a dramatic and objecti-
fied (rather than internalized) kind. His close communion with the
Creator makes him a spectator at creation—in a scene generated by
the most audacious display of metaphor that ever came from Cooper's pen.

Cooper first strikes a note of chaos as he stages his mighty scene,
blending the tremors of earthquakes with the sounds of volcanic
eruption, then describing a seething upheaval from within, a spew-
ing out of primal matter: "internal fires" rush forth in streams of
flame, and molten earth emerges from the ocean. It is a dramatic
version of what Meister Eckhart terms *bullitio* (the boiling over of
forms from the Godhead that constitutes creation), enacted in one
locale for the purposes of Cooper's narrative, a bursting outward
that results in the appearance of a new world. What Cooper gives
us is, as it must be, instant creation—as long before in *The Last of
the Mohicans* he had evoked romance from the instant ruins of Fort
William Henry.[19] That it is a second creation in no way diminish-
es its grandeur: the "stupendous fact" is that "nature had made
another effort, and islands had been created . . . in the twinkling of
an eye" (160–61). Out of all the people on earth "Mark Woolston,
alone," had witnessed "this grand display of the powers of the elements" (179).

In a state of wonder and curiosity Mark explores the vast territory around him, discovering inlets and islands that had not previously existed. Cooper makes him a combination of Columbus and
Adam, grateful discoverer and joyous namer—and once compares
his feelings with those Herschel must have had when he "established the character of Uranus" (180). Like Columbus, Mark kneels
on the beach and gives "thanks to God." Like Adam, he names the
geographic features of his "new world": a channel becomes the
Armlet, a harbor the Oval; on the first morning after creation he
finds more than twenty springs—fresh water, which he regards as "a
direct gift from heaven" (164–70). His initial feeling of "adoration
and reverence" at the splendor of his surroundings becomes a high
and almost mystical spirituality; he now communes with the Creator not through traditional forms but directly, with an ardent
"yearning of the soul" (167, 173). Considering his solitude, it is
understandable that Mark comes to worship the Creator through

the creation he has witnessed coming into existence. It is also understandable that he longs for his wife and casts himself finally in the role of Adam rather than that of Columbus. He would surrender the rest of the world, he thinks to himself, "for the enjoyment of a paradise like that before him, with Bridget for his Eve" (182). When Bridget arrives, she confirms their sense of themselves by naming the plain on which they will live Eden.

141

Telling
the
World
Over
Again

There is no doubt that an admonitory tone afflicts the final section of *The Crater*. As Cooper muses on the increasing dissension in the growing colony he warns that "everything human" moves toward excess, that "those who would substitute the voice of the created for that of the Creator" should recall "their insignificance and tremble" (444, 459). To look closely at Cooper's effort to capture the world in narrative, however, is to see that what robs the colony of its original purity is not demagoguery or mobocracy but the ownership of property. Even before the "serpent of old" (in the form of sectarian ministers, a lawyer, and a newspaper editor) comes to "this Eden of modern times," the forces of the novel are at cross-purposes. The colonists fear attack because they might lose their property; Mark (witness at creation now Governor for life) does not want to abandon the Reef, largely because "there was too much property at risk" (272). Cooper's unswerving faith in property as a principle of social order is reaffirmed in the character of his protagonist, Adam the namer turned Adam the property owner: Mark Woolston believes "that civilization could not exist without property," without people taking a direct personal interest in both its "accumulation and preservation" (300). Moreover, Bridget will shortly inherit "an amount of property that, properly invested, would contribute to the wealth and power of the colony, as well as to those of its governor" (286).

What we have finally in *The Crater* is Eve as heiress, Adam committed to the accumulation of property, and Eden growing in wealth—all supposedly undone by the messy politics of equality. But the force that subverts a narrative begun as a parable of genesis is the sovereign regard for property—disguised, as it is, by a litany of Cooper's complaints and fears. Put another way: Cooper champions the very thing that breaks his narrative in two. His colony, let us note, is never a utopia: the mélange of roles and issues in the novel brings on a confusion very different from the geometrical coolness of utopian communities. Moreover, such communities traditionally banish private property as a matter of principle. Although the vitality of the creation chapters marks achievement worthy of note, *The Crater* suffers from internal contradictions and a consequent lack of continuity. With no apparent understanding that an emphasis on property sets the conditions for its failure, Cooper has no way to deconstruct his fable according to expectations previously set up, no way to bring it to graceful fruition or compelling disappointment. He trusts his homily rather than trusting his tale. Thus, with his new world tattered by time, he sinks it back into the Pacific with no witnesses present, not Mark Woolston, and certainly not the reader.

Cather . . . and *Death Comes for the Archbishop* Significant to the fiction of Willa Cather is an initial sense of human diminishment and disorientation in the face of a boundless and not-yet-completed locale. Not that Cather invented such a reaction to alien confrontations: in differing accents and with different emphases, it had long been part of the imaginative response to the American continent. The paintings of Thomas Cole and Asher Durand comfortably portray human figures dwarfed by the grandeur of nature. From a different perspective, in his poem "The Prairies" (1834), William Cullen Bryant writes of "the encircling vastness" of the terrain, "boundless and beautiful," then adds that "Man hath no part in all this glorious work." And in Lydia Maria Child's *Hobomok* (1824) we find a structural formula that incorporates both the idea of "fixing" a beginning and that of beginning by negation. "In most nations," Child writes, "the path of antiquity is shrouded in darkness, rendered more visible by the wild, fantastic light of fable; but with us, the vista of time is luminous to its remotest point. Each succeeding year has left its footprints distinct upon the soil, and the cold dew of our chilling dawn is still visible beneath the mid-day sun."[20] "Chilling dawn" may be ambivalent; but it properly anticipates the "sensations" of Child's Puritan narrator, who, as he approaches the shores of Massachusetts in 1629, finds himself "lost and bewildered" in "a new world" of "almost unlimited extent": "I viewed myself as a drop in the vast ocean of existence, and shrunk from the contemplation of human nothingness."[21]

Recognizably similar in mode and manner, Jim Burden's awareness of all that is absent on the Nebraska prairie in *My Ántonia*

(1918) gives him a sense of being "erased," "blotted out," taken "over the edge" of the world. What Cather adds to the basic contrast of immensity and diminution of self is the idea of incompleteness. Whereas the narrator of *Hobomok* finds familiar religious and political attitudes in the struggling Plymouth Colony, Jim Burden finds "nothing but land: not a country at all, but the material out of which countries are made." The task of Cather's narrative is to bring the prairie within the "jurisdiction" of her narrator's imagination, to fashion a country out of material almost threatening in its lack of form. An even more extreme formlessness emanates from the mesa plain in *Death Comes for the Archbishop* (1927). Despite its appearance of great antiquity, the plain nonetheless looks incomplete; as if, "with all the materials for world-making assembled, the Creator had desisted, gone away and left everything on the point of being brought together, on the eve of being arranged into mountain, plain, plateau." In this case, with the locale "still waiting to be made into a landscape," it is (again) the task of Cather-the-artist to complete the act of creation.[22]

From the prairie and the Southwest come the stimuli that lead Cather to imagine the world from the beginning. And if the elemental harmony of the Southwest can yield spiritual health, the bleakness of the Nebraska prairie can threaten despair before it generates fruition. The nascent fear in Jim Burden's early description of the prairie is confirmed by Mr. Shimerda's suicide, even as it is tempered by the nostalgia of a narrative voice committed to memories that cohere in the bountiful figure of Ántonia. Without such a mediating vision, however, Cather's early fiction abounds in fatalities brought about by the unrelieved blankness of the locale. The Bohemian protagonist of her first story, "Peter" (1892), shoots himself in the manner of Mr. Shimerda. A Russian woman in "The Clemency of the Court" (1893) drowns herself "in a pond so small that no one ever quite saw how she managed to do it."[23] More elaborate than these stories, "On the Divide" (1896) features a succession of brutal metaphors that dramatize in absolute terms the plight of the seven-foot Canute Canuteson. Choosing liquor rather than suicide, Canute travels "through all the hells of Dante," with the "skull and the serpent . . . always before him, the symbols of eternal futileness and eternal hate." He has seen the prairie "smitten by all the plagues of Egypt," ravaged by drought, by rain, by hail, and by fire; "and in the grasshopper years he had seen it eaten as bare and clean as bones that the vultures have left." Throughout this story

Cather insists (to the point of rhetorical indulgence) on "the eternal treachery of the plains," which every spring turn green "with the promises of Eden."[24]

Not until *O Pioneers!* (1913) did Cather fashion a character with a deep commitment to the land and its promise. To the same Divide she brings Alexandra Bergson, whose faith and determination virtually force the land into yielding the riches she believes it to possess. In "A Resurrection" (1897), Cather had indulged in a flurry of *firsts* to establish the literal newness of her locale—noting that Brownsville was "the first town" on the Nebraska side of the Missouri river, that Martin Dempster was "the first child" born there, that he had witnessed the digging of "the first grave" and heard "the first telegraph wire" bring "the first message" across the river. Hazarding a tentative and more resonant *first* to establish Alexandra's special relation to the land in *O Pioneers!*, she writes that "for the first time, perhaps, since that land emerged from the waters of geologic ages, a human face was set toward it with love and yearning." What had been forbidding to others seems "beautiful" to Alexandra, "rich and strong and glorious."[25] Crucial to her faith is a sense of a glorious future latent but stirring under the high ground of the Divide. The accomplished early chapters of *O Pioneers!*, in which Alexandra virtually weds the land, pose the question of survival and success sharply; the contours of the narrative enlarge to include an ancillary story of destructive human passion only after Alexandra has won a living from something that is bleak and new. Susan J. Rosowski defines the basic impulse of *O Pioneers!* perceptively when she terms it Cather's "creation myth," located "not as an event in time but as a feeling."[26] To this perception I would only add that myth yields history in this novel, just as beginnings yield consequences. For "the history of every country," Cather writes, "begins in the heart of a man or woman." Protagonist of a creation myth, Alexandra Bergson thus becomes an honored maker of history, just as Jim Burden's Ántonia is "a rich mine of life, like the founders of early races."[27]

Willa Cather's fiction of the American Southwest celebrates elemental beginnings as a source of nourishment and harmony. After expressing a fascination with the region in "The Enchanted Bluff" (1909), Cather established the terms of her vision in *The Song of the Lark* (1915). Tired of the quotidian pressures of her operatic career,

Thea Kronborg finds a sense of wholeness in the sun-drenched village of the Cliff Dwellers. She knows that these Ancient People "had felt the beginnings" of human endeavor. As centuries disappear in the clarity of her vision, Thea rejoices that she is united with "a long chain of human endeavor." A decade later (as she acknowledged), Cather "overcrowded" Godfrey St. Peter's residence in *The Professor's House*, then—with Tom Outland's story—opened the window and "let in the fresh air" from the Blue Mesa. The stone village Tom Outland discovers sits high on the mesa "with the calmness of eternity." Every day he feels fresh, vital, in touch with "solar energy in some direct way"; it was like "breathing the sun," breathing "the colour of the sky."[28] In both of these novels, contact with an original world figures as an interlude, bright with significance but inevitably subordinate to larger issues. In *Death Comes for the Archbishop*, however, Cather engaged the imaginative possibilities of the Southwest in a way that sustained an entire narrative, enveloping character, event, and history in a harmony of place and spirit.

What Cather brought to the composition of *Death Comes for the Archbishop* was a radical assumption about the accessibility and value of beginnings. She had, as we have seen, used beginning moments to release the flow of narrative in her novels of the prairie. In playing out these dramas, she characteristically defines the threatening conditions of an early world, then moves forward in time to tell of personal accomplishment and failure. As the land comes to embody human fulfillment, the outlines of the original setting slip functionally into the background. In *Archbishop*, however, she courts the elemental and sustains its presence in the narrative. Her description of the mesa plain that seems on the eve of being created is a case in point. Such metaphors put Cather-the-artist in a primary position of completing the Creator's work in and by means of her imagination. In the process, through a strategy of "temporal doubleness," as John N. Swift calls it, she keeps manifestations of an original world proximate to the ongoing events of her story.[29] Although time passes and Bishop Latour's apostolic labors come to fruition in the form of his Cathedral, Cather's vision of beginnings continues to inform the narrative.

The prologue of *Archbishop* features a dinner in a villa overlooking Rome and, conveniently, a mention of beginnings and of James

Fenimore Cooper. The setting is cosmopolitan and refined, as three cardinals—French, Italian, and Spanish—listen to the petition of an Irish-born missionary. When he introduces the idea of founding an Apostolic Vicarate in the territory of New Mexico, now, in 1848, part of the United States, the missionary meets only "tepid" interest. When he predicts that the region will soon be a diocese whose bishop will "direct the beginning of momentous things," the Italian cardinal murmurs that there have been "so many" beginnings (6). The Spanish cardinal, by way of polite conversation, speaks of wigwams and says that his knowledge of America is drawn primarily "from the romances of Fenimore Cooper, which I read in English with great pleasure" (11). When the missionary informs him that the Indians of the Southwest do not live in wigwams, the Spaniard replies that it does not matter: "I see your redskins through Fenimore Cooper, and I like them so" (13).

This sole mention of Cooper in *Archbishop* serves an appropriate purpose. Not only is it difficult for the European cardinals to appreciate the size of the new territory or the opportunity of a fresh beginning in a remarkably early world; Cooper's work is no guide to seeing the American Southwest. The opening paragraphs of book 1 offer a reprise on this fundamental problem of *seeing*: as the newly appointed Bishop, Jean Marie Latour, rides through the arid country of central New Mexico three years later, he loses all sense of direction amid the miles of "conical red hills." The image of a "blunted pyramid," Cather writes, "repeated so many times upon his retina," evokes the sense of wandering in a "geometrical nightmare" (18). Only when he sees the cruciform tree is he able to feel at ease with his surroundings. In keeping with the general strategy of her narrative (as she preferred to call *Archbishop*), Cather here associates novelty with tradition, conical red hills with Egyptian monuments, then resolves Latour's confusion with the primary symbol of his religion, that of the Cross. This Bishop of gentle French birth must learn to see his territory directly, to experience a quality of landscape, atmosphere, and local culture for which the heritage of the classical world does not prepare one—any more than do the romances of Cooper. But the Cross exists in living vegetation, a natural part of the landscape to which Latour has journeyed.

Presented by means of subtle shifts in perspective as both old and early, Cather's setting is consistently proximate to creation. Not only is the locale "still waiting to be made into a landscape" (95). On a missionary journey Latour sees mountains bright with sunlight through vistas of rain and thinks that "the first Creation morning might have looked like this, when the dry land was first drawn up out of the deep, and all was confusion" (99). Later, with Jacinto, he takes refuge from a snowstorm in a cave known only to the Indians and is puzzled by a vibration that comes to his ears like the humming of bees or the roll of distant drums. Familiar associations, however, again fail to interpret the primal nature of the reality: listening through a fissure dug out by Jacinto, the Bishop hears far below the flowing of a vast underground river, "a flood moving in utter blackness under ribs of antediluvian rock" (129–30). In the prologue, the visiting missionary had struck a foreboding note of the elemental when he described New Mexico as a place where the floor of the world is "cracked open" into canyons and arroyos (7). Through this particular crack in the floor of the world Bishop Latour listens to "the sound of a great flood moving with majesty and power" and knows that he is hearing "one of the oldest voices of the earth" (130).

Primal, antediluvian, anterior to human endeavor, such images and impressions pervade the atmosphere of Cather's narrative, providing a bizarre reenactment of Genesis to the astonished senses of Bishop Latour. Moreover, *Archbishop* reinforces this sense of ultimate beginnings during the course of Latour's missionary labors, moving away from it with metaphors that suggest century-like strides only to subside gracefully into the unmolested world that is the encompassing matrix of the story. A passage describing Latour's first trip to Ácoma suggests the elliptical nature of this technique. "In all his travels," Cather writes, "the Bishop had seen no country like this." Thus we have (once again) a locale totally new, totally alien to the experience of the by now well-traveled Bishop. By means of a synoptic view of religious history, however, the following brief sentence invests this desolate scene not only with a sense of the familiar but of fruition: "From the flat red sea of sand rose the great rock mesas, generally Gothic in outline, resembling vast cathedrals" (94). A region absolute in its novelty has quickly given way to suggestions of the red sea, of an emerging Gothicism, and of the shapes of cathedrals—something dear to the heart of every bishop, something the narrative will later assemble in actuality, Roman monument from native stone. And just as quickly Cather brings us to the passage in which the mesa looks as if the Creator

147

Telling
the
World
Over
Again

had desisted with everything on the point of being formed into mountain, plain, plateau. It is no wonder that Bishop Latour always remembers this journey to Ácoma; he has ridden through epochs, entertained a vision of the future, and retained a sense of being present on the eve of creation.

The history of Latour's diocese is made functionally interlocking by Cather, a human analogue to the immanence of the locale. What we might think of as stages in time—Indian, Spanish, Mexican, and American—manifest themselves simultaneously. As the native inhabitants, the Indians remain close to the ancient secrets of the land. It is, we recall, the Indian guide Jacinto whose knowledge permits Bishop Latour to hear the sound of the underground river. Mute and enigmatic, Indian history seems to the Catholic mind of Latour to have taken the form of vital—albeit inaccessible—tradition, which can be sensed only by this relationship of the Indian and the land. Traveling with his staunch friend Eusabio is for Latour "like traveling with the landscape made human." The white man's way, he realizes, is "to assert himself" in any environment, "to change it, make it over a little (at least to leave some mark or memorial of his sojourn)." The Indian way, on the contrary, is to pass through a country "and leave no trace, like fish through the water, or birds through the air" (232–33). Such harmony with nature—always a cardinal virtue in Cather's work—becomes an impressive aspect of native tradition, the result of respect for the land that has nourished Indian life and religion "from immemorial times" (294).

The Spanish have also contributed to the history of the territory. The legacy of the early Franciscan missionaries is apparent throughout *Archbishop*, encompassing the heroism of Junipero Serra and the destructive hedonism of Friar Baltazar. Insofar as they were men of courage and simplicity, martyrs who planted seeds of faith long neglected but capable of growth, the Spanish friars have a place of honor in the consciousness of the Bishop and thus in the narrative itself. But the Spanish influence has a secular as well as a religious dimension. After celebrating Mass for the Indians, Father Vaillant finds that they will not bring their children to be baptized because of grievances against the Spaniards that have remained in their hearts for generations. More than two centuries have passed since the Spanish expeditions moved through the country, but vestiges—physical as well as emotional—remain in the present. On Eusabio's breast hang "very old necklaces of wampum and turquoise and coral—Mediterranean coral, that had been left in the Navajo country by Coronado's captains when they had passed through it on their way to discover the Hopi villages and the Grand Canyon" (220). History is thus present for the Indians both as inherited distrust and as ornament.

149

Telling
the
World
Over
Again

The Mexican and the American contributions to the history of the territory, though more recent, also impinge on the fabric of Cather's narrative. Powerful and arrogant in Cather's presentation, the figure of Padre Martínez represents the Mexican defiance of authority with which Latour must deal. "We have a living Church here," boasts Martínez: "Our religion grew out of the soil, and has its own roots. . . . The Church the Franciscan Fathers planted here was cut off; this is the second growth, and is indigenous" (147). Such a challenge from the worldly, self-educated Martínez would be serious indeed, if he were not portrayed as an impressive anachronism.[30] For at this point in the 1850s, as Latour senses, Martínez embodies a force rapidly becoming "impotent, left over from the past" (141). Moreover, in this narrative any religion that does not carry with it an aura of beginnings cannot prosper; second growths, no matter how flamboyant, lack the sustenance of origins.

Already under the dominion of the United States, the Mexicans in *Archbishop* are fighting a losing battle of power and politics. Padre Martínez not only defies Rome and Bishop Latour; he hates the Americans. And his hatred tallies with the attitudes of other Mexicans—the civilized Manuel Chavez, for example, who is "never reconciled to American rule," the boy José, who vows never to be an American: "They destroyed our churches when they were fighting us," José tells the Bishop, "and stabled their horses in them" (186, 27). Characterized by American domination and Mexican distrust, the chronological present in Cather's narrative can still seem *early* from a national perspective. Between Santa Fé and the Pacific coast the country is "not yet mapped." And the indomitable scout Kit Carson, who is said to carry the best map of the country in his head, is illiterate simply because he has traveled West "ahead of books" (76). Even Kit Carson, however, is not exempt from the interlocking issues of history: he becomes the Bishop's "misguided friend" when he leads American soldiers against the final bastion of the Navajo people. In the prologue, the Irish missionary had termed the American government progressive and seen its jurisdiction over

New Mexico as beneficial for all. In the narrative proper, however, American policy destroys the old orders without bringing a compensating sense of the new.

The special feature of Cather's presentation of history in *Death Comes for the Archbishop* is that nothing is left behind; along with the landscape, past and present merge into the foreground of the narrative and provide what David Stouck calls an "ever-present continuum."[31] Bishop Latour can see conical sand hills as blunted pyramids, can travel with an Indian who knows secrets of the land and wears Mediterranean coral, can discover the legacy of the Franciscan friars, can meet a priest who declares independence from Rome, can befriend an American scout who has moved West ahead of society, and still feel that he is witnessing the first day of creation. All is present, all is proximate, not so much *in* as *to* his consciousness. Adding to what Susan J. Rosowski has identified as a principle of "simultaneity" in Cather's work is Latour's profound awareness of his own tradition.[32] For Cather's Bishop, unlike the bluff, outgoing Father Vaillant, is distinguished in manners and intellect, schooled in the culture he embodies. Even his sportive remarks about Vaillant's soup come from an inbred manner of viewing reality. "I am not deprecating your individual talent, Joseph," he says to his friend-turned-chef, but "a soup like this is not the work of one man. It is the result of a constantly refined tradition. There are nearly a thousand years of history in this soup" (39). To the eyes and ears of this connoisseur of soup Cather brings the phenomena of her Southwest.

The effect of simultaneity in *Archbishop* owes much to Cather's manner, her *style*—in the most inclusive sense of the word. In a letter to *Commonweal* in 1927, Cather described the measured effort that went into the making of her narrative: she had long wanted to do something "in the style of legend," something "without accent"—"absolutely the reverse of dramatic treatment." In the Golden Legend, the martyrdoms of saints are given no more emphasis "than are the trivial incidents of their lives," as if the dominating reality of the spirit puts all human experience on the same level. "The essence of such writing," she continued, "is not to hold the note, not to use an incident for all there is in it—but to touch and pass on." Assisted by the detail and straightforward tone of William Joseph Howlett's *Life of the Right Reverend Joseph P. Machebeuf* (1908), Cather fashioned her account of missionary life in the Southwest with a disciplined lack of highlighting or "accent."[33] Her characterization of Father Vaillant epitomizes the fusion of style and substance that is the essence of this technique. Whether he is converting Indians near Tucson or having an audience with Pope Gregory XVI, the Bishop's assistant remains the same man of joyous faith. Cather admitted that she was "strongly tempted" to make Vaillant's audience with the Pope "stand out too much."[34] But her character remains the creature of her unaccented style in the Papal presence as he does elsewhere. Father Vaillant "added a glow" to whatever human society "he was dropped down into." A Navajo hogan, a huddle of Mexican huts, or a group of Cardinals at Rome—"it was all the same" (228). Similarly, Cather's style—which sacrifices the dramatic, refuses "to hold the note," and makes "all the same," proximate and vital to the narrative. Commenting on Cather's style generally, Wallace Stevens wrote "that it is easy to miss her quality" because "she takes so much pains to conceal her sophistication."[35] Such a judgment applies to the quiet audacity of *Archbishop* in a precise way.

151

Telling
the
World
Over
Again

One of the major problems confronting Bishop Latour is the magnitude of the area to which he has been assigned. To impress his superiors with the importance of his petition, the missionary in the prologue had described the territory of New Mexico as larger than all of Europe, excepting Russia. What Latour finds upon his arrival in Santa Fé is that no one has reliable information about the extent of his diocese, not even the Commandant at the Fort or Kit Carson at Taos. A year later, Latour's diocese is still "an unimaginable mystery to him" (81). And following the Gadsden Purchase in 1853, a vast additional area comes under his charge on orders from Rome. Although trips of several hundred miles are commonplace in his missionary life, the conference required to settle matters of jurisdiction with Mexican bishops requires Latour to travel almost four thousand miles.

The practical duties of missionary life thus attest to the fact of distance in this fictional world. And Cather repeatedly translates distance into a pervading sense of space. Not only does Bishop Latour travel in a territory of indeterminate boundaries; the atmosphere around him is suffused with the embracing reality of the sky. To the conventional observation that the sky is the roof of the world, Cather adds that "here the earth was the floor of the sky."

Filled with motion and change, the sky becomes "the landscape" one remembers, the "world one actually lived in" (232).[36] Such statements, of course, suggest the lofty nature of the spiritual life in a story that celebrates missionary efforts. To succeed in their work, the Bishop and Father Vaillant must abide in the realm of the spirit. But Cather's language does more than equate sky and spirit: by making the sky part of the landscape, it creates an illusion of boundless space that serves to augment the sense of beginning generated by the narrative. In American writing, space (most often projected as the West) signifies the future, opportunity yet to be realized. It is the condition of human efforts at beginning, and it inheres in the fabric of early, incomplete worlds.

Befitting the ambience of the narrative, the Bishop and Father Vaillant plan confidently for the future. Problems of distance yield to possibilities of space. Throughout *Archbishop*, the stimulus for narrative movement derives from a need to fill a spiritual void, to carry Christ into the emptiness of the desert. "Not since the days of early Christianity," Father Vaillant once says, has the Church had such opportunity to lift the human spirit (210). Repeated allusions to the work of the early Church enforce the idea that missionary labors in the New World are themselves authentic beginnings. Indeed, personal experience with the arid region into which he has come brings Bishop Latour to see the hardships of Franciscan martyrs as even more demanding than those of the early Christian martyrs. For the Spanish friars "endured *Hunger, Thirst, Cold, Nakedness*, of a kind beyond any conception St. Paul and his brethren could have had. Whatever the early Christians suffered, it all happened in that safe little Mediterranean world, amid the old manners, the old landmarks" (278). It is a significant idea for the Bishop to entertain, betokening the manner in which experience has come to measure and even counter tradition in his life. As heir-by-proximity to the work of the Spanish friars, Latour faces a task as large as his opportunity. Both equal the unmapped dimensions of his diocese.

Although *Death Comes for the Archbishop* is patently not structured around scenes of crisis, yet the disparity between old and new, between his heritage and his surroundings, twice sounds the depths of Bishop Latour's emotional being and intensifies the issues of the narrative. If the first instance tests profoundly his missionary zeal, the second vindicates his life and work in terms resonant of all that has gone before.

Latour's visit to the grim rock of Ácoma precipitates the most abrupt change of mood to be found in *Archbishop*. Riding toward the mesa, the Bishop finds its loneliness appealing to the imagination: it strikes him as a tangible figure of the Rock upon which Christ founded his Church. But the church building at Ácoma, fortresslike and inappropriate to the surroundings, depresses him strangely. As he knows, it was built under the direction of the sup- posedly great missionary, Friar Juan Ramirez, more than two hun- dred years before. The carved beams of the roof had been dragged almost fifty miles by Indians; every stone and every "handful of earth" had been carried up to the church-site on the barren mesa "on the backs of men and boys and women." The adjacent cloister, thick-walled and cool, opening on an enclosed garden, "must have required an enormous labour of portage from the plain" (101–102). Whose needs, the Bishop wonders uneasily, had this church been built to serve? At Mass in this Old World structure forced onto a primal rock, Latour loses faith in the efficacy of his *mission*: overcome with a sense of "inadequacy and spiritual defeat," he feels "as if he were celebrating Mass at the bottom of the sea, for antediluvian creatures; for types of life so old, so hardened, so shut within their shells, that the sacrifice on Calvary could hardly reach back so far" (100). Suddenly he is a Frenchman lost "in the desert," thrust back into "the stone age, a prey to homesickness for his own kind, his own epoch, for European man and his glorious history of desire and dreams" (103).

Incisive in its thrust and definition, this language is a stern application of the logic of Cather's story. The Bishop's initial perception, that of Ácoma as an embodiment of the founding of the Church, is unmediated by history; it is thus healthy and positive. The combination of church and cloister, however, forces Europe into his consciousness and destroys his feeling of being close to the origins of his religion. One might think that by understanding the anomaly between these buildings and the simple needs of the spirit, the Bishop would be even more resolute in his determination to work for the natives—if only by way of atonement. But Cather allows no such formula to emerge. If the church speaks of Europe, the cloister shuts out any view of the stone mesa top, admitting to the eye only garden (now desiccated) and "turquoise sky"—so that "the early missionaries might well have forgotten the poor Ácomas . . . and believed themselves in some cloister hung on a spur of the

Pyrenees" (102). Trapped by the controlled perspective of this cloister and church, the Bishop loses touch with origins, both primal and religious. And the loss is devastating to his spirit. As the prisoner of a history that has betrayed its source, he can no longer see the Ácomas as Christians: they recede in time, on an inverted evolutionary scale, until they become shell-like creatures with whom a nineteenth-century man has no affinity. The undeniable message of the cloister at Ácoma is corrosive in character. It brings a bewildered Bishop Latour to the nadir of his missionary life.

Cather gives no details concerning Latour's restoration of spirit. But she is not yet finished with Ácoma. Immediately after the Bishop's perilous adventure she inserts the story of Friar Baltazar, priest at Ácoma in the early eighteenth century, a man who "took a great deal of care to make himself comfortable on that rock at the end of the world" (105). In studied, laconic prose, Cather writes of his self-indulgent tyranny over the superstitious Indians. The macabre climax of the tale features the lavish dinner given by Baltazar to impress four neighboring missionaries—an unrelenting caricature, as critics have noted, of the dinner in the Sabine Hills from which the narrative takes its start. While the guests enjoy Baltazar's gardens and the coolness of his cloister walls, the "naked rock outside" on which the Indians live is almost "too hot for the hand to touch" (108). The clumsiness of the native servant—ironic baptism of rich brown gravy over the head of one guest—evokes Baltazar's wrath, his hurling of a wine mug, and the fatal collapse of the serving boy. That evening, with guests departed and Baltazar's silence a terrifying part of the ritual, the Ácomas throw their Friar off the mesa, three hundred and fifty feet to his death.

Strategically placed, "The Legend of Fray Baltazar" serves as a commentary on Latour's malaise of spirit, a tragic example of what can happen when the habits of the old world blind one to the existence of the new. That the tale is told to the Bishop by Padre Jesus de Baca, a childlike priest "with a quality of golden goodness about him," enforces the contrast between simplicity and pomp, selflessness and vanity (86). Understandably, Cather's Bishop undergoes his version of a dark night of the soul. From Rome to Ácoma is a mighty journey—made possible only by the proximity of an original and transcending faith.

The second extended contrast between heritage and surroundings, valedictory in tone, signals the triumph of Cather's early world. Many friends had expected Bishop Latour to spend his retirement years in France, and he had considered such an arrange- ment himself. When he visits the Old World after many years, however, the Bishop finds himself "homesick for the New" (274). As she sets the conditions for the conclusion of *Archbishop*, Cather formulates the difference between New World and Old with equa- tions that have characterized American writing since its inception: youth stands against age, lightness against weight and density—as they had, for differing purposes, in the work of such writers as Irv- ing, Hawthorne, Henry James, and Mark Twain. Invested as attitudes in the consciousness of Latour, such contrasting terms demonstrate how completely the missionary has become dependent on the atmosphere he has breathed for almost forty years. Because "there was too much past," he can no longer respond to the beauty of Clermont as he once did. At bottom is his "feeling that old age did not weigh so heavily upon a man in New Mexico" as in France. Mornings, particularly, bring an "ache" to his breast—for he recalls that in New Mexico "he always awoke a young man"; only when he began to shave (and thus faced the mirror) did he become aware that "he was growing older." Not even the company of scholars and the pleasures of art can compensate "for the loss of those light-hearted mornings of the desert, for the wind that made one a boy again" (274–75).

The harsh lines of Cather's beginning world have, we see, been softened by experience into beguiling aspects of youthfulness. A morning mood, refreshing, rejuvenating, almost Thoreauvian in character, prevails against the European past. That Bishop Latour feels "nostalgia" for New Mexico during his sojourn in France suggests how thoroughly Cather has substituted a feeling of youth-of-place for memories of boyhood. A note of rhapsody pervades her language as she describes Latour's surrender to the New World: the Bishop returns deliberately, contentedly, because of "something soft and wild and free," something that "lightened the heart, softly, softly, picked the lock, slid the bolts, and released the prisoned spirit of man into the wind, into the blue and gold, into the morning, into the morning!" (276). At least this once, Cather hardly writes without "accent." The model of saints' lives may have served her well; but finally she rejoices in the liberating appeal of an atmosphere that one can breathe "only on the bright edges of the world" (275).

The culmination of Bishop Latour's work is the Cathedral that is to be his tomb. Built of local stone, constructed with a reverence for setting, this structure seems "to start directly" out of the hills behind it "with a purpose so strong that it was like action." Cather gives the Cathedral a dual function in her narrative: while it expresses the Bishop's affiliation with his surroundings, it likewise affirms his identity as a European. His wish to erect a monument signifies that he comes from a culture known (as we have seen) by its inclination "to leave some mark or memorial" of its passage. But when the Bishop sits, "wrapped in his Indian blankets," and admires the unity of Cathedral and background, he becomes a part of what he sees (271). With this tableau vivant, Cather completes her landscape. At sunset the hills framing the Cathedral turn a living red, suggesting Sangre de Cristo, the blood of Christ. The juniper tree in the form of the Cross had dispersed Latour's "geometrical nightmare" many years before. Now, with thoughts of sacrifice again evoked by the setting of the Cathedral, Cather's Southwest expands to include a final manifestation of the origins of Christianity.

Arriving with the buffalo, living to see the railroad running into Santa Fé, the Bishop, as Cather writes, "had accomplished an historic period" (273). Even the wooden houses that distressed Latour in Ohio have gradually come to New Mexico, and the narrator seconds the protagonist's judgment by commenting that "the year 1880 had begun a period of incongruous American building" (271). Additionally, the death of friends such as Kit Carson and Father Vaillant brings to the Bishop the poignant sense of being a survivor of what many had witnessed.

As these examples suggest, the narrative takes careful account of external time as it draws to a conclusion. Nonetheless, it continues to flatten out internal perspective and subsume background and foreground into an immediate present. Cather controls her now fully shaped materials by moving their accumulated substance *into* the consciousness of Bishop Latour. As an aging man, the Bishop observes that there is "no longer any perspective in his memories." What Cather calls "calendared time" has ceased to be a factor in his life. Released from the sequential nature of reality, "he sat in the middle of his own consciousness; none of his former states of mind were lost or outgrown. They were all within reach of his hand, and all comprehensible" (290). Such an account of the Bishop's wandering mind safeguards even as it asserts the presence of everything that has gone before and thus serves the narrative with a retroactive significance. The imaginative authority of *Death Comes for the Archbishop* derives from its relation to vital sources of beginning. Cather's achievement is that now, at the end, nothing has been lost, nothing has been outgrown; all is proximate—and fully comprehensible.

157

Telling
the
World
Over
Again

From the Beginning to Now: Some Words About Faulkner

During a question period at the University of Virginia in the spring of 1957, a member of the audience asked William Faulkner if he recalled any character or incident or idea that brought him to write *Absalom, Absalom!*. Frequently during these classroom sessions Faulkner admitted (or professed) an inability to recall specific matters about novels written many years before. But on this occasion he replied with one quick word: "Sutpen." With *Absalom, Absalom!* as the much-studied evidence, we can see that Faulkner's memory was as clear as his answer was concise. Assembled with the help of what he called "other characters I had to get out of the attic to tell the story of Sutpen," *Absalom, Absalom!* develops from the central conception "of a man who wanted sons and got sons who destroyed him."[37] Faulkner makes the focus of his narrative emphatic from the opening chapter in which Rosa Coldfield sits in the midst of history, participant in and repository of the past, and talks, lectures, and chatters repetitively to Quentin Compson about a man who *"came out of nowhere and without warning,"* who rode into town on a "Sunday morning in June in 1833 . . . out of no discernible past and acquired his land no one knew how and built his house, his mansion, apparently out of nothing."[38]

What Rosa evokes for Quentin's edification is a character with affinities to the figure of the mysterious stranger, "a man," she insists yet another time, "who rode into town out of nowhere" (10).[39] Her perception is validated by local residents who looked up from the gallery of the hotel on that Sunday morning, "and there the stranger was . . . already halfway across the square when they saw him," both the man and his horse "looking as if they had been created out of thin air"—a man's face "that none of them had ever seen before," a name "that none of them had ever heard," and an "origin and purpose which some of them were never to learn" (23–24). But this new arrival is neither explained by tradition nor contained by stereotype: his absolute presence blocks perspective and transforms the figure of the stranger from the realm of familiar mystery to that of scary metaphysics. For the negative terms and phrases that introduce Sutpen give him the force of a character who has come directly from creation. They also point to the source of energy in Faulkner's narrative—in which characters who are creatures of history try to account for a character who seems to have been created ex nihilo, "out of thin air." After absorbing the aura of the elemental associated with Sutpen and his wild Negroes, Quentin, "in the long unamaze . . . seemed to watch them overrun suddenly the hundred square miles of tranquil and astonished earth and drag house and formal gardens violently out of the soundless Nothing . . . creating the Sutpen's Hundred, the Be Sutpen's Hundred like the oldentime Be Light" (4). Tortured and audacious, Quentin's vision epitomizes Faulkner's strategy of imagining the world over again in *Absalom, Absalom!*.

As the long narrative sequence in "The Old Man" carries a man and a woman through a flood to emerging land (complete with snake), then to a birth and to primitive attempts at commerce, so, in their own way, the compulsive labors of Thomas Sutpen enact in caricature the story of Genesis—with a suggestion of Greek tragedy and an overlay of Darwin. "He named them all himself," Quentin hears from Mr. Compson, "all his own get [including his slave daughter, Clytemnestra] and all the get of his wild niggers after the country began to assimilate them" (48). Much earlier, before the eyes of its astonished citizens, this Adam with a Design brings his wild slaves into Yoknapatawpha County, fighting with them, working with them, "stark naked except for a coating of dried mud"— once called "absolute mud" (26–27). In both a literal and a metaphorical sense, Sutpen rises from "absolute mud." Quentin's apocalyptic vision of "Be Sutpen's Hundred" may foreshorten Faulkner's mode of telling the world over again in *Absalom, Absalom!*, but it captures the abruptness of creation and the violence inherent in imagining Sutpen.

The implications of imagining Sutpen reach expansively into Faulkner's narrative and provide it with what David Minter calls its "inclusiveness"—its capacity to enrich "the prehistory" of Yoknapatawpha County with an assemblage of characters and issues.[40] Perhaps the most memorable reverberations brought about by Sutpen's presence can be seen in Quentin's later conversations with

Shreve McCannon at Harvard—conversations about the South in which Quentin, as Faulkner observed to Malcolm Cowley, lamented "the passing of an order the dispossessor of which he was not tough enough to withstand." What he "feared" even more was the fact "that a man like Sutpen, who to Quentin was trash, originless, could not only have dreamed so high but have had the force and the strength to have failed so grandly."[41] As a character virtually surrounded with accounts of Sutpen's portentous arrival and subsequent activities, Quentin broods over the meaning of Sutpen for the South. For once Sutpen has *entered* history with his mansion and his marriage and his service in the Civil War (for which he earned "a citation for valor" from Robert E. Lee), he can never be erased or returned to nowhere; this man who somehow got his land from Ikkemotubbe must be reckoned with as a force moving through time, relentless, tragic, transforming the shape of the present and (to Quentin) threatening that of the future (13).

159

Telling
the
World
Over
Again

Floyd C. Watkins has remarked that in the attitudes of their protagonists toward property *Absalom, Absalom!* and *Go Down, Moses* are "mirror images of each other."[42] The point is well taken. Whereas Sutpen grew up (amid violence and vulgarity) in western Virginia where there were no such things as property lines and deeds to land, Isaac McCaslin was born into a world of privilege and ownership. The land in the Virginia mountains, Quentin explains to Shreve, "belonged to anybody and everybody," and the man who would say " 'This is mine' was crazy" (179). Ike reaches back to the Civil War, to Christopher Columbus, and finally to Adam, as he circles toward the same idea in *Go Down, Moses*. Only when Sutpen moves to the Tidewater region with its plantations and slaves does he learn that to possess power and prestige "you got to have land and niggers and a fine house" (192). Only when Ike reads the ledger entries in the commissary does he learn the demoralizing cost of ownership. Watkins reminds us that Faulkner twice characterizes Sutpen's move as a fall (although there seems to be no Eden to have fallen from) and concludes that "if Sutpen falls from a primitive world, Ike McCaslin would like to do just the opposite to regain communal anonymity."[43] In my terms, if one character joins—and even embraces—history, the other attempts to secede from it.

On the opening page of *Go Down, Moses*, as I have noted, Faulkner tells us that Isaac "owned no property and never desired to." Scorned by Lucas Beauchamp for not having insisted upon the

McCaslin inheritance, insulted finally by a cranky Roth Edmonds (in "Delta Autumn") for being old and monotonous, Isaac takes the case against ownership to its ethical extreme. Whatever one's view of his "innocence," he remains the character who extends the issues of the novel to a radical dimension: by means of Isaac's stance, Faulkner projects in high relief what he calls the agony of "a whole land in miniature"; by means of Isaac's hop-skip-and-jump logic, Faulkner implicates the world in a family problem.[44]

Toward the end of "The Bear," an eighteen-year-old Isaac sees an enormous snake, "the old one, the ancient and accursed about the earth." Redirecting words once used in tribute to nature by Sam Fathers, Isaac salutes the snake by saying "Chief . . . Grand-father," thereby associating Ikkemotubbe and Carothers McCaslin with the eternal source of evil. The ludicrous spectacle of Boon Hogganbeck laying claim to a tree full of squirrels follows immediately. In the final words of the story, Boon shouts at Isaac, "Get out of here! Dont touch them! Dont touch a one of them! They're mine!"[45] Thus, Faulkner concludes with a synoptic meditation on evil and a comic view of the serious matter of owning nature—something that seems instinctive and innocent, yet insistent and troubling, in this childlike brute of a man.

In the chapter on property in his *Two Treatises on Government,* John Locke argues that money and ownership have brought the world to its present sorry condition—far different from what it was originally. For, "in the beginning," he concludes, "all the World was *America,* and more so than that is now."[46] The essential American narrative, the story that attempts to tell the world over again, is a version of Locke's statement: in a variety of ways, it reaches to the "beginning" and delivers us to the "now." And in doing so it cultivates a radical dimension that defines the self in its relation to innocence and experience, to the nation and to the world.

Part
Three

5

Inexhaustible Beginnings

Original World, Original Self   In "A Yankee in Canada," the
first parts of which were published in *Putnam's Magazine*
in 1853, Thoreau writes of his visit to that northern nation
in 1850. Contemplating the walls of Quebec, he wonders
momentarily why a country so "wild and unsettled" seems
older than the United States, then concludes that the
answer lies in the antiquity of Canadian institutions, in
what he calls "the rust of conventions and formalities."[1]
Left over from the feudal system, the all too visible
machinery of these aristocratic enterprises makes it
impossible to forget the government in Canada; as is the
case in England and Europe, one "cannot be wholesomely
neglected" (83). Although the "purity and transparency" of
the air are commendable, one is constantly made aware of
the government (34). Every day "it parades itself before
you . . . every day it goes out to the Plains of Abraham or
to the Champ de Mars and exhibits itself and toots"
(83–84). One must, I think, admire the word *toots* in this
context—irreverent, onomatopoetic, unit of sound that
mocks the pageantry Thoreau endures from his Yankee
perspective even as it heralds a fundamental statement

about the value of human existence. For the result of such governmental omnipresence, Thoreau tells us, is that the individual is "not worth so much in Canada as in the United States." An American, he believes, "is advantageously nearer to the primitive and the ultimate condition of man" (82–83).

A number of critics have commented on Thoreau's testy view of Canada, the jaundiced impatience signalled at the outset by his observation that what he "got by going to Canada was a cold" (3). Caustic, with a humor thumped in reflexively at the end, this offhand remark is only half of the opening sentence: the prior half, at once concessive and cutting, informs us that Thoreau might have little "to say about Canada, not having seen much." But no matter the narrowness that leads this tourist to dismiss a past and a present very different from those of New England. No matter the myopia that leads him to reduce Quebec to "a nation of peasants" (82). Thoreau with a cold is still Thoreau, an American who assumes there is an advantage to being near the "ultimate condition of man." And of course his conviction is not unique: transformed by a different set of considerations, the *absence* that Mr. Evelyn celebrates in *Margaret* (and that Henry James characterizes as *bleakness* in his study of Hawthorne) is the condition of Thoreau's cranky allegiance to the individual in the United States. Thoreau's parochialism, like that of Mr. Evelyn (and of James), makes his values all the more apparent.

More than a decade earlier, in his lecture "Being and Seeming," Emerson had declared (with detectable irony) that in this world of pretense and display there was no competition for the "low-levelled aim, simply *to be*."[2] A year later, he assessed the matter of unadorned existence in blunt metaphysical terms. "Being costs me nothing," he wrote in his journal in 1839: "I need not be rich nor pay taxes nor leave home nor buy books for that. It is the organizing that costs."[3] Emerson could carry such a value-laden conviction into various aspects of his life: his trips abroad, for example, allowed him to measure the cultivated "organizing" of England much as Thoreau had appraised the imported institutions of Canada. In *English Traits* (1856) he lists the "innumerable details" comprising the scene around him—not only the cathedrals and castles, the military splendor, the "servants and equipages," but the fields "combed and rolled till they appear to have been finished with a pencil instead of a plough." England is a garden, he writes: "Nothing is left as it was made."[4] On the shores of the upper Mississippi River, by way of contrast, everything remains as it was made; one is confronted with "interminable silent forest," with "forest behind forest." In the American West, Emerson wrote to Carlyle during a lecture tour in 1851, one finds "the raw bullion of nature," with social values "not stamped on it."[5] Thoreau, ever-biased toward genesis, admired a similar rawness and "continuousness" in the Maine wilderness, a place where nature had not been shaped to provide a preserve for kings, where, oxymoronically, "moss-grown and decaying trees" lived in "perpetual youth."[6]

Better able to value the advantages of different cultures than Thoreau ever was, Emerson acknowledged the attraction of an England made to order even as he deferred to nature unmarked by human endeavor. Yet his commitment to an existential "I" remains unqualified. Following the statement that *being* costs him nothing, he adds an astonishing sentence: "And the moment I *am*, I despise the city & the seashore, yes earth and the galaxy also."[7] If Thoreau's American is "advantageously" close to a prime or original human condition, Emerson's "I" incarnates a radical beginning. For any being that simply *exists* necessarily exists as (and at) a beginning, disdaining (in Emerson's terms) the need for "organizing" and even the galaxy, radiating possibility out of the nakedness of its existential state. "No power of genius has ever yet had the smallest success in explaining existence," Emerson wrote in his essay on Plato.[8] It is the ultimate negative condition, an ontological "point" that erases the phenomenological world.

In a journal entry of 1838 Thoreau uses similar terms to describe the consequences of an induced transcendent experience. If "I consult consciousness for a moment" with ears and eyes closed, he writes, I find that "all walls and barriers [are] dissipated"; the "earth rolls from under me," and "I float" (or "heave and swell") like a thought on "an unknown & infinite sea, without rock or headland." It is a place without demarcation of any kind, a wonderland in which riddles are solved and the ends of straight lines meet, a paradise in which "I am from the beginning—knowing no end, no aim. No sun illumines me,—for I dissolve all lesser lights in my own intenser and steadier light." Although Thoreau begins with an "If," his description reads more like the account of a down-home experiment than a hypothesis—almost as if he can call up a mystical experience by putting his hands over his ears, closing his eyes, and consulting "consciousness for a moment." He is playing at paradox in this passage, sporting with the idea of riddles solved and straight lines curving to meet, indulging the spectacle of "eternity and space gambolling familiarly through my depths."[9] But he is undeniably committed to a *via negativa* (complete with a vast and barren geography) as the mode of transcending the perspectives and limitations of the finite world.

What is distinctive, and thoroughly American, in Thoreau's description is his culminating emphasis on the self. Accounts of mystical states traditionally insist on a suspension of sensory awareness, a forgetting of the outer world. Concomitantly, they speak of moving beyond the limiting consciousness of self. Thoreau, according to convention, blocks out the surrounding world of sounds and sights. Rather than moving away from or beyond his consciousness, however, he isolates it, consults it, and discovers a *self* that commands the universe. It is this puckish yet imperious self that Emerson describes in an essay written shortly after Thoreau's death in 1862. Emerson sees his friend's life as a series of ongoing renunciations that made him "an iconoclast in literature," a "protestant *à l'outrance*," a "willing hermit." The evidence, he feels, is not hard to come by: for Thoreau "was bred to no profession; he never married; he lived alone; he never went to church; he never voted; he refused to pay a tax to the state; he ate no flesh, he drank no wine, he never knew the use of tobacco. . . . He had no talent for wealth, and knew how to be poor without the least hint of squalor or inelegance. . . . He had no temptations to fight against; no appetites, no passions, no taste for elegant trifles." A few paragraphs later Emerson concludes (and I bless him for his phrasing), "No truer American existed than Thoreau."[10]

As the manuscript of this essay shows, Emerson had originally ended one of the sentences in his negative catalogue with the words, "how near to the old monks in their ascetic religion."[11] He later deleted the phrase, perhaps because Thoreau's devotion to self-exploration made his asceticism pointedly different in motive from that of the monks of old. But Emerson expressed an attitude both provocative and profound with the phrase he first wrote, then deleted. From his contemporary he had stripped away alliances with society and religion, emotion and appetite; what remained was not a monk but an American, the unadorned and essential Thoreau, whose most radical quest was to recover the integrity of creation. Following the classic *via negativa*, the mystic arrives at a sense of an Original Being. Following their own negative way, Thoreau and Emerson proclaim the discovery of an Original Self.[12]

Invoking the Infinite   Replete with metaphors of renewal that commend the idea of stripping away for an unburdened start, much of the best-known work of Emerson and Thoreau courts the absolute with an air of triumph and necessity, pressing the infinite hard upon the finite, the eternal upon the temporal. The result is a rhetorical strategy at once negative and imperative that overrides a sense of human limitation with commanding assertion. The convictions of Meister Eckhart have a special resonance in this context, not only reminding us of the Neoplatonic strain that informs the ideas of these New England writers but suggesting the analogous ways in which theologian and poet, centuries apart in time, seek to imbue the finite with the infinite. Eckhart's belief that creation and the existence of the creator are simultaneous phenomena, for example, assumes a spiritual world of perpetual *nows* in which the absolute can never be excluded from any given moment precisely because it "always exists." In Eckhart's terms, God is present to individuals wholly, completely, "as he is in the eternal now." And there is "not more than the one now": for the "now" in which the first man was created, and "the now in which the last man will have his end, and the now in which I am talking, they are all the same in God." Accordingly, one who was "always united" with God "could never grow old." His happy fate would be to dwell "always anew in a now without ceasing."[13]

Emerson and Thoreau adapt the beguiling idea of not growing old to their own purposes. In "The Protest" (1839), Emerson argues (and promises) that one who ignores the opinions of the world in favor of "impulses from within," who permits "no horizon to fall on the illimitable space," will have "immortal youth."[14] In "Walking" (1862), Thoreau conflates the limitless and the limited with typical audacity when he declares that a person who made "infinite demands" on life "would always find himself in a new country"— "surrounded by the raw material of life."[15] To know a Divine Presence within, Emerson declares in "Doctrine of the Soul" (1838), is to know the "infinite scope" of the human spirit; at that point of

awareness one has not "a few possessions for a short time"—the
common predicament of humanity—but "entire existence."[16]
Thoreau shares a compatible vision: contemplating the antithesis of
time and paradise in his *Journal* in 1853, he records his desire for an
eternal morning, for woods where the thrush "forever sings," for "A
New Hampshire everlasting and unfallen."[17]

What these writers speak for with their conceits of eternal nows,
immortal youth, and everlasting mornings, is the wonder of existence ennobled by the infinite. As similar as their commitment to
an absolute *now* (and to a shaping family of metaphor) might be,
however, the identifying difference between the disquisitions of
Eckhart and the essays of Emerson and Thoreau should not be
overlooked. From a specific medieval perspective, Eckhart focuses
on an eternal moment, on the simultaneous existence of the Godhead, the Word, and the act of creation (what he calls a boiling-over
of Being—"*bullitio*" to "*ebullitio*"). From a specific nineteenth-century perspective, Emerson and Thoreau evoke the ideas of timelessness and limitless space to extol the potential of a existent self
apart from (ontologically prior to) the repetitive measures of a languid world. Considered thematically, this is an opposition frequently seen in American writing of the nineteenth and twentieth
centuries (provocatively embodied in the figure of the negative
character). But I am speaking less of a theme than of an impulse or
mode that is the *condition* of a theme, of an attraction toward a primal moment that evokes Thoreau's statement about an American
being "advantageously nearer to the ultimate condition of man"
than is an Englishman; that brings such writers as Emerson and
Wallace Stevens to prize unalloyed "being" and Melville (in chapter 44 of *The Confidence Man* [1857]) to compare the effect of an
original character "to that which in Genesis attends upon the
beginning of things"; that leads Jack Kerouac (much later, in *On the
Road* [1957] to pursue God as the ineffable "IT" on the momentum
of an orgasmic prose that reaches "into the holy void of uncreated
emptiness."[18] Because it enables one to apprehend existence out of
a consciousness of present encumbrance—Thomas Paine's "subsequent circumstances" in metaphysical guise—the disposition to
invoke the absolute generates a powerful sense of beginning, timeless, pure, inexhaustible in its possibilities.

As I shall note in the following chapter, the American need for
beginnings has long depended on assumptions of inexhaustibility,

frequently fuzzy and ill-defined but invariably compelling, to sustain an image of uniqueness and national greatness. A sense of the inexhaustible guarantees the future, gives purpose to the present, and subordinates the past. In the early work of Emerson, it takes authority from a joyous (if sometimes exacting) denial of limitation.

From the time of Stephen E. Whicher's *Freedom and Fate: An Inner Life of Ralph Waldo Emerson* in 1953, responsible studies of Emerson have stressed the developing nature of his life and work. Critics have come to understand him in a variety of ways—as a writer who moved from optimism to stoic acceptance, for example, or from transcendental dualism to a grudging empiricism, or from idealism to an incipient pragmatism. No matter the diversity of judgment, the conclusion of inquiries that trace the course of his ideas and methods of composition is that Emerson was a writer whose ideas evolved, changed—in contexts personal, societal, and philosophical.[19] Whatever one's assessments of fashion and achievement in scholarship, it is clear that we should not try to read Emerson as if he wrote everything on the same afternoon.

My purpose is not to survey the contours of Emerson's work once again but to point out (first here, then in the final section of this chapter) recurrent manifestations of a beginning impulse that cluster in his early lectures, in *Nature* (1836), and in *Essays, First Series* (1841), and to note his significant attempt in the vexed essay "Experience" (1844) to project the promise of beginnings into the future rather than to derive them from the absolute. Not that Emerson's early reach for beginnings came with uniform ease; and not that it remained in all instances identical. Although a fundamental strategy of stripping away is common to all who celebrate beginning moments, modulations occur because of forms and occasions of discourse. It is one thing to inscribe reflections concerning unadorned being and the grandeur of an existential "I" in one's journal, quite another to package them into performances for audiences and readers who inhabit a quotidian world of aspiration and disappointment. As efforts to demonstrate both the necessity and the problem of invoking the infinite, Emerson's early work enacts scenarios of entrapment and freedom, inertia and movement, which exhibit a dramatic awareness of what he later called "the odious facts."[20] Repeatedly in these public forums Emerson characterizes the finite world in metaphors of imprisonment: sounding like a literate cousin of Huckleberry Finn, he speaks not of the "smothery" ways of society but of bonds and shackles, prisons and jails, of being harnessed by one's conforming consciousness. Repeatedly, his language measures the consequences of being lifted into youth or weighted down by age—of incorporating energy or succumbing to mass.

Two provocative formulations of what was necessarily an ongoing effort to envision the informing power of the infinite can be seen in works that critics of Emerson have frequently paired for study—"The Protest" (delivered as a lecture in 1839) and "Circles" (1841). Generating the dialectic of "The Protest" is the premise that the youth, any youth, is born at odds with society, that a "dissonance" (both "involuntary and necessary") exists between the two. Emerson moves quickly to set the terms of his argument with a negative absolute: "Nothing" that has been accomplished, he writes, satisfies the youth, who rebels instinctively at "the bonds of the finite," who yearns for "the perfect, the illimitable" ("P": 93). It was a rhetorical strategy he used with equal resolution in the final paragraph of "The Over-Soul" (1841) to praise the unique potential of every human being: "Before the immense possibilities of man," begins his sweeping generalization, "all mere experience, all past biography, however spotless and sainted, shrinks away. . . . We not only affirm that we have few great men, but, absolutely speaking, that we have none; that we have no history, no record of any character or mode of living that entirely contents us."[21] In "The Protest" the situation of the youth is ominous: if he felt that he "dwelled in Eternity," his antipathy to limitation would vanish in the (subjective) disappearance of limitation itself; but he (like the rest of us) lives in a seductive world of time that lulls him into compromise, that requires "a lover of the infinite" to remain fully human. In such a world, he finds it difficult to remain true to "the bounding pulse of virtue" ("P": 93–94, 89). His aversion to "the prison-like limits of the Actual," his dedication to "the unshackled Ideal," all too often give way before custom and the treachery of his senses; he trims, compromises, decides that his opposition was "unadvised," and thus "goes down stream to darkness and to death" ("P": 94, 99).

Joel Porte and Barbara Packer have pointed out the personal context in which Emerson developed the specific argument of "The Protest."[22] Unfriendly and even hostile reaction to the "Divinity School Address" of the previous year had surprised and distressed

Emerson, causing him to assess the difficulty of maintaining one's commitment to the infinite in the midst of social dictates and blandishments and bringing him, as Packer says, to "invent a new myth of the Fall."[23] "The Fall of Man," he writes in "The Protest," is "the first word of history and the last fact of experience" ("P": 86). As one comes to expect from Emerson, this sobering conclusion is cogently phrased. But one also expects, in 1839, his idiom-of-the-infinite, transcendent and pure, to overcome the relational phenomena of history and experience. From a different perspective in "Man the Reformer" (1841), for example, he bemoans the ways in which the abuses of commerce ravage the prayers of childhood and the dreams of youth and thus deliver one into "the harness of routine and obsequiousness." In this case one's course is obvious: to avoid such a fate one must "begin the world anew."[24] And in "The Over-Soul" he asserts confidently that the soul "contradicts all experience," "abolishes time and space," and transcends both our addiction to vice and our wavering faith ("OS": 387).

In "The Protest," however, the issue is not so easily resolved: for an Emerson in perilous encounter with the world finds that the Fall consists not only of social imperatives but of "old age," of an "ossification of the heart," of "fat in the brain" ("P": 89). One is thus implicated in one's own Fall, beset, as Packer observes, with "a kind of lassitude" that makes it virtually inevitable.[25] Even in this troubled essay, however, the infinite retains its capacity to arrest one's indulgent slide into the constraining fabric of society (though Maurice Gonnaud judges the solution in "The Protest" to be less the result of invoking the illimitable than of a tranquil optimism).[26] Because "the Saviour is as eternal as the harm," Emerson proclaims, the world is to be saved "by obedience to the soul," the source of life for all. Specifically, "The Redemption from this ruin is lodged in the heart of Youth" ("P": 90). For if one is supported by "new impulses from within," if one heeds neither the praise nor the censure of the world, if, finally (as we have seen), one "suffers no horizon to fall on the illimitable space," then one has "immortal youth"—a condition that signifies the possibility of triumph over limitation and conformity, even as it provides a perspective for measuring the somber fact of the Fall ("P": 100).

Buoyant and brave in its formulations, "Circles" (1841) orchestrates similar ideas about human existence and transcendent possibility into cosmic opposition.[27] Emerson is at his most Whitmanesque in this essay: at the end he endorses "abandonment" as "the way of life"; at an earlier point he says that because he is "only an experimenter" the reader should neither value nor discredit what he does, "as if I pretended to settle any thing as true or false. I unsettle all things. No facts are to me sacred; none are profane; I simply experiment, an endless seeker, with no Past at my back."[28] The thesis of "Circles" is that in this "fluid and volatile" universe everything can be outdone, that human life is, or should be, a series of "self-evolving" circles ("C": 403–04). It was a figure for portraying spiritual growth that took protean form in Emerson's early work. In "The Over-Soul" the writer characterized the soul as "creating a world before her, leaving worlds behind her. She has no dates, nor rites, nor persons, nor specialties, nor men" ("OS": 388). With a dubious sense of occasion, he articulated the same concept of inevitable progression to a congregation celebrating the completion of their new church in East Lexington, Massachusetts, in 1838: "Round every thought of ours," he told the assemblage of believers, "is already dwelling a greater thought, into which after some time we enter, and find it in turn circumscribed by a higher truth."[29] Transforming his conviction to an appraisal of graduating personal loyalties in both the 1841 and the 1847 versions of the essay "Love," he suggested the impermanence of a single attachment and recognized the quest for new fulfillment that succeeds each ripening of joy.

At the outset of "Circles" Emerson tells us that "the eye is the first circle," a tribute both to sight and to the centrality of the "I," the expanding self, as the architect of horizons ("C": 403). *Generalization*, a highly empowered term, is the means by which we draw new circles around old ones, encompassing them, graduating beyond them. When Emerson praises the achievement of "great-eyed [and certainly "great-I'd"] Plato," he has no higher praise than to call him "the broadest generalizer."[30] For all thought and religion, all manners and morals, are "at the mercy of a new generalization." As one consequence, "a man's growth is seen in the successive choirs of his friends"; "there is no virtue which is final; all are initial" ("C": 406, 411). In context, such cool statements of impermanence are not so distressing as they might appear to be; indeed, they are designed to be symptoms of a deep and developing faith.[31] For generalization, as Emerson defines it, "is always a new influx of the divinity into the mind" ("C": 407). Inspired and infinite, tantamount to creation, it is a surge of life that takes us on a never-completed journey toward a "principle of fixture or stability in the soul," a principle (superior to the created world) containing all circles. One can, of course, never draw the ultimate circle: even so, as the youth in "The Protest" yearned for "the unshackled Ideal," the inspired drawer of circles strives for "the Unattainable, the flying Perfect" ("C": 403).

Underlying (and giving special punch to) the argument of this essay are assumptions of a pre-Einsteinian world about the opposition of energy and matter—or mass. For standing against generalization (energy) with its vibrant rush toward Truth is a condition of torpor or sluggishness much like "ossification" in "The Protest" and "repose" in "Intellect" (which follows "Circles" in *Essays: First Series*), a disposition toward the inert (matter) that threatens to set in after any new circle has been drawn; stubborn and difficult to overcome, it enervates the spirit, dulls perspective, and thus tends "to solidify and hem in" life ("C": 404). We experience it most frequently as "old age," a state of mind and body that manifests itself as "conservatism, appropriation, inertia" and seems at times "the only disease" ("C": 412). To borrow a phrase from "The Protest," old age "decline[s] creation," refuses to seek "the way onward" ("P": 87). At his peremptory best in "Circles," Emerson declares that "we grizzle every day," then adds with a snap, "I see no need of it" ("C": 412). For divine moments abolish not only sequence but "our contritions":

I accuse myself of sloth and unprofitableness day by day; but when these waves of God flow into me, I no longer reckon lost time. I no longer poorly compute my possible achievement by what remains to me of the month or the year; for these moments confer a sort of omnipresence and omnipotence which asks nothing of duration, but sees that the energy of the mind is commensurate with the work to be done, without time.   ("C": 411)

Generalizing is thus an act of being and beginning, pure, originary. Transmuted by the spiritualized physics of Emerson, it becomes a form of energy that triumphs over the inert. At such a moment time disappears; at such a moment "the past is always swallowed and forgotten" ("C": 411).

Whicher observes that in "Circles" Emerson begins to take cognizance of the "inexorable" effect of time and not simply the impact it has on an individual moments of inspiration.[32] The point is well taken (though it should not obscure the developing dualism of Emerson's vision): because time and evolving perspectives corrode the idea of the Eternal Now, the possible inevitably gives way to the actual, pre- or transtemporal perspectives to temporal—with an expanding awareness of succession and loss (and for some writers a legacy of nostalgia). As a human being living through periods of crisis, private and public, Emerson could not but be aware of the effects of time. Yet his capacity to offset limitation with a sense of original hope remains locked into the rhythms of his style. And the manner in which he deploys his consciousness of time and his vision of eternity sets the dialectic of individual essays.

As we have seen in "The Protest" and in "Circles," the distinctive thrust of a rhetoric aware of temporal constraint is to restore us to a state of possibility—the ultimate gift to the self. In these works and from such radical perspectives as that of "Doctrine of the Soul" (which commends the idea of the "newborn in his world beginning all as all had never been"), the homilist-in-Emerson brings us to a perception of experience as misspent possibility: what we have done pales before the vision of what we might do—or, perhaps more accurately, what we do pales in the light of what we are.[33] All such perceptual victories over limitation are divinely inspired, uplifting cadences that ennoble life. But life also has its downside, the ever-waiting tendency to submit to repose. Thus in "Intellect" Emerson tells us that ideas "catch us up for moments into their heaven," until we lose the rush of "rapture" and find it convenient to adjust and compromise. Between the spontaneity of truth and the concessions of repose, he goes on to say, "man oscillates" like a pendulum.[34] The metaphor of oscillation prefigures the later metaphor of the "double consciousness" in "Fate": "A man must ride alternately on the horses of his private and his public nature," Emerson concludes in this exacting essay; thereby he learns that because of a dual element inherent in circumstance "whatever lames and paralyzes you, draws in with it the divinity, in some form, to repay." "Matter and mind," he proposes, "are in perpetual tilt and balance."[35] Thus, with rhythmic and arhythmic measures, with push and pull alternations, the genetic, environmental, and social limits that beset us throughout life are convertible to renewed possibility. The final dimensions of Fate are not to be measured.

In moods triumphant or melancholy, the dialectical patterns of Emerson's early essays thus remind us that the finite must look to the infinite for well-being and renewal. When in general but dramatic terms he brings the infinite to the rescue of the human being constrained by custom (when, that is, he can envision a beginning), he forges a scenario of hope, inspirational and insistent. When he faces experience as an irrefragable fact, concrete, temporal, impossible to transform into coherent spiritual drama, he casts his ideas into a more stoic idiom. Thus his concern for vision, for an awareness that can transform the temporal to the eternal, natural phenomena to primal spectacle. In "History" (1841) he heightens the status of observer to that of august witness, nocturnal sublimity "verifying some old prediction," with the commanding assertion that one "who has seen the rising moon break out of the clouds at midnight has been present like an archangel at the creation of light and of the world."[36] If cosmology here is jumbled for the occasion, the idea of having an angelic seat at creation is nonetheless dazzling.

Ascending to Creation   Central to Thoreau's work is a vision of the infinite compatible with that of Emerson yet distinct in its postures of discovery and yearning. Not only does this disciple of self-exploration wish for "A New Hampshire everlasting and unfallen" and assert that "infinite demands" on life will put one "always" in a new country. As Frederick Garber and H. Daniel Peck have demonstrated, his concern for origins, for "earliness" as a point of purity, a source of creativity, pervades both his Journal and his first book, *A Week on the Concord and Merrimack Rivers* (1849).[37] And in *Walden* (1854), focusing his call for purification on human life, Thoreau postulates renewal as a re-originating of the self, envisions for the vibrant individual the promise of "perpetual morning," and tells us (with his genius for microcosm) of witnessing the beginning in miniature—sand foliage taking form on the railroad bank. It was "the creation of an hour," Thoreau writes, something that brought him into "the laboratory of the Artist who made the world and me," who was "still at work, sporting on this bank . . . strewing his fresh designs about."[38] What Andrew Delbanco calls the "sanctifying fervor" of *Walden* includes Thoreau's attachment to the root meanings of words (*extra-vagrance*, *mal-aria*), to significations that suggest "a pure point" of origin behind centuries of linguistic change. For Thoreau, Delbanco concludes, words "carry traces of God." The evidence behind Sherman Paul's pungent remark that at Walden Thoreau tested the idea of "beginning from scratch" leads us to see that it was an astonishing case of radical "scratch"—performed in a variety of ways.[39]

But it is in his dedication to walking, and specifically to climbing, ascending, that we find some of the most arresting evidence of Thoreau's affinity for beginnings. Blending metaphorical and literal insistence in "A Walk to Wachusett" and the more strenuous "Ktaadn," Thoreau describes the opportunities and perils evoked by journeying toward an early and ultimately original world.[40]

"A Walk to Wachusett," Frederick Garber observes, is "perhaps the most consciously literary" of Thoreau's ascents. Garber is both accurate and generous in his appraisal: a more dyspeptic critic might have termed the essay "conspicuously" literary.[41] For Thoreau's account of a walking excursion to the summit of Mt. Wachusett in the summer of 1842 (first published in the *Boston Miscellany* in January 1843) not only parades stock features of the sublime but ready allusions to Homer, Virgil, Samuel Johnson, and Wordsworth. Thoreau likens himself and his traveling companion, Richard Fuller, to Rasselas in search of enlightenment, wonders if "other Homers frequent the neighboring plains," and learns from reading Virgil that "Rome imposes her story still upon this late generation."[42] Likewise prominent in the essay are ready-made applications of individual actions to human experience: the insouciance of settlers in crude new villages, for example, teaches us that each person's "world is but a clearing in the forest"; mounting hills and descending into valleys is "perfectly symbolical" of the ups and downs of life (141, 150). At once tentative and overinsistent in its fashioning of materials, "A Walk to Wachusett" is the production of a writer laboring assiduously if somewhat unevenly at his craft.

Despite its amateurish qualities, however, this early travel sketch employs strategies of metaphorical perception characteristic of Thoreau's courtship of beginnings. The tone and manner are distinct from those of *Walden* or of the ascents in *A Week* or of the journal entry (of 1838) in which the writer sports with paradox en route to "an unknown and infinite sea." But the fundamental *moves* of "A Walk to Wachusett" anticipate those of Thoreau's mature work and

afford a perspective for examining the patterns of the more challenging "Ktaadn."

A progressive series of departures—from society, from history,
and from nature in familiar guise—takes the travelers in "A Walk"
from the accoutrements of a civilized world to a region at once desolate and august. They journey through a village that "had, as yet,
no post-office, nor any settled name" (141). Although the town of
Lancaster evokes the memory of Mary Rowlandson's captivity in
1676 and the mayhem of King Philip's War, the serenity of a July
afternoon makes those events seem "as remote as the irruption of
the Goths" (149–50). Finally, as they proceed through a forest and
arrive at the summit of Wachusett, Thoreau and Fuller find nature
transformed, the trees increasingly "dwarfed, till there were no trees
whatever" (142). The effect is one of distancing—journeying
through a nameless terrain, draining history of immediacy, ascending to an elevation, however "slight" (as Thoreau admits), that is
"infinitely removed from the plain": "when we reached it we felt a
sense of remoteness, as if we had traveled into distant regions."[43]
Thoreau presents the summit of Wachusett as a point of purity,
"simple even to majesty," a domain in which "gods might wander, so
solemn and solitary, and removed from all contagion with the plain"
(143–45).

Because "A Walk" is more an exercise in stripping away than a
full-blown encounter with the absolute, the summit of Wachusett
serves as a post for observing the world from which Thoreau and
his companion have (temporarily) withdrawn. As they survey "successive circles of towns," one rising above another, and watch people traveling along highways or going into houses for the night,
Thoreau concludes that Wachusett is "the observatory of the State.
There lay Massachusetts, spread out before us in its length and
breadth, like a map" (147).

It is a map to which Thoreau returns with didactic purpose as his
journey ends. Having resumed "the desultory life of the plain," he
counsels, "let us endeavor to import a little of that mountain
grandeur into it." Let us remember that "there is elevation in every
hour . . . and we have only to stand on the summit of one hour to
command an uninterrupted horizon" (151). "A Walk to Wachusett"
is a pleasant and anticipatory concoction. What it achieves with its
pattern of withdrawal and return is a perspective for refreshing the
self (the return to the world having been built safely into the with-

drawal). What it forgoes is the effort to test the traveler by means of a dramatic encounter with the presocietal, the pre-experiential, to escort him back as someone who has confronted creation rather than as a teacher who has been to summer school. That kind of challenge is the dangerous work of "Ktaadn."

At the end of August 1846, Thoreau left Walden Pond on a trip to the backwoods of Maine, specifically, as he says in a pun blending geography and purpose, "to mount Ktaadn"—an Indian word signifying "highest land." The record of his journey displays a virtual anthology of beginning moments, progressively radical, from details of early history to the starkness of creation. Thoreau is close enough in time to capture a *first*—in the manner of Thomas Prince (who remembered the first Puritan death in Boston), George S. Hillard (who honored the first Pilgrim to step on Plymouth Rock), and many others in the eighteenth and nineteenth centuries: Ktaadn, he writes, was "first ascended by white men in 1804" (3). But he also has proximity to a variety of worlds uninscribed by history— clearings and woods where the immigrant may begin "life as Adam did," an unexplored region where one encounters "the virgin forest of the New World" (14, 83). Ultimately, he confronts a forbidding elevation composed of "Matter, vast, terrific," something not simply prior to but alien to human efforts to domesticate or measure out (70). As one might expect, the map Thoreau has carried with him, the latest edition of "Greenleaf's Map of Maine," turns out to be woefully inadequate in these early worlds, "a labyrinth of errors" (15). As he proceeds up the Penobscot river, he must find his way through a maze of woods and lakes and primeval terrain without directions from a commercial publisher.

"Ktaadn" provides an eloquent example of how a negative structure functions in a carefully wrought essay—stripping away social trappings and assumptions and finally testing the limits of negation itself as it registers the perilous experience of intruding on an original world. And the experience is indeed perilous. Thoreau observes with understated accuracy that "it is difficult to conceive of a region uninhabited by man" (70). That is, however, precisely what this visitor to primal regions must do, and find language to do, in "Ktaadn." Thus he resorts both initially and in retrospect to negative forms that relieve us of our preconceptions and force us to gaze (as he does) at "pure Nature," at "form and fashion and material" that defy human classification, at Earth 'made out of Chaos and Old Night": "Here was no man's garden, but the unhandselled globe. It was not lawn, nor pasture, nor mead, nor woodland, nor lea, nor arable, nor waste-land. It was the fresh and natural surface of the planet Earth, as it was made forever and ever." Canceling out our most comfortable and value-laden attribution, Thoreau tells us that this was not even "Mother Earth." It was simply Nature in its "primeval" state, Nature "untamed and forever untameable," Nature (he adds portentously) "not bound to be kind to man" (69–70).

Although this matter of denying attributions, pseudo-Dionysian in its negative insistence, is crucial to the central drama of "Ktaadn," some commentary on the essay attempts to impose familiar terms on "Chaos," to cast the "unhandselled globe" (that is, a globe that will not extend a greeting) into a different but recognizable version of an American mythos. In exploring Thoreau's transactions with history, for example, John Hildebidle finds that in moving back to a "primeval prehuman timelessness" in "Ktaadn," Thoreau uses history to defeat time—in effect making the past destroy itself. It is a provocative and perceptive observation. But when Hildebidle proceeds to identify this point of timelessness as "the Eden of the eternal present and eternally wild, an Eden that is no garden . . . an Eden that can have no Adam," his attribution converts the alien into the familiar and cushions the impact of Thoreau's radical encounter.[44] For at the climactic point in his essay Thoreau is not writing about Eden, with or without Adam. He is writing about or *trying* to write about "no man's garden," about something that is not even "waste-land"—and, as Stephen Adams and Donald Ross, Jr., have shown in their meticulous study of Thoreau's methods of composition, the "many interlinings" and alterations in this section of "Ktaadn" reveal his struggle to do so.[45]

As recorded in "Ktaadn," the movement to an original world proceeds by fits and starts. Steven Fink points out that Thoreau took at least some pains to make his essay reader-friendly—deleting a number of literary allusions from the rough draft, adding both useful information and evocative details of the wilderness for the benefit of travelers and sedentary readers, creating what Fink terms "a more informal and practical relationship between author and reader."[46] Perhaps for this reason, the writer pauses to describe logging camps, huts, graves, and the "germs" of villages even after his party arrives at what seems "a wholly uninhabitated [sic] wilderness" in which (arresting trope) "the air was a sort of diet-drink" (16). Importantly, he visits the Scotsman McCauslin, who burns wood prodigally (whole logs four feet long to boil water for tea) and accompanies the party as a guide. The crossing of North Twin Lake, however (the river now a "connecting link" between numerous lakes), serves as a passage into a region mythical and ultimately surrealistic, a passage facilitated by language that negates standard traces of humankind in nature. From this "noble sheet of water," Thoreau writes, one receives the impression that a new country is "fitted to create." Following this knowing generalization, he adapts the standard rhetoric of exploration to his own purpose: "There was the smoke of no log-hut nor camp of any kind to greet us, still less was any lover of nature . . . watching our batteau from the distant hills; not even the Indian hunter was there, for he rarely climbs them, but hugs the river like ourselves. No face welcomed us but the fine fantastic sprays of free and happy evergreen trees, waving one above the other in their ancient home" (35–36).

Concomitant with this acknowledgment of what is not present comes the travelers' realization that they have lost the river in the lake and must undertake "a voyage of discovery" to find it. Once found, discovered in its new manifestation, it floats them upstream, "over unmeasured zones of earth, bound on unimaginable adventures" (37–38). The preparatory part of the voyage is over: Thoreau and his companions have moved past history, have entered a fairy-tale world in which water begins "to partake of the purity and transparency of the air," in which fish, the "product of primitive rivers," cascade down falls, glistening like "jewels" or "bright fluviatile flowers." The sight brings the writer to a better understanding of "the truth of mythology, the fables of Proteus, and all those beautiful sea-monsters." Put to "terrestrial use," he comes to see, history is "mere history." Put to "celestial" use, it is "mythology always" (58, 54).

Appropriately, at the portal of this mythic and surreal world, the travelers leave their extra baggage behind, a stripping away of social trappings before the advent of primal reality: from this point on, "there was not the slightest trace of man to guide us" (56). Appropriately, too, Thoreau faces the most elemental and threatening scenery (if one may call it that) when he is alone, stripped of the society of his companions. He climbs to a locale "bare of all vegeta-

tion but lichens, and almost continually draped in clouds." By grab-
bing the roots of firs and birches, he pulls himself up ("and I mean
to lay some emphasis on this word *up*") the course of a torrent, "per-
pendicular falls of twenty or thirty feet," then walks in the bed of
the current, "ascending by huge steps, as it were, a giant's stairway,
down which a river flowed" (60). In an increasingly grotesque and
inverted environment in which negation surrenders to the alien,
Thoreau works his way ("scarcely less arduous than Satan's anciently
through Chaos") up the mountain peak—"scrambling on all
fours over the tops of ancient black spruce-trees, (*Abies nigra,*) old
as the flood," then walking, actually walking, "some good rods erect
upon the tops of these trees." With a note of irony he resorts to
familiar language to summarize an outlandish experience: "This
was the sort of garden I made my way over"; it was "certainly the
most treacherous and porous country I ever travelled" (60–61).

The climax of what becomes a solitary invasion of an inchoate
world stands before the traveler. The following day Thoreau climbs
"alone" over gigantic rocks tumbled haphazardly against each other,
realizing that they are "the raw materials of a planet," that he is tra-
versing "an undone extremity of the globe," that his mountain-top
destination in the clouds is "among the unfinished parts of the
globe, whither it is a slight insult to the gods to climb and pry into
their secrets." The threat of this primal world to the self is imminent: "deep within the hostile ranks of clouds," able to see only an
occasional "dark, damp crag," Thoreau envisions such figures as
Atlas and Prometheus and thinks that "Aeschylus had no doubt visited such scenery as this. It was vast, Titanic, and such as man never
inhabits" (63–64). And it takes a toll on the spectator: for at this
point, "Some part of the beholder, even some vital part, seems to
escape through the loose grating of his ribs as he ascends. He is
more lone than you can imagine. . . . His reason is dispersed and
shadowy, more thin and subtile like the air. Vast, Titanic, inhuman
Nature has got him at a disadvantage, caught him alone, and pilfers
him of some of his divine faculty." Indeed, Nature warns him back,
tells him in "relentless" measures that if he should "freeze or starve,
or shudder" his life away, "here is no shrine, nor altar, nor any access
to my ear" (64). If society conventionally oppresses and weighs
down the individual, if an evening on Mt. Wachusett enables one to
ascertain the limitations of the finite, this ascent to creation threat-

ens to disassemble the self back (through mythology) to creation-stuff.

No one reads "Ktaadn" carefully without being struck by Thoreau's extravagant presentation of a self-confronting primal matter. And both the quantity and quality of interpretation testify to the implications of the encounter.[47] Most commentators see it as a supreme point of peril—an apparently unexpected moment of "desolation and derangement," as Cecelia Tichi puts it, an existential and pure "contact" unmistakably beyond "the control of the redemptive imagination," in Frederick Garber's terms.[48] Ronald Wesley Hoag expresses an opposing judgment that finds in the experience a confirmation of a Transcendental faith in the unlimited.[49] Other critics, among them H. Daniel Peck and Bruce Greenfield, supply provocative contexts for the climactic passage in "Ktaadn" and for the essay as a whole—Peck by pointing out the difference between mountaintop experiences in *A Week* and in "Ktaadn" (two texts on which Thoreau was working contemporaneously), Greenfield by making Thoreau's journey part of a tradition of visualizing the American continent (and American West) as empty—in this case "awaiting his discovery."[50]

Adams and Ross's examination of draft manuscripts of "Ktaadn" reminds us helpfully that Thoreau was writing after his experience on the mountain, reconstituting it as a text. The attempt "to recreate that experience in writing," these critics find, led Thoreau to experiment with the role of myth in shaping narrative, to use mythology and fire according to conventions of romantic travel-writing. One result is that at the center of this essay nature "assumes and maintains mastery"; another is that Satan appears "not as Milton's villain but as the archetypal rebel and adventurer that the romantics pictured."[51] Only such figures as Satan, Prometheus, and Atlas—products of the human imagination questing to fashion the story of genesis—can be associated with this ultimate terrain.

Thoreau's strategies of language as he recounts the various stages of his excursion to Ktaadn lead Greenfield to assess the extent to which seeing "virginity" or emptiness in the American landscape was a matter of cultural perception or a response to "objective, geographical conditions." In general terms, of course, the relation of "seeing" to extra-mental reality has been an enduring epistemological question—entertained by philosophers and poets, addressed by historians and scientists, considered by all who inquire how the mind processes and makes sense of what it sees. In its nineteenth-century American manifestation, it becomes a question of the priority of a specific kind of vision.[52] Certainly, something "objective," some qualities of the American terrain, evoked exclamations of spaciousness and earliness on the part of a variety of writers. But just as certainly, Greenfield suggests, a cultural disposition, definably Euro-American, brought explorers such as Lewis and Clark, Zebulon Pike, and John Charles Fremont to see the West "both as the country of the Mandans and as an empty, claimable landscape."[53] As one well-read in such journals of exploration, Thoreau seems to have shared the common view "of Euro-American expansion into the continent." "Ktaadn" is the evidence—a "typical account of an exploratory journey," heavily indebted to Thoreau's reading. Moving one step farther, Greenfield concludes that "Ktaadn" is a record of Thoreau's "attempt at an absolute discovery of a definitive America."[54]

With this one final assertion, however, Greenfield (like Hildebidle before him) modifies the thrust of Thoreau's narrative. At a number of important junctures in "Ktaadn," as we have seen, negatives strip away standard associations—orthodox use of established rhetorical structure. But alone on an alien mountain top, confronted with "solid cold" and clutter that made him think "it had rained rocks," Thoreau encounters a world not only pre-domesticated but pre-pure and pre-beautiful, a "specimen" of creation inchoate, in the "process of formation" (63, 61). Faced with what Frederick Garber calls "inert possibility" (rather than possibility humanized into potential), Thoreau abandons many of the conventions of style that made Americans comfortable with what they were not.[55] Accordingly, the climax of "Ktaadn" does not yield an America of any kind, Greenfield's excellent reading notwithstanding. What Thoreau gives us is a more radical beginning than that, beginning as intimidating spectacle.

Only while descending the mountain can Thoreau begin to portray his experience in more familiar terms. Only "when coming down" does he "fully" realize that he has confronted "primeval, untamed, and forever untameable *Nature*" (69). Only when he no longer has Primal Matter literally in his face does he rejoin his companions and regain possession of a vital negative rhetoric. "I found my companions where I had left them," Thoreau writes, almost as if these other travelers had been frozen in place during his solitary experience on the mountaintop. It is at this point, in the transitional "Burnt Lands" section, that some of the most memorable phrases in "Ktaadn" occur—"Chaos and Old Night," "Matter, vast, terrific," "a specimen of what God saw fit to make this world" (70–71). Almost immediately afterwards Thoreau is able to celebrate the Maine wilderness—that is, to become the Thoreau we know and claim—by saying that "These are not the artificial forests of an English king. . . . Here prevail no forest laws, but those of nature. The aborigines have never been dispossessed, nor nature disforested" (80). Coming back in stages from his encounter with creation, as he had moved toward it in stages, he reintroduces himself to the world (and to the reader) by describing the "inexpressible tenderness and immortal life of the grim forest," by honoring Nature ever springlike and perpetually young, by envisioning a place where men could "live forever, and laugh at death and the grave" (81). It is a signature statement, the absolute once again pressing on the relative, the infinite imprinting the finite.

As "Ktaadn" moves to its conclusion, Thoreau's re-entry into the world becomes a return to the present, a move that incorporates history as well as nature, time as well as space. Thoreau mentions Columbus and Vespucci, proceeds through the "very America . . . visited" by Cabot, Gosnold, Smith, and Raleigh, and reveals his enduring thirst for exploration by observing (with habitual flair) that we "have discovered only the shores of America" (81).[56] From a perspective finally set in and by the present, he reminds us "how exceedingly new this country still is"; sixty miles north of the railroad and the military road in Maine, "virtually unmapped and unexplored," stands the "virgin forest of the New World" (83). With its intermittent patterns of withdrawal and return, punctuated by a rendezvous with creation, "Ktaadn" demonstrates Thoreau's persistent and almost brash dedication to beginnings. In this case, the writer's portrayal of a beginning both radical and perilous stands opposed to those supported (in much American writing) by benign evocations of an untouched New World.

The Infinite and the Future Henry James, Sr., described Emerson as a man who "brought you face to face with the infinite in humanity."[57] Nowhere does this pungent observation find more dramatic verification than in *Nature*, the book that sets an agenda for envisioning "the possibilities of man." And nowhere does it meet greater challenge than in "Experience," the essay that obscures the infinite, then scrambles to recapture it in the form of an undefiled future. With "access to the entire mind of the Creator," Emerson declares in *Nature*, one becomes "the creator in the finite," an originating self capable of fashioning one's own world through purification of the soul (*N*: 41). In "Experience," on the contrary, he observes that "temperament puts all divinity to route," leaving us lost in illusion yet finally capable of "passage into new worlds" by means of expectation and hope ("Ex": 475, 492). Each of these notable texts testifies to Emerson's allegiance to beginnings, those empowered by the infinite, those made possible by what is yet to come.

The fundamental movement of *Nature* is toward an apprehension and consequent assimilation of the infinite. Throughout, Emerson directs us to a graduating perception of *existence*—ultimately made possible by an awareness of primordial ideas. An intelligent understanding of the physical laws of nature introduces one to "the counsels of creation," in the context of which one "feels by knowledge the privilege to BE." At this significant point "Time and Space relations [ever the antagonists in dramas of the infinite] vanish" (*N*: 27). Liberated from the approved geometry that constrains human life, one is able to doubt the existence of matter and thus fasten attention (in Emerson's billowing language) "upon immortal necessary uncreated natures, that is upon Ideas. . . . We ascend into their region, and know that these are the thoughts of the Supreme Being." Emerson then adapts words from Proverbs 8 to make knowledge of the infinite and of beginning-ness one: "These are they who were set up from everlasting, from the beginning, or ever the earth was. When he prepared the heavens, they were there; when he established the clouds above, when he strengthened the fountains of the deep. Then they were by him, as one brought up with him. Of them he took counsel" (*N*: 37).

The logic of Emerson's argument, mystical in its quest, practical in its procedure, is unassailable. His language reaches its highest point of intensity when he terms ideas of God "necessary" and "uncreated" and concludes that consorting with such eternal being transports us "out of the district of change." Having assimilated what Eckhart would term the eternal Now, "we apprehend the

absolute" and in so doing "become immortal." "As it were, for the
first time, *we exist*" (*N*: 37). Anticipating the insistence on an original self and the conflation of the limited and limitless in such later
chapters of *Nature* as "Prospects" and "Idealism," Emerson at the
outset recommends what we do not have—"an original relation to
the universe"—a statement worn smooth by familiarity but deeply
revolutionary in its implications (*N*: 7). His first chapter brings us
to the celebrated (or notorious) "transparent eye-ball" metaphor
and a medley of ideas from various journal entries. "In the woods,"
he tells us, is "perpetual youth" and spiritual safety:

> Standing on the bare ground,—my head bathed by the blithe
> air, and uplifted into infinite space,—all mean egotism van-
> ishes. I become a transparent eye-ball. I am nothing. I see all.
> The currents of the Universal Being circulate through me; I
> am part or particle of God. The name of the nearest friend
> sounds then foreign and accidental. To be brothers, to be
> acquaintances,—master or servant, is then a trifle and a dis-
> turbance. I am the lover of uncontained and immortal beauty
> (N: 10)

With these words Emerson epitomizes the transcendent thrust
of his early work. Standing between the finite and the infinite, the
"I" (the human being) connects the two realms in a prototype of the
incarnation. In accord with mystical convention, the "I" dissolves to
a transparency, a "nothing"; and with Emerson's characteristic
emphasis on perception (and the "I" to "eye" homophone generating a compatible meaning) the transparency can be figured both as
an "I-ball" free from worldly egotism and an eye-ball receptive to
"currents of the Universal Being," capable of seeing and therefore
being "all," a particle of divinity. The analogy to other metaphors of
aspiration in his work is obvious—albeit with a mighty difference.
For what Emerson describes in *Nature* is tantamount to drawing
the grandest circle (in a moment of all-seeing), making the ultimate
generalization. To appropriate a line from Emily Dickinson, Emerson's "business is circumference," now on an infinite scale. To attend
to such all-consuming business is necessarily to leave behind relations (of all kinds), reducing them to trifles and even disturbances.
The transparency that sees all and is nothing becomes "the lover of

uncontained and immortal beauty"—negative concepts, negative words, that strip the world away from the naked "I."

No matter the Neoplatonic vapors that permeate *Nature*, Emerson makes it clear that man does not live by idealism alone. "Idealism," as he says, "is a hypothesis to account for nature by other principles than those of carpentry and chemistry." If it simply denies the existence of matter it leaves the "demands of the spirit" unsatisfied. Put bluntly, "it leaves God out of me" and makes me a vagrant in "the splendid labyrinth of my perceptions" (*N*: 41). The assumptions of idealism are therefore a *means* in *Nature*; they provide a philosophic structure convenient to the end. And the end, as stated in "Prospects," is "the redemption of the soul," which will restore the world to its "original and true beauty" (*N*: 47). Throughout *Nature*, Emerson's accent is on the restoration of an original spiritual condition to be achieved by assimilating the infinite.

Given Emerson's predilection for transcendent beginnings, the very title of "Experience" signals an encounter with a recalcitrant subject. The consequence is not simply a work personal and confessional in tone, as David Van Leer correctly describes it, but a series of meditations alternatively dismayed by the eclipse of the absolute and buoyed (tentatively so) by the hope that the future may reveal the consonance the world so badly needs.[58] The essay opens into a series of hallucinatory states bereft of boundaries, *mid* positions from which we can discern no "extremes." "We wake," Emerson writes, and find ourselves with stairs above and stairs below, unable to shake off a "noonday" lethargy—as when "night hovers all day in the boughs of the fir-tree." Gliding "ghostlike" through the "swim and glitter" of life, unable to locate a beginning (or an end), we live at the mercy of temperament that shuns divinity and leaves us bewildered creatures of time rather than creators in the finite—to recall a central trope from *Nature* ("Ex": 471).

The startling premise of "Experience"—underlying Emerson's discrete observations—is that *existence*, more precisely a recognition of our existence, registers the fact of the Fall. What was the source of energy (the ontological condition by means of which a human being could find redemptive power) in *Nature* and earlier essays is here contaminated, its purity tainted: "It is very unhappy, but too late to be helped," Emerson writes, "the discovery we have made that we exist. That discovery is called the Fall of Man" ("Ex": 487).

In "The Protest" he had declared that the Fall is "the first word of history and the last fact of experience"—but this fateful statement came from a perspective that allowed the writer to discount both history and experience by visualizing society as seductive and youth as redemptive. In "Experience," Emerson lacks the luxury of transcendent perspective: as deadly as they once seemed, society, repose, and old age are no longer the principal culprits; we exist—therefore we are fallen.[59]

Yet "Experience" struggles toward the promise of harmony in a fragmented world as it recontextualizes the life-affirming metaphors of such essays as "Circles" and "The Protest." The task is not an easy one: for the animating potential of ever-broader generalizations and of immortal youth becomes in "Experience" a troubling "succession of moods" anchored in "quicksand" and the more conventional hope of finding "symmetry" amid the follies and defects of society as a whole ("Ex": 476). Nonetheless, despite the melancholy quality of these observations, Emerson posits a fixed center within us, as he had done in "Circles," then moves with recognizable authority to a version of the figure of "oscillation" he had used in "Intellect." Something unchangeable, he concludes, something that "ranks all sensations and states of mind," persists through our "flux of moods." In every human being consciousness is "a sliding scale, which identifies him now with the First Cause, and now with the flesh of his body; life above life, in infinite degrees" ("Ex": 485). Preceding and virtually generating this acknowledgment of allegiance to spirit and to flesh is a well-known passage (culminating with the words "this new yet unapproachable America I have found in the West") to which Stanley Cavell has devoted careful and perplexed attention. Noting the names Milton and Columbus among the many others in "Experience," Cavell suggests that the loss of Eden is something embedded deeply in the essay and that finding a new world in the West is rehearsing "something Columbus did, repeating it otherwise than in *Nature*."[60] The suggestion is encompassing, loaded with implication for the philosophical stances of "Experience" and *Nature*. Cavell then puzzles over why "this new America [is] said to be unapproachable" in a way that diffuses the question but generously leaves it open.

What I wish to emphasize in Emerson's passage is the effort to project the promise of a future. Have patience, the essayist enjoins us: for underlying the disjunctions of the day "is a musical perfection, the Ideal journeying always with us, the heaven without rent or seam." This promise of unity shapes life "into an expectation or a religion." Gradually, we become aware of "a new and excellent region of life," tranquil and eternal, of "flashes of light" and "sudden discoveries" that are "felt as initial" and promise a sequel. "I did not make" this "realm of thought," Emerson continues:

> I arrive there, and behold what was there already. I make! O no! I clap my hands in infantine joy and amazement, before the first opening to me of this august magnificence, old with the love and homage of innumerable ages, young with the life of life, the sunbright Mecca of the desert. And what a future it opens! I feel a new heart beating with the love of the new beauty. I am ready to die out of nature, and be born again into this new yet unapproachable America I have found in the West."   ("Ex": 484–85)

To appreciate the precise wording of these concluding sentences (and thus the final form of "Experience"), it is worthwhile to note their source in Emerson's journal. Concerning the objective reality of the "new & most bright region of life," Emerson's journal entry is emphatic:

> "Two things: 1. I do not make it, I arrive there & behold what was there already. I make? O God, No! I clap my hands in infantine joy & happy astonishment before the first dread opening to me of this August Magnificence, old with the love & homage of unnumerable Ages, young with the life of life, the sunbright Mecca of the Desart [sic] of Infinite Power.
> 2. It affirms continuance. It gives the first assurance I have had of permanence not by indicating continuance but increase. Love, Desire are born in my breast—and all signs of enlargement. Instantly the world in which I had lived for so long becomes an apparition & I am brave with the celestial blood that beats in my heart whilst I worship the new beauty, & I am ready to die out of Nature and be born more fully into the new America I have found in the West.
>
> (JMN 8:237–38)

In the transition from journal to essay Emerson sharpens the focus of his description by omitting the conventional terminology of a mystical void ("dread opening," "Desart of Infinite Power"), by replacing the important but unwieldy notion of "enlargement" with a succinct mention of "future," and by making the idea of rebirth absolute—"born more fully" becomes "born again." He also adds the provocative term *unapproachable* to the description of his new America, suggesting that from the gathering perspective of actual composition, in the process of writing "Experience," he saw formidable difficulties in reaching (or realizing) a region already "found" (or perceived).

In examining the phrase "dying out of nature," we should remember that "nature" in "Experience," is not "nature" in *Nature*. The baffled opening paragraph of the later work asks rhetorically if "some fit of indigence and frugality in nature" attended our birth so that we were given a paucity "of her fire" and an abundance "of her earth." Although we have sufficient energy to conduct our lives from day to day, "we have no superfluity of spirit for new creation" ("Ex": 471). In the passage from "Experience" cited above, being *ready* to die out of (not *dying* out of) an impoverished nature is a gesture of willingness to leave the uncreative world of today; being *ready* to be born into (not *being* born into) "this new yet unapproachable America" is a metaphor of desire for a harmonious world of the future. This world previously described as "a new and excellent region of life," is now figured more precisely as "the West" (traditional American direction for the future); and it is "found" by an Emerson who can envision it although it is not (yet) available to him or to citizens of the present, whose lives, at best, are "melted" into expectation or religion.

"Experience" is an essay fraught with irony. As Jerome Loving observes, it turns Emerson's "transcendences into transitions."[61] Dominating its modulations of tone (ranging from numbness to bright surprise) is the alarming fact that experience itself isolates us from others and from the reality of our own emotions. Not even the death of his young son can make suffering vibrate in Emerson's life; like everything else, the loss proves "caducous"—transitory, something that drops away.[62] More localized, hide-and-seek ironies spring from this realization and emphasize the difference between lived-in present and envisioned future. Given the meager surroundings described at the outset, for example, the dictum "The mid-world is best" seems an acceptance of life as it is, a recognition that a "temperate zone" harbors thought, spirit, and poetry. Yet the America Emerson presently envisions is the exhilarating antithesis of this "narrow belt": it brings him to "clap [his] hands in infantine joy and amazement" ("Ex": 480–81, 485). The idea of *discovery* likewise carries a double edge: after expressing delight at having arrived at a "realm" he did "not make" but "found," the writer confronts "the discovery" (the fatality) of our existence, collective finding at this point, Adam superseding Columbus ("Ex": 487). And in his conclusion, he dissolves the distinction between "thinking" and "doing" scrupulously observed throughout the essay, even as he wraps the slogans of a pep rally around carefully-nourished convictions of previous years. Between the heartening "we shall win at the last" and the stirring (or forlorn) "up again, old heart!" is a reminder to be suspicious of the deceptive priorities of time and a characteristic dismissal of quotidian activities in favor of the "sanity and revelations" of the inner life. In the context of Emerson's discussion, "hope" (expectation) allows one to measure the unworthiness of the temporal, while intuitions sustain one on the "passage into new worlds" rather than on the route to the infinite. Ridicule or defeat means nothing, concludes an Emerson committed to *realms* and *regions* abundant with hope and therefore possibility: justice will triumph; "and the true romance which the world exists to realize, will be the transformation of genius [thinking] into practical power [doing]" ("Ex": 492).

The idea that experience estranges us from our emotions proceeds from the lack of the infinite in Emerson's reckoning. For, crucially and typically, his conception of the self existing vitally (that is, creatively) in the world depends on a sense of the surging power of the infinite in the finite, an ability to apprehend *being* "coetaneous" with creation. With no access to an ontological beginning, the mood of Emerson's prose registers our lost claim on possibility. Unwilling, finally, to cast his argument into so bleak a mold, he looks to the future rather than to the infinite to retrieve the inexhaustible.

Emerson had moved provocatively toward an idea of successive human beginnings in a journal entry of 1838. The entry begins on a note of portable contemplation: recalling an evening walk "to receive the fair inscriptions of night," Emerson describes a scene of natural beauty, then makes it his own by saying "It is all music." Whenever he finds a fundamental unity amid discrete phenomena, I think it is fair to say, Emerson invokes a language of startling power. Thus, by way of an allusion to John Martin's painting of creation in an 1827 edition of *Paradise Lost*, he employs the metaphor later used in "History" and likens the moonlit scene to the spectacle of an archangel witnessing creation. Significantly, his journal entry does not stop at this climactic point but extends the basic trope of creation into a synoptic parable of life. Thus, "he who has been in love has *assisted* at a new and second morning"; he "in whose soul Art has been born has seen a greater day"; and "finally (where indeed there is no final,) he who has through weary experience of sweet & smart in life attained to know character, & to worship that slow secular divine product, has beheld a worthier creation, that great day of the feast" (JMN, 7:10).[63]

By alluding to creation in the context of Milton's epic, Emerson's journal entry associates the absolute beginning and the beginning of human experience. From the loss of paradise comes a graduating series of creative moments made possible by experience, specifically those of love, of art, and (by means of "weary experience of sweet & smart") of the knowledge of character—a quality defined by Emerson in "Character" (1844) as "nature in the highest form," capable of sustaining hope while the world waits for "fulfillment" ("Char": 502, 507). Most importantly in his journal entry, Emerson ennobles the concept of character and thus the finite by defining it oxymoronically as a "secular divine product." The analogous effort of "Experience" is to secularize the infinite and project it as possibility into a luminous future. Such a transformation in Emerson's manner of conceiving (and ameliorating) the plight of the human being beset by the world proved to be a protean legacy for a later and literal America, one no longer quite new and no longer unapproachable.

6

The Politics
of Inexhaustibility

Whitman and the Future   To understand the character of
Whitman's dedication to the future, it is helpful to juxta-
pose his perspective on the nation's potential with that of
Thomas Paine. The argument of *Common Sense* led Paine
to define the nation-to-be as a blank slate on which the
future could be written. A century later, Whitman found a
way to wipe the slate clean whenever events corroded the
promise of America. In his Preface to the Centennial Edition of *Leaves of Grass*, he assesses the "morbid facts of
American politics and society," as he had done before in
such poems as "Wandering at Morn" and "To the States"
("Are those really Congressman? are those the great
Judges? is that the President?").[1] Because he views the
prior experience of the nation as "preparation, adolescence," however, his optimism remains intact. Replete
with disappointment, the first century of American independence nonetheless becomes for Whitman a series of
"trial-voyages and experiments of the Ship, before her
starting out upon deep water." "Only now and henceforth"
will the nation enter on its "real history" (748, 754).
Whereas Thomas Paine's sense of a beginning in 1776 is

supported by events taking place around him, Whitman's in 1876 takes form despite (virtually in the face of) the "general malaria of Fogs and Vapors" that envelops the national scene (748). Both writers structure time in a way that privileges the future, although their attitudes toward the past understandably differ. Paine rejects a monarchical past outright so that Americans can "begin the world over again." His vision of a beginning is radical: he wants the Revolution. Whitman, on the other hand, embraces the post-Revolutionary experience of the nation, good and bad, past and present. His vision of a beginning is tactical: he wants the original promise of democracy restored. The unwholesome matters to which he refers are therefore presented as "passing incidents and flanges of our unbounded impetus of growth—weeds, annuals of the rank, rich soil—not central, enduring, perennial things" (748). All that has happened is propadeutic, a series of lessons leading to commencement. Whitman, in other words, repeatedly casts what is not worthy of American democracy into postures of experiment and adolescence that have, as he says, set the stage for the "real history" of the nation. His tactic of deferring to unfulfilled potential is both appropriate and effective: for he is celebrating the anniversary of the beginning Paine had championed, "the first Centennial of our New World Nationality," and his commemorative stance pays tribute to the event even as it projects original promise into the future (745).

In subordinating rather than rejecting the past, Whitman sustains the vision that informed his poetic life. "I have lived in fresh lands, inchoate, and in a revolutionary age, future-founding," he wrote in the 1876 Preface (753). It is a synoptic appraisal of the manner in which he orchestrated the American experience. The most ebulliently Adamic of our poets, Whitman is the only American writer who dates his work from the beginning of the republic: the title page of the third edition of *Leaves of Grass*, for example, proclaims "Year 85 of the States"; below, in parenthesis, is "(1860–61)." In that third edition, "A Boston Ballad" is subtitled "The 78th Year of These States," while "Europe" (untitled in the 1855 edition, as are all twelve poems) bears the inscription "The 72d and 73d Years of These States."[2] And in "Full of Life Now," the final work in the "Calamus" section of *Leaves of Grass*, the poet announces both his age and that of the nation: "I, forty years old the Eighty-third Year of the States" (136). (The year of reckoning is always 1776.) These are, to be sure, external details, but they suggest the extent of Whitman's commitment to the United States as a phenomenon worthy of making one start time over again.

With his unceasing attraction to the idea of beginning as a draft on the future, Whitman was able to survive the Civil War as no other American writer did. As we know, the War and the assassi- nation of Abraham Lincoln shocked him greatly; one has only to read the poems from "Drum-Taps" (among them "The Wound- Dresser," with its graphic images of "the crush'd head" and "the amputated hand") to see how he incorporated the wounds of the nation into his imagination (310). Yet even in these poems there are poignant signals of resurrection coupled with the idea (in the opening stanza of "Over the Carnage Rose Prophetic a Voice," for example) that love can transform national difficulties into national achievement:

> Over the carnage rose prophetic a voice,
> Be not dishearten'd, affection shall solve the problems of
> freedom yet,
> Those who love each other shall become invincible,
> They shall yet make Columbia victorious. (315)

The future tense in these lines signals deferred but undaunted hope. The word "yet" takes on a burden of expectation that becomes heavier in the twentieth century—with each additional deferral, and each accompanying "yet."

Alone among his contemporaries Whitman called the war years "the real parturition years," the years of the birth of the country— moreso, he came to believe, "than 1776–'83" (570). Dismayed at the lack of fulfillment in his beloved nation during the postbellum years, and no longer dating poems in the year of the republic, he turned ever more resolutely to a vindicating future by casting both the past and the present into a variety of subordinate postures. In his Preface to *As a Strong Bird on Pinions Free* (1872), for example, he describes the "vulgar material and political present" as but "the preparatory tuning of instruments by an orchestra" (743). In the earlier "To the States" (1860) he pictures the nation sleeping through "a filthy Presidentiad," mercifully oblivious to the "scum floating atop the waters," but sure to awake, refreshed by slumber, to new hope (278). And in "Wandering at Morn" (1873), finding the country "coil'd in evil times," with "craft" and "treason thrust upon it," he takes heart at the sight of a thrush feeding its young. For if, he reasons,

> worms, snakes, loathsome grubs, may to sweet spiritual songs be
>   turn'd,
> If vermin so transposed, so used and bless'd may be,
> Than may I trust in you, your fortunes, days, my country;
> Who knows that these may be the lessons fit for you?
> From these your future songs may rise in joyous trills,
> Destined to fill the world.   (399–400).

Worms to song, sleep to wakefulness, tuning-up to harmony—such tropes measure the resilience of Whitman's identification with what he termed "still-to-be-form'd America" (748). The United States, Whitman wrote in *Democratic Vistas* (1871) depends for "her justification and success (for who, as yet, dare claim success?) almost entirely on the future."[3] The more failure he saw, the more future he appropriated. He stands repeatedly at a moment of beginning, secure in his conviction that there is ample *time* to realize the promise of democracy, that—as he said in "A Backward Glance" (1888)—"the strongest and sweetest songs yet remain to be sung" (574).

Emerson's effort to annex the future rather than the infinite in "Experience" thus finds a self-propelling advocate in Whitman. The younger writer's assertion that he had been "simmering, simmering, simmering," and that Emerson brought him "to a boil" does not of course point to "Experience" or to any specific essay but to what Whitman sees as an energizing consonance of vision.[4] Central to *Leaves of Grass* from its first appearance in 1855 is an idea of endless growth and boundless possibility, with the self the vital agent of expansion. As Richard Pascal observes, the self for Whitman "was an independent, Godlike shaping force, not a creature of history."[5] Accordingly, "Song of Myself" insists on the spectacle of a transcendent self

moving forward then and now and forever,
Gathering and showing more always and with velocity,
Infinite and omnigenous. . . .   (60)

In whatever terms it emerged ("See ever so far, there is limitless
space outside of that, / Count ever so much, there is limitless time
around that" [82]), Whitman's profound and romantic assumption
about the democratic *self* possessing the future coincides with the
tendency of Emerson and Thoreau to invoke inexhaustible
realms—be they of time, spirit, or internal space—endlessly available for realizing human potential. Thoreau will invariably walk
West, Emerson will inevitably invoke youth, and Whitman (as we
see) will continually levy on the future—and never will there be less
West, less youth, or less future. Although the spectacle on which he
looked out in 1871 was "appalling," the atmosphere choked with
"hypocrisy," he remained confident of "results to come."[6]
    In a variety of forms, the idea of the inexhaustible pervaded
American thought and culture in the nineteenth century. A hard-
headed politician like Daniel Webster could say in 1850 that the
principle on which our government is based "seems to be indefinitely expansive," happily so in the way it makes the citizens of new
territories participants in "a new creation, a new existence."[7] Almost
half a century before, in his first inaugural address, Thomas Jefferson articulated his conviction that the new United States was "the
world's best hope" by describing a country "with room enough for
our descendants to the thousandth and thousandth generation."[8]
Even when we allow for a ration of presidential licence in this
remark, an immense and virtually immeasurable amount of "room"
(and therefore opportunity) remains. From the vantage point of
1801 the future could seem as big as the country, not inexhaustible
in an absolute sense, to be sure, but so indefinitely vast as to pass for
the same thing. People who shared President Jefferson's view would
perforce feel themselves at a beginning just as surely as one who
permitted (in Emerson's terms) "no horizon to fall on the illimitable
space." A sense of openness, of possibility, of boundless space and
time, characterizes both the transcendental and the historical formulations: it brought Whitman in 1872 to celebrate a "modern
composite Nation, formed from all, with room for all, welcoming
all immigrants . . . no limit here to land," to opportunity, to prod-

ucts (741). Out of such assumptions of inexhaustibility has come the American romance with beginnings, the habit of looking to the future for fulfillment. Characteristically, Americans never feel so confident as when they are about to start, about to embark, about to enter on a road or path or voyage. And so long as the frontier and the Adamic ideal could embody this assumption, the American dream (as it was fondly called) could be set securely in the future—where it had always had a home.

Perceptions of the Frontier   By assorted and uneasy consensus, the greatest factor in generating a sense of beginnings in nineteenth-century America was the frontier, an ever-advancing frontier that beckoned a "mighty stream" of hopeful emigrants, as James Hall wrote in *Letters from the West* (1828). According to its popular image, the frontier bred beginnings not so much recurrent as continuous. William Gilpin may have been oversimplifying in his *Mission of the North American People* (1873) when he pictured farmers planting on the "outer edge of the settlements" for a year, selling out and advancing twenty-five miles for another season, selling again to move further West—or, if they settled permanently, giving way to others who "rush from behind, pass to the front, and assail the wilderness in their turn."[9] But Gilpin, the first territorial governor of Colorado, was merely adopting a perspective (cherished by Americans) that has for its sanction the fluidity of the frontier at various stages of development. Frederick Jackson Turner's famous assessment of the significance of the frontier in American history takes full account of this perspective: as Turner said in 1893, the frontier had afforded the conditions for "perennial rebirth"—and this despite the fact that the farmers whom Gilpin portrays in generalities must have had their share of backaches, disappointments, and outright failures.[10] So long as the frontier existed, Americans could incorporate into their thinking the possibility of shedding history, of starting fresh, of making something new rather than adding to something old. As the distillation of more than a century of westering hope, Turner's interpretation (in the words of Henry Nash Smith) "makes all American history a constantly renewed process of transcendence, resulting in the continual production of New Men, democrats, Westerners."[11] By positing a transcendent quality to the frontier experience,

Turner thus affirms the American sense of beginnings in its most seductive historical form.

A belief in the dynamic quality of the frontier thus contributed to the identity of a nation that knew what it was not and prided itself on its youthful vigor. According to Turner's reckoning, however, the identifying contribution of the frontier vanished in geographical fact during the final decades of the nineteenth century: "The frontier has gone," said Turner in 1893, even as he formulated its transcendent significance. As we can see from our present perspective, a number of important things seem to have followed in its wake. But not, as the evidence shows, the American need for beginnings. And not the American habit, ingrained, coexistent with the life of the nation, of looking for beginnings where we had always found them. "The Frontier has become so much an integral part of our conception of things," the novelist Frank Norris wrote in 1902, "that it will be long before we shall all understand that it is gone."[12] The evidence of the twentieth century confirms this perception and suggests further the strategies we have adopted in an effort to keep what we no longer had.

Over the past decades, a number of scholars have contributed to our understanding of the frontier as cultural construct and metaphor (as what Charles Altieri might call a primary structure of desire). I stand indebted to the work of Henry Nash Smith, Edwin Fussell, Richard Slotkin, Patricia Limerick, and Paul A. Carter, to name but a few.[13] My particular interest in the frontier as a phenomenon that has lost its power to inspire a valid sense of beginnings, however, leads me to mention specifically the far-ranging thesis of Walter Prescott Webb's *The Great Frontier* (1952). Crucial to Webb's definition of a frontier is a body of land with untapped resources that changes the ratio of land, precious metals, and commodities to existing population and thus makes for what Webb calls "boom" times. Such a situation, he works carefully to show, came into existence around the year 1500 with the European discovery and subsequent exploitation of the continents of North and South America. Because of the accumulating wealth that far surpassed population growth, the continued appropriation of land in increasingly remote areas, and (I would add) the unblinkable reality of distance between European centers of authority and productive colonial outposts, new institutions evolved, gradually and erratically, to be sure, but unmistakably, as a response to developing conditions:

in the realm of economics, capitalism; in the realm of politics, democracy; in the realm of religion, Protestantism. The common denominator of these new institutions was individualism—or, to put the matter another way, the new institutions were expressions of a growing (and almost necessary) individualism.[14]

For more than four hundred years, Webb continues, the Western world has partaken of boom times and an expansionist climate fostered by a frontier larger than the continent that originally benefited from it. But we have not fully understood the boom for the "abnormal" occurrence it has been: because it has flourished so long in comparison to cycles we ordinarily track or to individual life spans, we tend to consider its various manifestations as normal, almost natural—to regard Protestantism, capitalism, and democracy, that is, as normative rather than as "exceptional institutions" that were boom-born and boom-fed. According to Webb's argument, the centuries of a world frontier have passed, never more to return. As a consequence, individualism and its accompanying institutions face new challenges in a world that no longer supplies conditions for their sustenance. "There is no plural," Webb concludes, for the word *frontier*.[15]

Such a conclusion, however convincing (and Webb makes it very convincing), has never stopped Americans nurtured on and still in need of a sense of beginning. For the American frontier, as we have seen and as Edwin Fussell has demonstrated in convincing detail, has always had a metaphorical as well as a literal life.[16] Although it was now gone in fact, the frontier in the twentieth century continued to survive in beguiling metaphor out of our persistent need to envision ourselves as beginning. When we had a frontier, we had a bright future; to have a bright future (so goes the inverted logic), we must have a frontier— adjusted, pluralized, almost, at times, legislated, to work its inexhaustible magic on our lives.

It is not, however, in twentieth-century literature that we find strategies of beginning-by-metaphor most insistently invoked. Caught up in their need to refract the discordant realities of a modern world, a number of American writers paid scant tribute to the idea of an inexhaustible frontier: countermetaphors of a wasteland and of a lost generation, born in the aftermath of World War I, stood dramatically against those of horizons unlimited. Novels such as *An American Tragedy* (1925) and *Native Son* (1940) offer troubling parables of constriction that portray the collapse of space and opportunity for protagonists, one white and one black, whose lives are shaped by forces beyond their control. *Walls* preside over Dreiser's novel—those of "the commercial heart" of a city, those of a factory, and finally those of a prison. In the context of these ambivalent symbols of wealth, exclusion, and confinement, Clyde Griffiths's effort to flee "southwest," toward "open space" (at the end of book 1), leads him by ironic patterns of replication to death row and the electric chair. Bigger Thomas's command of space in *Native Son* is virtually nonexistent. Seeing a plane in the air, Bigger wishes he could fly—and drop bombs on whites; watching *Trader Horn* and *The Gay Woman* in a neighborhood theater, he plans a robbery while he is subjected to two-dimensional stereotypes concocted by Hollywood.[17] His fantasies, at once impotent and thrust upon him by a world he fears, are overwhelmed by the stark realities of his life—from the rat he battles in the family bedroom as Wright's novel opens to the rat he envies (because it can disappear into a crack between buildings) when he is being hunted block-by-block on Chicago's south side. Bigger Thomas is so completely devoid of sovereignty, so shut off from considerations of spatial reality during his trial and subsequent weeks on death row, that he defines himself in terms of what he did rather than with conventional indicators of who he is. Saul Bellow's Augie March can introduce himself by saying "I am an American, Chicago born." Bigger says, "What I killed for, I am," an existential statement that is frightening to Bigger's lawyer but liberating to Bigger because it stipulates a self unaffected by confinement and impending execution. For the penal system to work well, Foucault contends, all parties including the offender must see a punishment as natural, something that serves individual and social interests.[18] In *Native Son*, officials of the court have no doubt that Bigger's conviction serves society; and the many visitors to his cell do their best to convince the prisoner that his ordeal will lead him to eternal life or be an object lesson for social reform. With his final statement, however, Bigger steps beyond all rituals and rationalizations. In defining himself he creates himself; he goes to his death intact in his freedom, no longer vulnerable to an outside world, and without a frontier.

At times more ambivalent than their twentieth-century counterparts, some nineteenth-century writers evinced a prescient skepticism about the gospel of endless expansion. Even Whitman—the apostle of beginnings—surrenders to macro-perceptions of bleak-

implication, Lydia Maria Child's "Chocorua's Curse" (a tale from
the 1820s by a champion of minority rights) depicts the escalating
Part violence between a Native American tribe and white settlers fol-
Three lowing the death of an Indian boy who unknowingly eats poison set
out by a settler to kill a marauding fox. And Cooper's early work, let
us recall, sounds a note of cultural foreboding. Consider: in the first
of the Leatherstocking novels, *The Pioneers* (1823), Chingachgook
dies; in the second, *The Last of the Mohicans* (1826), Uncas dies; and
in the third, *The Prairie* (1827), Natty Bumppo, a character "form'd
for the wilderness," dies. By 1826 Cooper had written a two-part
requiem for the Mohican nation. By 1827 he had signaled the
demise of the frontier. The comic pessimism of Willa Cather's later
"El Dorado: A Kansas Recessional" (1901) offers a picture of outright failure in the West. The story chronicles discouragement and
disappointment in a western Kansas town filled with a family
named Gump—Apollo Gump, Aristotle Gump, Ezekiel Gump,
Isaiah Gump, DeWitt Gump, Chesterfield Gump, Almira Gump,
and even Venus Gump (an undeveloped precursor of Faulkner's
Eula Varner). The denouement of the story features a "recessional,"
a move back east—to "God's country."[19] In Cather's work, western
Kansas is a tough sell.

As these examples suggest, the writers I discuss have frequently
encouraged us to reconsider conventional ideas of the West and the
frontier in American history and have thereby eschewed formulas
that spill out a guaranteed future. But these, of course, are not the
only voices to be heard: those of our political leaders, sincere and
assured in their promises, have appropriated the idea of a
metaphorical frontier and of "new beginnings" most publicly to give
us the nourishment we crave. Indeed, Americans in modern times
(undoubtedly like human beings at all times) have tended to support politicians who can pledge a future convincingly, in terms they
know, understand, and trust.

I have already mentioned Henry Wallace's *New Frontiers*, which
portrays the United States as a robust eighteen-year-old boy ready
to start in a new direction. The importance of Wallace's analogy can
hardly be overestimated: had he likened the nation to an aging or
even to a middle-aged man, the argument of his book would have
been thwarted. As it stands, however, his eighteen-year-old boy

(who, he says, has been "playing in the sand pile since 1920") has both the potential and the need to begin.[20] Whether the date was 1876 or 1934, the United States seemed ready to embark, as Whitman might say, on its "real history."

Wallace's call to begin is not an isolated example. In his inaugural address, John F. Kennedy invoked the term "New Frontier" as he spoke of the need to get the nation "moving" again. The task, as he said, would not be finished in the first hundred days, nor in the first thousand—"but let us make a beginning." Shrewdly, with a resonance of which he was perhaps unaware, President Kennedy brought the idea of a beginning out of the metaphor of the New Frontier and thus inspired the nation—definitely, if all too briefly. Sixteen years before, Franklin D. Roosevelt had surveyed the postwar world and announced that "new frontiers of the mind are before us" in a letter requesting Vannevar Bush, then Director of the Office of Scientific Research and Development, to define more precisely what they might be. Published in 1945, Bush's highly regarded study bore the title, *Science, the Endless Frontier*. A collection of his essays appeared during the following year with the title *Endless Horizons*.[21]

What Wallace, Kennedy, Roosevelt, and Bush endeavored to give the nation was a future into which it was about to move, opportunities it was about to explore, prospects it had yet to realize—and, as a consequence, the hope and confidence that come with a sense of beginning. Significantly, each of them invokes the term *frontier*, something no European leader would do if only because the word *frontier* (as both Turner and Webb point out) has consistently denoted in Europe the line between two sovereign countries—what Americans would call a *border*—and thus has not been convertible to the same metaphorical purposes. Indeed, Vannevar Bush goes so far as to promise an "endless frontier," the ideal circumstance, surely, for the American mind. Now this is recognizably the metaphorical world of Emerson and Thoreau, limitless and inexhaustible, grafted onto scientific endeavor— without, however, a literal frontier to sustain its transcending quest. It is likewise a metaphorical world sponsored by the federal government for the good of its citizens, not one evoked by a radical individualism for the good of oneself. As Vannevar Bush says in both of the books to which I have alluded, "It has been basic United States policy that Government should foster the opening of new frontiers. . . . It is in keeping with the American tradition—one that has made the United States great— that new frontiers shall be made accessible for development by all American citizens."[22]

With an authority based on notable achievement, Bush speaks in these volumes for the possibilities of scientific progress in the 1940s and beyond, choosing insistently the vehicle of a frontier in which to couch his discussion. At times one might think he had been reading Fenimore Cooper: the "pioneer spirit is still vigorous within this nation," Bush wrote to President Roosevelt on July 5, 1945 (the Fourth had fallen on Sunday; otherwise, he might have drafted an Independence Day letter): "Science offers a largely unexplored hinterland for the pioneer who has the tools for his task."[23] "Associative" or computer indexing will give us what he calls "endless trails"; memory banks evoke a vision of "horizons unlimited." What Bush has in mind is far-ranging and prescient, a version of the information superhighway envisioned fifty years later. "Wholly new forms of encyclopedias will appear," he writes,

> ready-made with a mesh of associative trails running through them, ready to be dropped into the memex and there amplified. The lawyer has at his touch the associated opinions and decisions of his whole experience, and of the experience of friends and authorities. The patent attorney has on call the millions of issued patents, with familiar trails to every point of his client's interest. The physician, puzzled by a patient's reactions, strikes the trail established in studying an earlier similar case, and runs rapidly through analogous case histories, with side references to the classics for the pertinent anatomy and histology.[24]

That Bush can conceive such possibilities for computer memory (*memex* replacing *index*, in his terminology) is a tribute to his manifest abilities as a scientist; that he couches his vision in terms of "trails" and "frontiers" is a tribute to the perennial attraction of such metaphors for the American mind. What President Roosevelt called for, Bush designed. And in *Endless Horizons*, he states the official view succinctly: "The opportunity for advancement" does not "necessarily vanish when the geographical frontier gives place to one that is entirely of a technical nature."[25]

When, not many years later, technology fulfilled President Kennedy's promise to the nation (and caveat to the world) by opening up the prospect of space travel and showing us—live—men walking on the moon, the role of science in providing a frontier substitute might have seemed assured. As former generations had once explored the vastness of a continent, so now we would begin to explore the vastness of space. But the exploration of space, astonishing as it has been, has failed to generate a viable notion of a new frontier, not simply because it has made Americans (and others) spectators at a public drama that yielded no transforming returns but also because it has contributed to the formation of a challenging new metaphor—that of the earth itself as a spaceship, our collective spaceship, with finite and diminishing resources that we must conserve and care for. Archibald Macleish expressed an increasingly widespread view when he wrote (in 1978, four years before his death) that "To see the earth as we now see it, small and blue and beautiful in that eternal silence where it floats, is to see ourselves as riders on the earth together."[26] And thus one of the most dramatic steps of modern technology fostered a perception contrary to that given by a frontier, antithetical to a sense of beginning that had depended on indefinite expansion, on transcendence. (It is interesting to note that in 1967 Vannevar Bush published a book entitled *Science is Not Enough*.)

From Jefferson's vision of a country in which there was "room" for our descendants to the thousandth and thousandth generation, we have come in less than seven thirty-year generations to a perspective like that of Oscar Newman in *Defensible Space* (1972), a cogent study of urban living and the psychological-architectural ways of discouraging aggression on the space we occupy in our daily lives. Precisely because so many Americans lack "room," *Defensible Space* is a book for the late twentieth century, a symptom, as the very title suggests, of our need to draw in, to defend what we have. Another symptom, I believe, can be seen in the contemporary emphasis on the Constitution—especially the Bill of Rights: whereas in the nineteenth century we celebrated the Declaration of Independence, in the twentieth we take refuge in the Constitution. Rather than assert our independence, we feel the need to defend it; rather than declare our rights, we find it increasingly necessary to protect them. We search now for justice, not transcendence, and look to the courtroom, not to the West, for satisfaction.

And yet Americans continue to yearn for openness, for a sense of abundant space and time. At times the effort seems misdirected and shallow: Webb notes the "plaintive" attempts to claim "new frontiers" in such fields as insurance and women's fashions.[27] At times it seems directed by a need to convey reassurance: concerned (as all chief executives must be) with the need to protect the future, President Gerald Ford commemorated the battle of Lexington in April of 1975 by saying that the American Dream was not dead— it was "yet to be realized." Six months later, Theodore H. White inverted the term *frontier*, turned it inside out to signify urban challenge, when he wrote that our "cities are the frontier of American government today."[28] The lesson of these final examples is both enlightening and melancholy: so long and so easily was the American need for beginnings, for hope, and for a future, fed on a national scale by the same formulas that we have continued to invoke them, with diminishing and confusing returns, as if they could nourish us forever.

One additional and perhaps decisive factor in draining the frontier of its charismatic appeal has been a fundamental change in our perception of the American continent and its development. Although (if we are not to be prisoners of the present) we should be able to understand why fifteenth-century Europeans, surprised at finding a sparsely populated landmass of undetermined size, considered this "new world" available for ownership, we stand five hundred years away from their assumptions. And given what archaeologists and historians have taught us about the inhabitants of pre-Columbian America and what we have learned about the experience of Native Americans in later centuries, we can no longer subscribe to the idea that European explorers sailed to an empty continent or that the American frontier moved into an empty West. Yet what has been American history's most influential hypothesis is predicated on this very notion of emptiness. In the opening paragraph of "The Significance of the Frontier in American History," Frederick Jackson Turner comes right to the point: "Up to our own day American history has been in a large degree the history of the colonization of the Great West. The existence of an area of free land, its continuous recession, and the advance of American settlement westward, explain American development (20)." Walter Prescott Webb, as we have seen, extends Turner's premise to include consideration of a world frontier vast in scope and duration. He, too, is explicit about his methodology: "As defined in this study," Webb writes, the frontier "was an empty land, a vacancy inviting occupants."[29]

I have no wish to try to diminish or even to carp at the achievement of Turner, Webb, and those who have examined American development in the light of their ideas; historians who disagree with Turner's interpretation have already issued resounding counterstatements that are part of the dialogue concerning the settling of the continent and of the West.[30] I do wish, however, to observe that the model of the frontier as a generator of beginnings was based on a perception now discredited. What we have learned subverts the validity of a reading of history that was linear in its bearing, powerful in its simplicity, and—as Louis Montrose has suggested in another context—gender-specific and imperial in its origins and development.[31]

Moreover, the voices of those we once regarded as the *other* tell us (now that we listen) of *their* view of the other (us). A sixteenth-century poem transcribed from Mayan hieroglyphs yields a mirror image of beginnings and of activities valorized by the Western world:

> They came from the east when they arrived.
> Then Christianity also began.
> The fulfillment of its prophecy is ascribed to the east . . .
> Then with the true God, the true *Dios*,
> came the beginning of our misery.
> It was the beginning of tribute,
> the beginning of church dues,
> the beginning of strife with purse-snatching,
> the beginning of strife with blow-guns,
> the beginning of strife by trampling on people,
> the beginning of robbery with violence,
> the beginning of forced debts,
> the beginning of debts enforced by false testimony,
> the beginning of individual strife,
> a beginning of vexation.32

Along with its medley of evils (from "purse-snatching" to "blow guns"), the modernity of diction in this poem reminds us that we are at the mercy of a translator—in this case, Ralph L. Roys in 1933. Whatever fashions of translation may inform the above lines, however, the litany of beginnings detailing one new outrage after another makes itself felt as an "outside" perspective that—importantly—bends our perception of the Spanish conquest back upon itself. Similarly, Jeffrey L. Hantman's examination of Native American views of "the Other" in the Jamestown colony yields a sense of space no longer mastered (and therefore linear) but curved reflexively so that we may see and, it is to be hoped, recognize, ourselves through the eyes of others.[33] It was comfortable to satisfy a national need for beginnings when "a vacancy inviting occupants" stretched before us; it is perplexing (as the circularity of this sentence suggests) to do so now that we know ourselves as people who required a comfortable way to satisfy a national need for beginnings.

Adam and Oedipus   Based on the carefully nourished sense of difference from Europe that I have noted in earlier chapters, the myth of the American Adam bore a celebratory and geopolitical alliance to beginnings. In the words of R. W. B. Lewis, the American Adam stood "emancipated from history," "prior to experience," the embodiment of a nation that had been blessed with "a divinely granted second chance for the human race, after the first chance had been so disastrously fumbled in the darkening Old World." John L. O'Sullivan, editor of the *United States Magazine and Democratic Review*, set forth the convictions that fostered such a perspective when he wrote (in 1839) of "our disconnected position as regards any other nation." "Our national birth," he continued, "was the beginning of a new history, the formation and progress of an untried political system, which separates us from the past and connects us with the future only; and so far as regards the entire development of the natural rights of man, in moral, political, and national life, we may confidently assume that our country is destined to be *the great nation* of futurity."[34] Although it served to emphasize the moral superiority of the American character, the model of Adam—especially an Adam poised to embrace the future—was in some ways unfortunate for a new nation to project, since the only thing Adam could do, and did, was fall. Nonetheless, the protean appeal of the Adamic concept carried it through the fashions and vicissitudes of a history it sought to shed: battered by time and deprived of its teleological matrix by the passing of the frontier and the secularization of American society, it continued to survive in attenuated popular forms because—I submit—it generated a sense of beginning and thereby offered a renewable purchase on the future.

Perhaps its most familiar transmutation has been an encompassing deference to youth. Although such an attitude is by no means limited to the United States, it comes easily to the American mind as a corollary of our former gratification at being a young nation. As early as August, 1776, Abigail Adams expressed some anxiety about the education of "the rising Generation."[35] In both the nineteenth and twentieth centuries a similar concern became a shaping force in thousands of families, many of them new to America. The pattern was as commendable as it was clear: motivated by a desire to provide a future they could not experience themselves, parents made financial sacrifices so that children could have a richer life in the land of opportunity. When those children became parents, they customarily acted in the same way. In effect, there was a recurring investment in the future. In later years the story takes a somewhat different turn: guilty at having made so imperfect a world, Americans seek to preserve the future for those who will one day inhabit it. One way or another, unspoiled or not-yet-spoiled, the future has been the promised land of the young. With time ahead of them, with a new honesty and an aversion to discredited patterns of behavior, "the rising Generation" in some recent variations of the story will not only inherit but envision their way into a glorious new era.

Such, in charitable essence, is the argument of Charles A. Reich's *The Greening of America* (1970), a book that took its posture of hope and superiority from an Adamic ideal that had claimed the future at the outset of our history. "There is a revolution coming," says Reich: "It will not be like revolutions of the past." Because it is a revolution in consciousness, "it will not require violence to succeed, and it cannot be successfully resisted by violence." Even now, it is "spreading with amazing rapidity" out of a belief that "beyond the industrial era lies a new age of man."[36] Millennial and messianic, *Greening* is, as Michael Novak points out, both "a record of a conversion" and "a new convert's program for missionary activity." Reich takes pains to instruct devotees how to carry the message of what he calls Consciousness III to "workers and older people."[37]

Insofar as his argument focuses on statism and professional and economic relationships of power (Consciousness II), Reich is in the company of those who derive their ideas from Marx. But as Joel Kramer observes, Reich also tells people in "an emerging class" that "society will be revolutionized" if they simply pursue their own goals and live (or drop out) as they wish.[38] And when he proceeds to reify Consciousness III, he sounds the chords of a vulnerable and parodic romanticism:

> The extraordinary thing about this new consciousness is that it has emerged out of the wasteland of the Corporate State, like flowers pushing up through the concrete pavement. Whatever it touches, it beautifies and renews: a freeway entrance is festooned with happy hitchhikers, the sidewalk is decorated with street people, the humorless steps of an official building are given warmth by a group of musicians. And every barrier falls before it.[39]

Add to this that bare feet and bell bottom jeans are good and that hydrogenated peanut butter is bad (which it is), and one sees the trivia in which this new beginning founders. To paint revolutionary (Adamic) features on the faces of people whose future is Consciousness III is to bestow a heavy burden on them.

Nonetheless, the number of Americans who wanted to believe Reich's message made the book a stylish success—gullible public paying tribute to naive author. And there are pensive moments when one can understand the phenomenon of its popularity. For there is something beyond the silliness, the condescension, and the myopia in *Greening* that tallies with a deep yearning for a better future. The book may promise a tarnished brass ring, but one is tempted to grab for the ring even so.

For better or worse, and perhaps inevitably, the spirit of *The Greening of America* continues to inform the efforts of other writers. Only two years after the appearance of what Reich sometimes called his "novel," Gilles Deleuze and Félix Guattari published the swirling transgenerational tour de force, *Anti-Oedipus: Capitalism and Schizophrenia* (1972), followed several years later by *A Thousand Plateaus: Capitalism and Schizophrenia* (1980). Although students of these eminent thinkers might not appreciate my pointing it out, what these two books present is a program (a "flow") for greening the world. The authors move from Marx to Nietzsche to Henry

Miller to D. H. Lawrence to William Burroughs to Allen Ginsberg, all of whom—with assistance from Kafka, Proust, and Joyce—
bump hard into Freud and rational analysis in a "nomadic" attempt
to destroy territoriality, repression, and the focus on self and family
(promoted by the State) so that we may follow the "flow of desire"
rather than the flow of capital to happiness. Capitalism, assisted by
its handmaiden, psychoanalysis, breeds schizophrenia (as does
Consciousness II in Reich's formulation)—and that is the condition in which we are forced to live. The new mode of "schizoanaly-
sis," however, leads to free-flowing desire formations that are anti-
authoritarian, anti-Oedipean, and anti-capitalistic. Citing Henry
Miller, Deleuze and Guattari adduce the idea that "desire is instinc-
tual and holy," that only by means of desire can "we bring about the
immaculate conception"—and "body forth a new world."[40] Not
everyone can go with the flow: a synoptic appraisal of the careers of
Jack Kerouac (in *Anti-Oedipus*) and of Herman Melville (in *A
Thousand Plateaus*) leads the authors to ask rhetorically "if the destiny of American literature" is not to be found in the crossing of
"limits and frontiers, causing deterritorialized flows of desire to cir-
culate, but also always making these flows transport fascising, mor-
alizing, Puritan, and familialist territorialities."[41] This interesting
speculation, derived conceptually if not rhetorically from D. H.
Lawrence, points to the difficulty of sustaining a beginning when
one is weighted down with social and domestic baggage. Taking
that as a given, it is surprising that no mention is made of Whitman
in these volumes, nor of Emerson, nor of Thoreau.

As different as are their ideas concerning the individual in society—Reich advocating the actualizing and Deleuze and Guattari
the abrogation of the monadic self—capitalism for these writers
stands as the primary obstacle to openness and possibility, to the
consummation of Consciousness III and to endless configurations
of desire (a thousand plateaus). For Reich, as we have seen, capitalism is both the creature and the creator of "the American Corporate State."[42] For Deleuze and Guattari, it is the authority (quin-
tessentially fascistic) behind a system of treatment that cripples the
psyche. Yet as Angela Miller's analysis of our national landscape
suggests, capitalism as manifested in the American corporation has
the capacity to absorb classic expressions of boundlessness. Critics
have frequently overlooked the ambivalence of Thomas Cole's *The
Oxbow* (1836), reading it as a straightforward glorification of "the

Edenic possibilities of the new nation." Together with the logo of the Chrysler Corporation, the painting was displayed in that spirit to advertise the *American Paradise* exhibition in 1987. The "linkage" of painting and logo, Miller remarks, affiliates the corporation with "the inexhaustible wilderness of the nineteenth-century imagination." With the wilderness depleted (as Cole's painting may portend), the idea of inexhaustibility finds by association and transference "a new home in corporate capitalism."[43]

The idea of a corporation seeking to in-corporate the inexhaustible by means of adroit advertising techniques would doubtless confirm the adverse view of capitalism held by Reich and Deleuze and Guattari. Amid the ideological ironies, as Miller leads us to see, it does constitute an attempt to acquire gilt by association. But Miller's perception goes farther, pointing through the mask of commercial strategy to a central feature of the American economic system—the perennial need for growth, "the worship of growth," as John Maher puts it, the virtual dependence on expansion.[44] We hear the refrain daily: the Gross National Product must grow if the nation is to be healthy; the Leading Economic Indicators must point upward if the economy is to flourish; the earnings of a given corporation must exceed expectations if its market valuation is not to suffer. The quantified demand for endless economic growth has replaced the myth of the inexhaustible wilderness as the source of the American dream.

Moreover, the idea that the government "should foster the opening of new frontiers" for all American citizens—as Vannevar Bush defined its "policy" at the end of World War II—required, to use a convenient trope, a flood of government spending.[45] One consequence was to conflate debt and growth, to institutionalize the national debt as the engine of growth. In the latter half of the twentieth century, the national debt (swollen not only by deficit spending for the military and so-called entitlement programs but by a general largesse to business and industry) replaced the geographical frontier as the purveyor of opportunity. We ran up the debt with anguished shouts of joy, lamenting its size, relishing its benefits, burnishing the present, and proroguing considerations of the future out of a belief (or at least a hope) that we could transcend problems with economic expansion.

From another perspective, this policy could be called not the greening but the greenbacking of America, a systematic practice of spending, not insuring, the future. In the final decades of the twentieth century Americans have found themselves at cross-purposes, still wanting to believe in some form of national inexhaustibility and a consequent promising future, but surprised that these inherited articles of faith no longer seem compatible with present-day realities. When a writer in the *North American Review* proclaimed in 1818 that "no people" ever faced the future "with such encouragements and advantages," he could infer that the promise of the present would yield a glowing future. When Margaret Fuller said in 1849 that "No country has ever had such a good future," she could assume that the promise of the future was inherent in the present.[46] We can no longer make such blithe assumptions and inferences. Wanting to have things both ways, we acknowledge that our policies are mortgaging the future, yet remain unwilling to modify attitudes that have made us what we are. We grow restive at the thought that our world might not be inexhaustible. We are disinclined to become citizens of a world of limitation.

Diminishment . . . and Possibility   "This is a middle-aged country now," Ellen Goodman remarked in her syndicated column in January 1993. Assessing the mood of the nation's capital during the rituals of President Clinton's inauguration, Goodman observed that hopes were sincere but tempered, made so by the "belated understanding of our country's problems." For the nation, she continued, faces a difficulty "that often comes at midlife: How do you make a fresh start in the middle?" How do you generate a sense of beginning when "you don't get a clean slate," when "waste sites" are "more visible than new frontiers?"[47]

Goodman's questions (and the resonant metaphors in which they are couched) lead us to consider the American need for beginnings in the light of what is no longer present in the nation we inhabit—a clean slate, a frontier, the promise of youth. We can no longer assume that "we have it in our power to begin the world over again" (as did Thomas Paine in 1776). We can no longer visualize a country with "room enough" for thousands of generations (as did Thomas Jefferson in 1801). We can no longer write off national disappointments as "preparation, adolescence" (as did Walt Whitman in 1876). All of these formulations depended on perceptions of unique opportunity, of measureless space and time, on what was originally a vital contrast between an Old World scarred by history and a New World cleansed of the past. Such beginning-oriented cadences, as Goodman suggests, no longer work their magic.

By no means, of course, have beginnings ceased to be a factor in human experience. Because (as I have suggested earlier) beginning moments echo, however faintly, the wonder associated with genesis, they continue to affect human conduct and aspirations in many ways. Whether one experiences a beginning (as with a religious awakening), commemorates a beginning (as with holiday celebrations), or stipulates a beginning (as with a resolution to stop smoking), one divides time into what is past and what is to come and looks ahead with fresh hope—with a personal version of a clean slate. Occasionally, in specialized cases, a sense of proximity to a radical beginning can convert rational inquiry into something akin to religious awe. After examining satellite photographs that yielded confirmation of the Big Bang theory of creation and suggested how galaxies could have been formed, one physicist reportedly said it was like "looking at the year 1." The absence of pattern in an extended list of prime numbers brought mathematicians Philip J. Davis and Reuben Hersh to point out that between 9,999,900 and 10,000,000 there are nine primes; in the next hundred integers, however, there are only two—10,000,019 and 10,000,079. In the presence of these two numbers, they attest, "one has the feeling of being in the presence of one of the inexplicable secrets of creation." Such an epiphany is the product of what Davis and Hersh call the "overwhelming desire" of mathematicians to "bridge the gap between the finite and the infinite."[48]

The excitement brought about by these latter perceptions, the sense of an almost mystical proximity to creation, derives from inquiry that is remarkable but restricted in its appeal, not likely to exhilarate a nation in need of beginnings that provide tangible promise for the future. Meanwhile, some surveys of economic data point to a long-term erosion of consumer confidence (despite occasional euphoric blips) and to consistently low rates of savings as evidence that Americans are living in a period of diminished expectations. No longer convinced that next year will bring a better job or that the next generation will see greater opportunity, many citizens question the capacity of business and government to provide an optimistic view of the future. Aware of their conflicting goals and indulgent aspirations, President Jimmy Carter once told the American people that they were suffering from a malaise. It was an accurate appraisal that was politically devastating. No President has expressed such a judgment since that time.

What no longer informs American life at the end of the twentieth century is a *collective* sense of a beginning based on some benign form of transcendence. We have sincere and formulaic calls for "renewal" of our policies and ourselves. We have the fashionable notion of "reinventing" government (a term derived from Garry Wills 1978 study of the Declaration of Independence, *Inventing America*). And we will doubtless have visions of "new beginnings" held out to us as a new century approaches, quick fixes, bubbles of confidence, novel visions of inexhaustibility. But our original perceptions of the nation and the future, those flawed but valuable pieties that gave us a profound sense of commencement, belong to a period of history that is gone. Loath to admit that fact, and frustrated by its implications, we may be (how can anyone be sure?) evolving fitfully, painfully, at times by indirection, toward a different sort of definition or paradigm to characterize ourselves as a nation. With its diverse voices, our literature remains a provocative cultural indicator, one worth attending to, not for solutions or easy formulas, but for the questions it is asking and its portrayals of what we are and might be in our frailties and aspirations. Indeed, the work of postmodern writers offers a remarkable range of responses to issues imbedded in the American experience—frequently expressed in modes that inspire a shock of recognition for those acquainted with our faith in beginnings.

We are still drawn, for example, to "firsts," to portraits of Adam, and to the idea of accessibility to radical beginnings. But we get such things with provocative mythic twists. Both John Hollander's "Adam's Task" (1971) and Nancy Sullivan's "The Death of the First Man" (1975) portray an Adam humanized, not Americanized, a solitary individual in postures of yearning, not of ahistorical triumph. And Gary Snyder's career-long exploration of myth and ritual, of history and wildness, enacts the idea of ongoing creation and inner growth as the source of fulfillment in life.[49] A number of late twentieth-century dramatic productions, moreover, challenge conventional ideas of the west and the frontier as phenomena in American history. Such works as Sam Shepard's *True West* (1980) and Beth Henley's *Abundance* (1992)—and a film such as Kevin Costner's *Dances with Wolves* (1992)—develop inverted perspectives that block the simple replication of myth on myth and encourage re-cognition of the past.

Both novels and personal narratives likewise adapt conventional means to enhance the authority of their statements. In the Prologue to *A Rumor of War* (1977), Philip Caputo uses familiar negative strategies to define both the kind of war fought in Vietnam and his sense of the individual as a social and ethical being in that war: "there were no Normandies or Gettysburgs for us," he writes, "no epic clashes that decided the fate of armies or nations." Having distinguished the fighting in Vietnam from battles honored in American history, Caputo continues with negatives of a deeper import:

> There was nothing familiar out where we were, no churches, no police, no laws, no newspapers, or any of the restraining influences without which the earth's population of virtuous people would be reduced by ninety-five percent. It was the dawn of creation in the Indochina bush, an ethical as well as geographical wilderness. Out there, lacking restraints, sanctioned to kill . . . we sank into a brutish state. The descent could be checked only by the man's inner moral values, the attribute that is called character.[50]

Those who lacked such a net "plunged all the way down," discovering, as Caputo knows, "a capacity for malice" they probably never suspected was in them.[51] In *Song of Solomon* (1977), Toni Morrison explores the patterns of love and consuming loneliness in a black middle-class family whose surname is Dead. That name, given inadvertently by a drunken Yankee soldier who was registering former slaves, is the central fact and metaphor of the novel. A quest for gold on the part of young Macon Dead becomes finally a quest of another kind: he must, as he sees, strip away the history of his family, a century of being identified as Dead, in order to find life.

Each of these narratives confronts the anguish of our history. Caputo's staccato negatives bring us once again to an image of the dawn of creation—converted now to a Conradian point of terror because of his assumptions about the natural state of the human being. Morrison's joyful strategies of negation include an explanation of how Not-Doctor Street got its name and the presentation of a unique character who lacks a navel as they encourage us to see that our country has declared a sizable portion of our population dead during a century of official freedom. In this novel, however, there is life before Dead—if one can reach it. By searching through a brutal past, one arrives at the consciousness of self and family filled with honor, magic, and love.

By surviving and (crucially) assimilating a succession of brutal experiences, the narrator of Ralph Ellison's *Invisible Man* (1952) achieves a personal sense of identity and freedom that includes (just as crucially) the capacity for love. Invisible Man's misadventures take him from a series of promising starts in life to—in each case—humiliation and chaos: his bizarre departure from college, for example, the explosion in the paint factory, the Harlem riots. A wondrously naive young man from the South, he repeatedly takes on roles endorsed by others. To be successful, he first determines to emulate Dr. Bledsoe, the President of the college; to impress those whom he meets in New York, he later decides (fleetingly) to be "*charming*—like Ronald Colman"; to possess the comforts of an orthodox ideology, he subsequently joins the Brotherhood.[52] Only when he realizes the depths of Bledsoe's treachery does he begin to struggle toward identity. "When I discover who I am, I'll be free," he thinks in the mechanical dreamscape of the factory hospital; "I yam what I am," he exclaims in gustatory excitement (Ronald Colman long forgotten) as he devours the hot buttered yams of a street vendor (185, 201). Even then, however, this narrator's naïveté leads him to a new career as part of the Brotherhood and to the experience of a more profound treachery.

Writing essays in exam booklets, scribbling against the pressure of time, several generations of college students have identified Invisible Man simply as I. M. Happily, the sound generates the sense. For in this up-tempo, allusive tale, with its audacious wordplay and modulations of tone, the narrator's awareness of who he is, of his homegrown black identity, becomes the condition of his rebirth. The outpouring of emotion at Tod Clifton's funeral triggers a painful transformation in his consciousness. While "the bell tolled again in the yard below," he realizes that the marchers, the music, the songs of lamentation signify "something deeper than protest, or religion"—"something for which the theory of Brotherhood had given me no name" (338, 342). "Could politics," he wonders, "ever be an expression of love?" (341). What emerges in his impromptu threnody is a half-angry tribute that answers this rhetorical question and tallies with the swirling emotions of the epilogue. Considered "politically," I. M. comes to see, individuals, even Tod Clifton, are "without meaning" (337).

Orchestrated by the ideas of the Declaration of Independence and the failures of American history, the epilogue to *Invisible Man* is a narrative version of traditional Fourth of July addresses, complete with a tribute to the spirit of the original document, a recognition of national shortcomings, and a final move toward a fresh beginning.[53] A sense that the "humiliations" of his life are part of his identity ("They were me; they defined me") leads I. M. to speak for the first time with sustained self-knowledge (383). Out of that knowledge, he "affirm[s] the principles on which the country was built" but "not the men who did violence" to them. Committed to independence and freedom, he speaks against tyranny and the "increasing passion" for conformity. "America is woven of many strands," he reminds us in the manner of an orator (which he is), all of which need to be recognized if we are "to become one, and yet many" (433, 435). He acknowledges not only that he has "been hurt to the point of abysmal pain" but that the process of recording his story has blunted his anger and left him with a divided perspective. Through a lens of his own, he now judges the world to be "concrete, ornery, vile and sublimely wonderful"; he is prepared to denounce and defend what he sees, to condemn and affirm, to hate and to love (435, 437–38). Gestures of stripping away to identity prepare him to leave his basement hole: having burned the papers in his briefcase (for light), he is now "shaking off the old skin" because there is "a possibility" he may have "a socially responsible role to play." His allegiance to the individual, his discovery that "in spite of all I find that I love," signifies his new relation to the world and a potential for beginning. And "who knows," he concludes, "but that, on the lower frequencies, I speak for you?" (438–39).

Additional food for thought can be found in *Generation X* (1991), surely one of the most forlorn novels in the whole of American literature. Awash in self-pity, Douglas Coupland's cadre of characters look out at a polluted world bereft of opportunity, appropriated by Baby Boomers (and prior generations) for their own aggrandizement. As citizens of this wearied world, the narrator and his friends work at "McJobs" and coat themselves with protective irony. Yet in an apocalyptic scene at the end of the novel Coupland converts his narrative to a parable of possibility.

The date is January 1, the year 2000. The scene is near the Salton Sea in southern California. Driving to Calexico on that day in that place, the narrator sees what he takes to be "a thermonuclear cloud," ominous and angry, "as high in the sky as the horizon is far away."[54] A votary of the end, he has been dreaming of that cloud "steadily" since he was five, "shameless, exhausted, and gloating." When "the roots of this mushroom" turn out to be farmers burning stubble off their fields, he is momentarily relieved, then transfixed by the blackness of the fields before him. It is an "absolute" black that seems "more stellar in origin than anything on this planet." It is "supergravitational blackness," a "marvel of antipurity" so profound and "blemishless that fighting, cranking children stopped squabbling inside their parents' mobile homes to stare," as did "traveling salesmen in their beige sedans, stretching their legs and eating hamburgers microwaved back at the 7-Eleven." For gazing at this inexhaustible blackness is "a restful unifying experience": "It made us smile at each other."

At this point two things happen: "a cocaine white egret"—a bird "I had never seen in real life before"—flies over the blackened fields and a dozen ("or so") mentally retarded teenagers tumble gregariously out of a nearby van and surround the narrator. The contrast between circling bird and passive fields, between arcs of white and stationary black, startles everyone into wide-eyed silence. And when the egret alters its course to swoop low over the astonished group, "We felt chosen." Before the bird lands in the field and pecks sustenance out of the inchoate blackness, its talons graze the narrator's head; he falls to his knees while one of the teenagers inspects his wound. Whereupon, all of the youngsters fall on him in an "adoring, healing, uncritical embrace," in a painful "crush of love" that was "no problem at all," that was "unlike anything I had ever known."

The details of this ultimate vision provide their own commentary—the power of blackness, the "jet-white" bird redolent of "the Ganges or the Nile" finding life in the burnt fields, the sacramental wounding of the hero by the bird, the twelve healing disciples, the final crush of love. Coupland has given us an eloquent creation story set on the first day of a new millenium.

"How do you make a fresh start in the middle?" asks Ellen Goodman. It is a difficult question to answer, one that might not be necessary to ask if Americans had not enjoyed such a long and comfortable romance with beginnings. From a different perspective, Jerome Loving characterizes the American experience as one of waking up "in the middle of the story and wonder[ing] why the Promised Land is full of broken promises."[55] His words echo the central question of Robert Bellah's *The Broken Covenant*, a study that not only explores the nation's "myth of origin" but reflects the struggles of a committed American who has suffered from the condition he analyzes. Troubled by social values in the mid-twentieth century, Bellah (as he says) eventually rejected most aspects of his "own society." His later attitude toward America (startlingly like that of Ellison's Invisible Man) "has embodied a tension—*odi et amo*—of affirmation and rejection," a tension made all the greater because the nation has been built "centrally on utopian millenial expectations"—the very things, I would say, that have spawned our dependence on and need for a unifying sense of beginning.[56] At present such a need is acute because (to make the point one final time) a particular matrix of circumstances delivered us as a nation into the world, nurtured us (by negation) on how different we were, brought us confidently to the "midlife" Goodman speaks of, then, inevitably, vanished, leaving us dependent on sustenance that was no longer there. The general diagnosis seems to be in: something is missing; something has been broken; and the means for restoring and repairing are not at hand.

We will, of course, live into the years ahead, no doubt with postures of perplexity and disenchantment, determination and hope. Over a clarifying period of time, it may be that scientific endeavors (as Vannevar Bush once thought) will contribute in some way to a sense of the inexhaustible and thus of a future and thus of a beginning. It may be, too, that the spiritual nourishment many people treasure will contribute to a realization of inner and endless growth. It may be, further, that the terms of current economic dialogue, with their emphasis on such matters as the Pacific rim and the effects of free trade agreements, will realign our relation to the world and thereby contribute new vistas of opportunity. And it may be, finally, that our literature, with its continuing visions of inconclusiveness and our need for a love that is deeper than politics, will contribute to a communal sense of beginning.

All contributions will be welcome.

Notes

1. Fixing a Beginning

1. Jeremy Belknap, *The History of New-Hampshire* (Philadelphia, 1784), pp. 1–2. William Boelhower points out that Jedidiah Morse, in his popular *American Geography* (1792), took pride in the "precision" with which Americans could trace their origins. See Boelhower, "Stories of Foundation, Scenes of Origin," *American Literary History* 5 (Fall 1993): 396–97.

2. Edward W. Said, *Beginnings: Intention and Method* (New York: Basic Books, 1975), p. 49.

3. Wallace Stevens's phrase occurs in his poem "The Idea of Order at Key West." Eusebius, *The History of the Church from Christ to Constantine*, trans. G. A. Williamson (New York: Penguin, 1983), p. 33. The two subsequent references to this edition are noted parenthetically in the text.

4. *The Collected Dialogues of Plato*, ed. Edith Hamilton and Huntington Cairns (Princeton: Princeton University Press, 1982), pp. 1162–63.

5. *Meister Eckhart: The Essential Sermons, Commentaries, Treatises, and Defense*, trans. with introduction by Edmund College and Bernard McGinn (New York: Paulist Press, 1981), pp. 85, 125.

6. Said, *Beginnings*, pp. 48–49.

7. John Daly Burk, *The History of Virginia, from Its First Settlement to the Present Day* (Petersburg, Va, 1804), p. 5.

8. George S. Hillard, "The Past and the Future," in *New England Society Orations*, 2 vols. (Boston, 1851), 2:160.

9. Henry David Thoreau, *A Week on the Concord and Merrimack Rivers*, The

Writings of Henry D. Thoreau (Princeton: Princeton University Press, 1980), p. 325.

10. Louis Montrose analyzes the manner in which European conceptions of gender affected colonialist attitudes toward appropriated lands in "The Work of Gender in the Discourse of Discovery," *Representations* 33 (Winter 1991): 1–41. For crosscultural perspectives on the term *discovery*, see Lynne Withey, *Voyages of Discovery: Captain Cook and the Exploration of the Pacific* (London: Hutchinson, 1987).

11. Williams devotes the opening chapter of *In the American Grain* (1925) to a meditation on Eric the Red. Morison's *The European Discovery of America: The Northern Voyages, A.D. 500–1600* (1971) examines the journeys and purported journeys of St. Brendan, Leif Ericson, Prince Madoc, and others.

12. Garrison Keillor, *Lake Woebegone Days* (New York: Viking, 1985), pp. 92–93.

13. Henriette Mertz, *Pale Ink: Two Ancient Records of Chinese Exploration in America*, 2d rev. ed. (Chicago: Swallow Press, 1972), pp. 1, 32–33; Frederick Turner, *Beyond Geography: The Western Spirit Against the Wilderness* (New York: Viking, 1980), p. 301.

14. Thomas Prince, *A Chronological History of New-England in the Form of Annals . . . with an Introduction Containing a Brief Epitome of the Most Remarkable Transactions and Events Abroad, from the Creation*, 2 vols. (Boston, 1736), dedicatory letter on unnumbered page. Subsequent references to the *Chronological History* are noted parenthetically in the text. See Michael Kraus, *A History of American History* (New York: Farrar, 1937), pp. 86–88, for an account of Prince's work. Haydn White discusses Voltaire's stance against figurative writing in history and the role of annals in providing a sense of continuity in *Metahistory: The Historical Imagination in Nineteenth-Century Europe* (Baltimore: John Hopkins University Press, 1973), pp. 53, 59.

15. Robert James Belford, *History of the United States, in Chronological Order, from A.D. 432 to the Present Time* (New York, 1886), p. iii.

16. Frank A. DePuy, *The New Century Home Book* (New York: Eaton and Mains, 1900), pp. 384, 385, 388.

17. Mark Twain, *The Innocents Abroad: or, The New Pilgrims Progress* (New York: New American Library, 1966), p. 190.

18. Nathaniel Hawthorne, "Main-Street," in *The Snow-Image and Uncollected Tales*, The Centenary Edition of the Works of Nathaniel Hawthorne (Columbus: Ohio State University Press, 1974), p. 66; *The Scarlet Letter*, The Centenary Edition of the Works of Nathaniel Hawthorne (Columbus: Ohio State University Press, 1960), p. 47.

19. Samuel Whelpley, *A Compend of History from the Earliest Times*, 2 vols. (New York, 1808), 1:10.

20. Whelpley, *Compend*, 2:131.

21. Because of the poverty of materials available, early historians of the American Revolution made liberal use of the British *Annual Register* for their accounts of the war. See David D. Van Tassel, *Recording America's Past: An Inter-*

pretation of the Development of Historical Studies in America, 1607–1884 (Chicago: University of Chicago Press, 1960), pp. 32, 39–40.

22. Belknap, *History of New-Hampshire*, p. iv.

23. Benjamin Trumbull, *A Complete History of Connecticut* (Hartford, 1797), p. iv.

24. David Ramsey, M.D., *The History of South-Carolina, from Its First Settlement in 1670, to the Year 1808*, 2 vols. (Charleston, 1809), 1:vii.

25. Belknap, *History of New-Hampshire*, p. iv.

26. Thomas Hutchinson, *The History of the Colony and Province of Massachusetts-Bay*, ed. Lawrence S. Mayo (Cambridge: Harvard University Press, 1936), p. 1; Belknap, *History of New-Hampshire*, pp. 1–2. Trumbull; *History of Connecticut*, p. 2; and Ramsey, *History of South-Carolina*, p. 1.

27. Burk, *History of Virginia*, pp. 3–5, 19.

28. Burk, *History of Virginia*, p. iii.

29. Francis J. Grund, *The Americans in Their Moral, Social, and Political Relations*, 2 vols. (1837; reprint 2 vols. in 1, New York: Augustus M. Kelly, 1971), 1:174. Grund continues by saying that "no mythological fable is blended with [America's] origin. Her children are not descended from the gods or the sun."

30. David Ramsey, M.D., *A History of the United States, from Their First Settlement as English Colonies, in 1607, to the Year 1808*, 2d ed., 3 vols. (Philadelphia, 1818), 1:39.

31. Abiel Holmes, *American Annals: or, A Chronological History of America from Its Discovery in MCCCCXCII to MDCCCV*, 2 vols. (Cambridge Mass., 1805), 1:iii, 2:237.

32. White, *Metahistory*, p. 60.

33. George Bancroft, *History of the United States, from the Discovery of the American Continent* (Boston, 1834), pp. 5–6, ii.

34. Russel B. Nye, *George Bancroft: Brahmin Rebel* (New York: Octagon Books, 1972), pp. 101–102.

35. Washington Irving, *A History of New-York . . . by Diedrich Knickerbocker*, Author's Revised Edition (New York, 1853), pp. 23–24. Subsequent references to the Knickerbocker *History* are noted parenthetically in the text.

36. See Jeffrey Rubin-Dorsky, *Adrift in the Old World: The Psychological Pilgrimage of Washington Irving* (Chicago: University of Chicago Press, 1988), pp. 101ff.

37. William L. Hedges, *Washington Irving: An American Study, 1802–1832* (Baltimore: Johns Hopkins University Press, 1965), p. 65.

38. James Kirke Paulding, *Letters from the South*, New Edition (New York, 1835), pp. 5, 7.

39. Claude Lévi-Strauss, *The Savage Mind* (Chicago: University of Chicago Press, 1966), p. 259.

40. Jeremy Belknap, *A Discourse, Intended to Commemorate the Discovery of America by Christopher Columbus* (Boston, 1792), pp. 5, 25–26.

41. *The Poems of Philip Freneau: Poet of the American Revolution*, ed. Fred Lewis Pattee, 3 vols. (Princeton: University Library, 1902), 1:89–90.

42. Jeremy Belknap, *Biographies of the Early Discoverers of America* (Boston, 1798), p. 19.

43. Prince, *Chronological History*, 2:78.

44. William Robertson, *The History of America* (Alston, Cumberland, 1809), pp. 80–81.

45. Charles A. Goodrich, *A Child's History of the United States: Designed as a First Book of History for Schools*, 2d ed. (Philadelphia, 1844), p. 9.

46. Isaac Taylor, *Scenes in America, for the Amusement and Instruction of Little Tarry-at-Home Travellers* (Philadelphia, 1825), p. 10.

47. Joel Barlow, *The Columbiad: A Poem* (Philadelphia, 1807), book 1, lines 7–8. Subsequent references to *The Columbiad* are noted parenthetically in the text. For a fuller account of these two poems and a third *Columbiad*, by the Englishman James A. Moore in 1798, see my "Three Columbiads, Three Visions of the Future," *Early American Literature* 27 (Fall 1992): 42–56.

48. Marie-Anne DuBoccage, *La Columbiade: où, La Foi Portée au Nouveau Monde* (Paris, 1756), "Neuvième Chant," p. 163. The lines in this poem are not numbered.

49. Roy Harvey Pearce, *The Continuity of American Poetry* (Princeton: Princeton University Press, 1961), pp. 59–69.

50. Wayne Franklin, *Discoverers, Explorers, Settlers: The Diligent Writers of Early America* (Chicago: University of Chicago Press, 1979), p. 13.

51. Emory Elliott, *Revolutionary Writers: Literature and Authority in the New Republic, 1725–1810* (New York: Oxford University Press, 1982), pp. 94, 115.

52. Cecelia Tichi, *New World, New Earth: Environmental Reform in American Literature from the Puritans Through Whitman* (New Haven: Yale University Press, 1979), pp. 115, 128.

53. Goodrich, *Child's History*, pp. 12–13. On the challenge America as new-found-land presented to the understanding, see Robert Lawson-Peebles, *Landscape and Written Expression in Revolutionary America: The World Turned Upside Down* (Cambridge: Cambridge University Press, 1988), especially "Prologue: An America of the Imagination," pp. 1–21.

54. Cotton Mather, *Magnalia Christi Americana, Books I and II*, ed. Kenneth B. Murdock (Cambridge, Mass.: Belknap Press, 1977), pp. 118–19.

55. Ramsey, *History of the United States*, p. 30; Ralph Waldo Emerson, *Essays and Lectures* (New York: The Library of America, 1983), p. 849.

56. Belknap, *Biographies*, p. 37.

57. Whelpley, *Compend*, 2:142. The quotations from Whelpley in the following paragraphs are from 2:142–43.

58. Samuel Latham Mitchill, *Address to the Fredes, or People of the United States, on the 28th Anniversary of Their Independence* (New York, 1804), p. 7.

59. Edgar Allan Poe, untitled comment in *Graham's Magazine*, 29 (December 1846): 312. Poe notes the suggestion by "Mr. Field" of the New York Historical Society on the same page.

60. George R. Stewart, *Names on the Land: A Historical Account of Place-Naming in the United States*, 3d ed. (Boston: Houghton Mifflin, 1958), p. 173.

61. Keillor, *Woebegone*, p. 94.

62. Martin Waldseemüller, *Cosmographiae Introductio* (Ann Arbor: University of Michigan Microfilms, 1966), p. 70. A xylographic print of Waldseemüller's first map is in the Indiana University Library: *The Martin Waldseemüller 1507 Hauslab-Liechtenstein Globular Map of the World on Which the Name AMERICA Appears for the First Time* (New York: Parke-Bernet Galleries, 1950).

63. See Harold Jantz, "Images of America in the German Renaissance," in *First Images of America: The Impact of the New World on the Old*, ed. Fredi Chiappelli, 2 vols. (Berkeley: University of California Press, 1976), 1:91–106, and William G. Niederland, M.D., "The Naming of America," in *The Unconscious Today*, ed. Mark Kanzer, M.D. (New York: International Universities Press, 1971), pp. 459–72.

64. Samuel Eliot Morison, *The European Discovery of America: The Southern Voyages, 1492–1616* (New York: Oxford University Press, 1974), p. 292. For a favorable estimate of Vespucci's endeavors, see Antonello Gerbo, "The Earliest Accounts of the New World," in *First Voyages of America*, 1:37–43.

65. Hugh Honour, *Romanticism* (New York: Harper and Row, 1979), p. 263. John D. Hazlett discusses the divided nature of Irving's attitude toward Columbus in "Literary Nationalism and Ambivalence in Washington Irving's 'The Life and Voyages of Christopher Columbus,'" *American Literature 55* (1983): 560–75. For discussions of Irving's presentation of Columbus, see John Harmon McElroy, "The Intergrity of Irving's Columbus" and James W. Tuttleton, "The Romance of History: Irving's Companions of Columbus," both collected in *Washington Irving: The Critical Reaction*, ed. James W. Tuttleton (New York: AMS Press, 1993), pp. 126–36, 137–48. See also my "American Literature Discovers Columbus," in *Discovering Difference: Contemporary Essays on American Culture*, ed. Christoph K. Lohmann (Bloomington: Indiana University Press, 1993), pp. 16–34. Claudia Bushman advances the idea that what Americans have thought of Columbus reflects what they have thought of themselves, in *America Discovers Columbus: How an Italian Explorer Became an American Hero* (Hanover, N.H.: University Press of New England, 1992); Joel Porte terms this study successful despite its "shallow scholarship and lame conclusions" (*New England Quarterly* 65 [December 1992]: 671–74).

66. Samuel Miller, "Discourse on Henry Hudson," *Collections of the New-York Historical Society, for the Year 1809* (New York, 1811), p. 263.

67. Philip Melancthon Whelpley, *New England Society Orations*, 1:115, 121; J. Prescott Hall, *New England Society Orations*, 2:4.

68. James Spear Loring, *The Hundred Boston Orators, Appointed by the Municipal Authorities and Other Public Bodies* (Boston, 1852), pp. 24–25.

69. Loring, *Boston Orators*, p. 156.

70. See, for example, Richard M. Weaver, *The Ethics of Rhetoric* (Davis, Cal.: Hermagoros Press, 1985); Robert Tarbell Oliver, *History of Public Speaking in America* (Boston: Allyn and Bacon, 1965); and Edward Griffin Parker, *The Golden Age of American Oratory* (Boston, 1857).

71. *The Works of Joel Barlow*, 2 vols., ed. William K. Bottorf and Arthur L. Ford (Gainesville, Fla.: Scholars' Facsimiles and Reprints, 1970), 1:4–11.

72. Henry Colman, *An Oration Delivered in Salem . . . at the Request of the Town* (Salem, 1826), p. 10; Edwin Forrest, *Oration Delivered at the Democratic Republican Celebration . . . in the City of New-York* (New York, 1838), p. 5; and Samuel Taggart, *An Oration Delivered at Conway* (Northampton, 1804), p. 1.

73. John Quincy Adams, *An Address, Delivered . . . at the City of Washington* (Cambridge, Mass., 1821), p. 31; *An Oration Delivered Before the Inhabitants of Newburyport, at Their Request* (Newburyport, 1837), p. 12.

74. Adams, *Oration*, p. 47; Forrest, *Oration*, pp. 13, 21; and W. M. Corry, *Against the Degradation of the States: An Oration Delivered Before the Peace Democracy, at Canton, Stark County, Ohio* (Cincinnati, 1863), p. 7.

75. Levi Woodbury, *An Oration, Pronounced at Lyndeborough, N.H.* (Amherst, 1816), pp. 3–4; Adams, *Oration*, p. 5; and Charles Sumner, *The True Grandeur of Nations: An Oration Delivered Before the Authorities of the City of Boston* (Philadelphia, 1846), p. 1.

76. Frederick Douglass, "Oration, Delivered in Corinthian Hall, Rochester," in *Black Writers of America: A Comprehensive Anthology*, ed. Richard Barksdale and Keneth Kinnaman (New York: Macmillan, 1972), pp. 93–101.

77. Margaret Fuller, "Fourth of July," in *Life Without and Life Within; or, Reviews, Narratives, Essays, and Poems*, ed. Arthur B. Fuller (Boston, 1874), p. 235.

78. Sacvan Bercovitch, *The American Jeremiad* (Madison: University of Wisconsin Press, 1978), pp. 141, 145–52. See also Rush Welter, *The Mind of America: 1820–1860* (New York: Columbia University Press, 1975), p. 396, and Howard H. Martin, " 'Style' in the Golden Age," *Quarterly Journal of Speech* 43 (1957), 374–82.

79. *Oration Delivered by J. Murray Rush, Before the Democratic Citizens of the Third and Fourth Congressional Districts of Pennsylvania* (Philadelphia, 1852), p. 4.

80. Cited in Loring, *Boston Orators*, p. 27.

81. Barlow, *Works*, 1:525.

82. John Lowell, *An Oration Delivered to the Citizens of Boston* (Boston, 1799), p. 3; Colman, *Oration*, p. 12; Douglass, *Oration*, p. 89; and Forrest, *Oration*, p. 23.

83. Barlow. *Works*, 1:526; Henry James, Sr., *The Social Significance of Our Institutions: An Oration Delivered by Request of the Citizens of Newport, R. I.* (Boston, 1861), pp. 3, 33; and Henry Wallace, *New Frontiers* (New York: Reynal and Hitchcock, 1934), p. 3.

84. Adams, *Oration*, p. 10.

85. Cited in Loring, *Boston Orators*, p. 158.

86. Among the many plays, poems, and fictional narratives that make use of the Fourth of July for individual and historical purposes, Ross Lockridge, Jr.'s *Raintree County* (1948) is one of the most achieved and wide-ranging. The story of a single day, July 4, 1892, the novel appropriates the anniversaries of national independence and Columbus's landing to its narrative design.

87. *A Gentleman of Much Promise: The Diary of Isaac Mickle, 1837-1845*, 2 vols., ed. Philip English Mackey (Philadelphia: University of Pennsylvania Press, 1977), 1:53. Subsequent references to Mickle's *Diary* are noted parenthetically in the text.

88. Mircea Eliade, *The Myth of the Eternal Return: or, Cosmos and History*, trans. Willard R. Trask (Princeton: Princeton University Press, 1954), pp. 51–62. Barry Schwartz examines the shaping of national memory in "The Social Context of Commemoration: A Study in Collective Memory," *Social Forces* 61 (1982), 374–402. For a detailed examination of historical perspectives in this period, see Michael Kammen, *A Season of Youth: The American Revolution and the Historical Imagination* (New York: Knopf, 1978).

2. Beginning by Negation

1. *The Letters of Ralph Waldo Emerson*, 6 vols., ed., Ralph L. Rusk (New York: Columbia University Press, 1939), 2:394–95.

2. Hector St. John de Crèvecoeur, *Letters from an American Farmer* (London, 1782), p. 46; Thomas Cooper, *Some Information Respecting America* (London, 1794), p. 53; for Noah Webster, see Richard M. Rollins, *The Long Journey of Noah Webster* (Philadelphia: University of Pennsylvania Press, 1980), p. 29.

3. Américo Vespucio, *El nuevo mundo: cartas relativas a sus viajes y descubrimientos*, Estudio preliminar de Roberto Levillier (Buenos Aires: Editorial Nova, 1951), p. 290.

4. Montaigne, "Of Cannibals," in *Complete Works: Essays, Travel Journal, Letters*, trans. Donald M. Frame (Stanford: Stanford University Press, 1957), p. 158.

5. See Edmundo O'Gorman, *The Invention of America: An Inquiry into the Historical Nature of the New World and the Meaning of Its History* (Bloomington: Indiana University Press, 1961). In *Witnesses to a Vanishing America: The Nineteenth-Century Response* (Princeton, Princeton University Press, 1981), pp. 3–6, Lee Clark Mitchell restates the premises of O'Gorman's idea, then proceeds on a searching study of what happened to America-as-place in the nineteenth century.

6. Bernard W. Sheehan, *Savagism and Civility: Indians and Englishmen in Colonial Virginia* (New York: Cambridge University Press, 1980), p. 21. Roy Harvey Pearce has written importantly on the impact of native Americans on a "civilized" consciousness in *The Savages of America: A Study of the Indian and the Idea of Civilization*, rev. ed. (Baltimore: Johns Hopkins Press, 1965) and in the later *Savagism and Civilization: A Study of the Indian and the American Mind* (Berkeley: University of California Press, 1988).

7. See Patricia Caldwell, *The Puritan Conversion Narrative: The Beginnings of American Expression* (New York: Cambridge University Press, 1983), esp. chapter 1. Additional perspectives on the idea of experience in America stripping away social encumbrances can be found in Peter N. Carroll, *Puritanism and the Wilderness: The Intellectual Significance of the New England Frontier* (New York:

Columbia University Press, 1969) and Annette Kolodny, *The Land Before Her: Fantasy and Experience of the American Frontiers, 1630–1860* (Chapel Hill: University of North Carolina Press, 1984).

8. Sylvester Judd, *Margaret: A Tale of the Real and the Ideal, Blight and Bloom* (Upper Saddle River, N.J.: Gregg Press, 1969), pp. 230–33. Because the novel, as she saw it, focused on the development of character "in a woman," Margaret Fuller considered *Margaret* "a harbinger of the new era"—*The Writings of Margaret Fuller*, ed. Mason Wade (New York: Viking Press, 1941), pp. 369–70.

9. *The Poems of Philip Freneau: Poet of the American Revolution*, 3 vols., ed. Fred Lewis Pattee (Princeton: University Library, 1902), 1:82. Freneau adds additional negatives out of his millennial conviction that the new Canaan shall excel the old: "No thistle here, nor thorn, nor briar shall spring"; "No fierce disease, / No fevers, slow consumption, ghastly plague."

10. Cited in Perry Miller, *Consciousness in Concord: The Text of Thoreau's Hitherto "Lost Journal" (1840–1841), Together with Notes and a Commentary* (Boston: Houghton Mifflin, 1958), p. 216.

11. *North American Review* 6 (1818): 238; *American Quarterly Review* 2 (1827): 509.

12. Marianne Moore, "England," in *Collected Poems* (New York: Macmillan, 1951), pp. 53–54.

13. James Fenimore Cooper, *Notions of the Americans: Picked up by a Travelling Bachelor*, The Writings of James Fenimore Cooper (Albany: State University of New York Press, 1991), p. 348; Margaret Fuller, "A Record of Impressions Produced by the Exhibition of Allston's Pictures in the Summer of 1839," *The Dial* 1 (July 1840): 73; and Horatio Greenough, *Form and Function: Remarks on Art, Design, and Architecture*, ed. Harold A. Small (Berkeley: University of California Press, 1957), p. 52. Greenough's essay, "American Architecture," was originally published in 1843 in the *United States Magazine and Democratic Review*. Nathaniel Hawthorne, *The Marble Faun: or, The Romance of Monte Beni*, The Centenary Edition of the Works of Nathaniel Hawthorne (Columbus: Ohio State University Press, 1968), p. 3.

14. Henry James, *Hawthorne* (London, 1879), p. 43.

15. George S. Hillard, "The Past and the Future," in *New England Society Orations* 2 vols., (Boston, 1851), 2:137.

16. *Edinburgh Review* 50 (October, 1929): 127.

17. Washington Irving, *A History of New-York . . . by Diedrich Knickerbocker*, Author's Revised Edition (New York, 1853), p. 49.

18. D. H. Lawrence, *Studies in Classic American Literature* (New York: T. Seltzer, 1923), p. 14.

19. Robert Clark notes the presence of negative definitions in nineteenth-century American writing in *History and Myth in American Fiction, 1823–52* (New York: St. Martin's Press, 1984), pp. 55–58.

20. Richard Helgerson, "Inventing Noplace; or, The Power of Negative Thinking," in *The Power of Forms in the English Renaissance*, ed. Stephen Greenblatt (Norman, Okla.: Pilgrim Books, 1982), p. 101. See also J. C. Davis, "The